Socializing the Sky

ORO Editions
Publishers of Architecture, Art, and Design
Gordon Goff: Publisher

www.oroeditions.com
info@oroeditions.com

Published by ORO Editions

Author: Robert Oxman
Project Manager: Jake Anderson

Book Design by CircularStudio
Pablo Mandel: design director
Micaela Carraro: layout

Typepset in Bau and Minion

10 9 8 7 6 5 4 3 2 1 First Edition

ISBN: 978-1-957183-95-4

Prepress and Print work by ORO Editions Inc
Printed in China

ORO Editions makes a continuous effort to minimize the overall carbon footprint of its publications. As part of this goal, ORO, in association with Global ReLeaf, arranges to plant trees to replace those used in the manufacturing of the paper produced for its books. Global ReLeaf is an international campaign run by American Forests, one of the world's oldest nonprofit conservation organizations. Global ReLeaf is American Forests' education and action program that helps individuals, organizations, agencies, and corporations improve the local and global environment by planting and caring for trees.

ROBERT OXMAN

Socializing the Sky

The Typology of Tower Clusters

ORO

ACKNOWLEDGMENTS

This search for knowledge began with an invitation by Moshe Safdie to attend the ceremonies for the opening of the Marina Bay Sands resort in Singapore in 2010. Not only was the architectural approach to the design of the building complex remarkably rich and interesting in its compositional approach, but the central building grouping of the complex—three hotel towers topped by a connecting horizontal plaza in the sky—provided a new architectural form of a special amenity for the hotel population.

This led me on a research process to attempt to understand where, how, and why, what I considered to be an innovative architectural and urban typology had begun to emerge internationally as a new architectural phenomenon. The architectural websites, particularly *Dezeen* and *ArchDaily*, among others, have provided a daily knowledge interface without which I would not have become engaged in what became a long process of research, formulation of a basic structure of the historical development of the new typology, and finally, the creation of a conceptual structure.

The availability of a library of research-based literature, as well as various volumes of professional literature, were an invaluable intellectual stimulus and aid in understanding a body of material which over my long period of research frequently appeared to lack a clear ordering set of concepts. Among the many works of brilliance and professional experience in my library there are many outstanding works. Jennifer Yoos and Vincent James's study of international experimental urban design projects, *Parallel Cities: The Multilevel Metropolis*, and Sarkis, Barrio, and Kozlowski's *The World as an Architectural Project* were a constant intellectual stimulus in my attempt to arrive at a thesis that might provide a substantial foundation for placing the architectural case studies in a broader theoretical framework. Works such as the Regional Plan Association's *Urban Design Manhattan* and Fumihiko Maki's *Nurturing Dreams: Collected Essays on Architecture and the City* not only provided important urban concepts to the work, but were also a constant source of inspiration, providing encouragement to intellectually approach the challenge of charting new forms of architectural/urban relationships. Moshe Safdie's writings have been for me a constant source of intellectual enrichment, and his recent work, *If Walls Could Speak: My Life in Architecture*, provided many insights on Marina Bay Sands and other works relevant to the research. Ingrid Böck's *Six Canonical Projects by Rem Koolhaas: Essays on the History of Ideas* made an insightful contribution to thought on foundational attempts to go beyond the traditional form of the skyscraper. I also learned much about skyscraper architecture from a large selection of works. Among these, of importance have been the research and other works of the Council of Tall Buildings and Urban Habitat (CTBUH).

Through this lengthy period of research, I discovered a body of projects and a group of designers whose names appear in the Dedication. I found these to be a typologically, functionally, and morphologically diverse body of works which were so intellectually rich that I was repeatedly encouraged to employ them as a justifiable foundation for the theoretical positions that are developed in this book. I must say that during my long period of research, I encountered many other examples of tower clusters. But due to the typological innovations of this particular group of works, I was stimulated to define their contributions to the typology. It is this process that is collectively documented in the addenda.

I found these contributions to be so important that I am still amazed by the privilege that I had to define the value, both intellectual and professional, that they have contributed. I will mention only two examples in order to clarify the potential importance to the future of urban high-density functional integration in tall buildings. Norman Foster's DJI Headquarters building is an example of the use of the tower cluster as a medium to enable the design of high-tech headquarters incorporating administration, research, experimentation, product design, exhibition, and other functions in the environment of the tall building. This remarkable achievement is in important contradistinction to Foster's other famous high-tech center in the US, the Apple Headquarters building. Another example of experimental architectural formal and material design attempting to optimize high-tech research and design in the environment of vertical urbanism is that of Zaha Hadid Architect's project for the OPPO Headquarters research, design, and administration functions in a vertical environment which can optimize communication between departments and individuals.

It should be emphasized that these achievements have important implications for the future cultural and commercial potential of vertical urbanism. The two examples which are mentioned are in China, where such experimental developments now appear to be frequent. The remarkable characteristic common to all of the case studies is that they recognize the structural organization of the tower cluster as a highly flexible organizational mechanism that can optimize a great variety of diverse functional requirements and connections. It is a framework that invites typological as well as other classes of innovation.

In order to illustrate rapidly developing innovative design phenomena throughout the world, I have attempted to find a broad selection of important examples. Given that this material has been gathered from such a broad palette of material, the process of identifying and recognizing the copyright characteristics of the material has been complex. The many firms and individuals who assisted in obtaining permission to publish illustrations have worked very hard to assist me in this process, and the quality of this publication is deeply indebted to them. Among the many persons who have undertaken this work with devotion and careful attention to detail are Osarieme Isokpan of OMA; Christopher Mulvey and Roxana Liu of Safdie Architects; Tom Wright of Foster and Partners; Liv of Zaha Hadid Architects; Isa Fahrenholz of Büro Ole Scheeren; and Marisa Espe of Steven Holl Architects.

It is with the greatest attention and care that I have attempted to obtain permission for publication of the illustrations in order to compensate the creative individuals who have produced the diagrams, drawings, and photographs. My primary medium of communication with the internationally dispersed body of photographers and artists has been email. Though all of them are known, their email has not always been available. Wherever I have missed that essential contact, I apologize and leave the door open for communication with oxman.robert@gmail.com.

Finally, to my creative daughters, Neri and Keren, who have reinforced me artistically, intellectually, and emotionally with love and patience throughout this lengthy period, I send my love and devotion.

CONTENTS

In gratitude for the typological genius
Of a unique and distinguished
Group of architects
Who enlightened this search for knowledge

REM KOOLHAAS *and* OMA

MOSHE SAFDIE *and* SAFDIE ARCHITECTS

PATRIK SCHUMACHER *and* ZAHA HADID ARCHITECTS

OLE SCHEEREN *and* BÜRO OLE SCHEEREN

NORMAN FOSTER *and* FOSTER + PARTNERS

STEVEN HOLL *and* STEVEN HOLL ARCHITECTS

PREFACE

Vertical Urbanism and Early Visions of the Tower Cluster and the Connected City

This work is part of that broad historical quest for an architectural medium—a typology of design—that might be capable of transferring certain urban social places to new locations within skyscrapers and above their traditional urban locations as an integral part of the ground plane. That is, *to socialize the sky*!

This is a brief report on the concentrated, and eventually successful, effort over time to achieve that goal. The book is based on current research regarding the discovery of such a potentially socializing urban architectural medium during the beginning of the twenty-first century.

The history of urban modernization over the last century and a half has been a process of typological, technological, and conceptual invention. The increase of building density due to the emergence of the elevator and the high-rise building has concomitantly propagated a new scale and organization of urban social and cultural facilities. Within this process of urban typological evolution there have occurred instances of highly generative concepts. Among these are the appearance of ideas of such a level of creative potential that they have provided the impetus for a totally new and unforeseeable stage of urban development.

Vertical urbanism is a concept that in recent decades has seen the emergence of a new syndrome of generative components. *Socializing the sky* refers to the possibility that certain of the traditional contents of the urban environment such as public space, public parks, urban squares, public transportation, and other major urban spatial functions which are inherently associated with the urban ground plane might eventually exist aboveground—even high aboveground within the uppermost realm of what are referred to as *skyscrapers.* Thus, it is the emerging phenomenon of vertical urbanism that creates the possibility of socializing the sky. It is the nature of this recent developmental process and its essential ingredients of urban and architectural components that we propose to identify, to define, and to exemplify.

What then is the instigator of vertical urbanism? Among the recent developments that have begun to provide glimpses of such processes of vertical urbanism has been the rapid crystallization of a new urban building typology that we term the *tower cluster*. Tower clusters are the dense grouping of multiple towers into formally integrated multifunctional complexes that can be read and experienced as an urban spatial entity. Multitower urban complexes are a historically well-recognized phenomenon. But it is the new density made possible with groupings of closely related tall buildings built as a single spatial, functional, and formal entity that is beginning to suggest the potential of a future vertical urbanism in which the tower cluster becomes the seminal and pivotal element of a new urbanism. In this age of an emerging vertical urbanism, the popular functions of the ground plane, including streets, squares, and circulation ways can be distributed vertically through groups of tower clusters, thus creating a new form of vertical urbanism.

It is the emergence of the tower cluster as a formally integrated, multifunctional, multitower building type that is producing the potential for this new vertical urbanism. It is tower clusters that are also providing a new scale and organization of urban spatial, social, and cultural amenities, and it is the potential linkage of tower clusters that can become the legitimizing foundation of this new vertical urbanism. While multitower developments composed of high-rise and low-rise buildings are well known in the history of modern architecture, it is the proximity of elements of the tower cluster and the principles of their relationships and rules of organization that establish a new architectural typology in which all of the tower cluster elements are formally integrated into *a monolithic order*.

Thus, the tower cluster is a whole of parts formally composed of multiple towers, but legible as an urban entity. The formal and functional integration of the components of the tower cluster are of such a scale that they provide a programmatic context for the introduction of urban amenities: the square, the plaza, the roof terrace, and so forth, which can vary in their location within the morphology of the tower cluster. However, in contrast to the historical location of cultural amenities such as public squares on the ground plane, within the tower cluster such urban amenities are frequently located aboveground, even at the highest roof level of the tower cluster. As a consequence, the emerging forms of tower clusters are beginning to provide a new functional logic of urban space and functions high above the baseline of the tower cluster. Among the objectives of this present work is to explicate and exemplify this inner logic of the tower cluster and its relationship to the potential *integration of urban amenities* within such complexes. Finally, we will attempt to explore what might be the potential and significance of the *horizontal connection of tower complexes* into a larger connected order of urban scale building elements. This has the potential to become the future city of a new connective vertical urbanism.

We can begin to define the component characteristics of the emerging building type of the tower cluster:

- It is composed of a formally integrated tight grouping of multiple high-rise elements such as towers, and there is an articulated connectivity between the towers;

- It is generally multifunctional, some elements of which are private functions such as housing units, or hotel rooms, and others of which are public functions such as commercial malls;

- It contains large-scale public urban spaces integrated within the complex of towers at various levels throughout the complex;

- Frequently these urban spatial elements of squares, plazas, and malls are located aboveground;

- This provides the possibility of urban connectivity via *streets in the sky* between the public spaces of tower clusters which might serve to achieve socializing the sky, or the foundation of a new connective vertical urbanism.

We will continue to refine this definition in succeeding chapters.

In the first two decades of the twenty-first century, the configuration of these design tendencies has begun to crystallize as a new urban type. The typological program has proven highly viable commercially, and after two decades has seen the success of several foundational projects. Currently, a new generation of multiple tower cluster projects is rapidly appearing in recent publications. By 2022, the typology has begun to appear in numerous projects throughout the world. This work is an attempt to define this design phenomenon by identifying its historical roots, its typological characteristics, and its design variables.

PART I

Introduction to the History and Sources of Vertical Urbanism

1.1 The Role of the Formation of Conceptual Structures in the Advancement of the Architectural Discipline

In architecture, the great achievements are those which are generative. Rather than merely the achievement of formal innovation, a generative design, or design concept, is one that historically leads to an evolving progeny. In generative designs these resultant designs are not copies of the original, but the continuing evolution of a related set of original ideas. This is the power of the generative. It influences future significant developments by creating a new structure of concepts. Rather than buildings alone, it is the evolution of such *conceptual structures* that advances architectural knowledge and contributes to architecture as a discipline.

In the following presentation we will introduce, define, and exemplify a new building type which has evolved over the past two decades. We will demonstrate this as a generative architectural type in that, by definition, it is intimately connected to the evolution of a body of new urban concepts and forms.

With the birth of the twentieth century and the evolving importance of urban development through advancing skyscraper design, the conceptual transposition between ground and sky enters the realm of visionary urbanism. From the emergence of the tall building as a central urban developmental building type in the late nineteenth century, and with its continued centrality, the skyscraper has profoundly introduced the duality of city and sky within the city of skyscrapers. The functions conventionally associated with the urban ground plane—urban space, pedestrian connectivity, public transportation, public parks, and so forth—have now begun to become conceptually drawn into the realm of the sky.

Left Pieter Bruegel the Elder, *Tower of Babel*, c. 1563. Museum Boijmans Van Beuningen, Rotterdam
Come let us build ourselves a city, and a tower with a top in the heavens

We begin with a schematic presentation of the concept of vertical urbanism, which is defined herein as the transposition vertically upward within groupings of towers of the major urban functions usually associated with the ground plane. Following this first chapter, we embark on the introduction of a new building type that we have named the tower cluster, and subsequently demonstrate that it is this new typology which is enhancing dramatic possibilities in the advancement of vertical urbanism as the new urban architecture of the twenty-first century. It is the clarification of the potential relationship of these two new conceptual structures, tower clusters and vertical urbanism, that is the objective of this work.

1.2 Vertical Urbanism as a Foundational Concept of Future Urbanism

A selection of theoretical projects, researches, and experiments from the twentieth century are presented, and their contribution of concepts and morphologies to the future of urban typologies is proposed. This will lead us to the past thirty to forty years, during which prominent examples of tower clusters and of vertical urbanism have emerged internationally. Current case studies of recent theoretically important works of tower clusters are identified in the relationship with evolving classes and conditions of vertical urbanism and the potential that this identifies as a future for urban development.

From the invention of the modern elevator by Elisha Otis in 1853, man's vertical aspiration skyward has rapidly gained momentum. In the second decade of the twenty-first century, people have become enamored of the term *skywalker*, even though it still, at least temporarily, hovers in the realm of science fiction. Perhaps a contemporary indication of the persistent potency of the concept can be seen in the needlelike supertall and superthin towers beginning to thread themselves into the sky around Manhattan's Central Park.

Louis Kahn, that master of the eternal, asked the brick what it wanted to be. The brick answered: an arch. What if we today asked the elevator a similar question? It can no longer be simply to go higher, to share in the envy of weightlessness. Today the answer must be to find a raison d'être for being in the sky, for becoming a skywalker. The logical meaning of such a future of being in the sky is to find the potential for the creation of a new form of urbanism, a vertical urbanism. In a new vertical urbanism, we will find the *medium* as well as the reason to be in the sky.

As we will see below, at the beginning of the twentieth century, the growth of density in the city and the dominance of the skyscraper as an urban building type began to be a prominent international realization of what the future city might become. As the prospect emerges for a new urbanism characterized by dense groupings of skyscrapers, a new and characteristic form of urban vision begins to become frequently visualized. The important elements of the urban ground plane—the pedestrian street, the roadway, major urban spaces, and others—begin to appear to be vertically elevated to high levels above the ground plane and integrated within the structure of towers. This becomes a frequent part of the visionary expression of the future city. New forms of urban activity spaces have come to be visualized as vertically elevated to identify new urban activity centers as the future of the skyscraper city.[1]

We refer here to this phenomenon by the generic nomenclature vertical urbanism. Among the objectives of this work is to identify how this significant urban concept develops through the twentieth century and begins to evolve significantly with the emergence of new forms of tall buildings designs at the end of the twentieth century and in the first two decades of the twenty-first century. It is this dominant vision of the realistic possibility of a vertical urbanism that is enhanced and interrelated with the gradual emergence of a new class of tower design. This work seeks to historically bring us to the threshold of realization of what has been, up until now, in the realm of the visionary.

1.3 Visionary Urbanism in Early Visions of the City of the Future

1.3.1 Ludwig Hilberseimer and the High-Rise City (Vertical City) Project 1924

Ludwig Hilberseimer (1885–1967) was a German architect and urban planner known today for his theoretical studies of new urban organizational models. He studied architecture in Germany and subsequently worked in several professional and governmental offices. In 1929 Hannes Meyer invited him to teach at the Bauhaus in Dessau. Motivated by the rapid urbanization of American cities, he began to develop theoretical studies of high-density cities, each of which was based upon unique organizational models. In 1938 he went to work with Mies van der Rohe at the IIT College of Architecture in Chicago, where he became the head of the department of urban planning. At IIT, he continued to work on his theoretical urban planning studies.

His most noted project was the High-Rise City (Hochhausstadt) of 1924, otherwise known as the Vertical City. This was intended to be a new model of organization for the development of high-density, high-rise cities. It is based upon an approach to mass dwelling as a major collective function to be accommodated and socially enhanced within the framework of the tall building. Thus, the design of the organizational model of the components becomes the major objective. Within this conceptual framework, the organizational design of the towers is an important part of the elements of the urban model.

High-Rise City is organized by a vertically stratified model of urban organization. A base stratum contains two primary functions of the high-density city. One is work functions such as offices, factories, and commerce.

The second function associated with the base is primary vehicular circulation. Dwellings are located above this base level in towers superimposed on the base volume. Pedestrian circulation is also superimposed on the work zones of the base in the form of "streets in the sky." Thus, High-Rise City is a true vertical city given its vertical superimposition of the essential functional elements of the metropolis (see illustration below).

1.3.2 Hugh Ferriss, *The Metropolis of Tomorrow*, 1929

Hugh Ferriss was a well-known architect and architectural delineator who worked in New York City during the first decades of the rise of New York as the first skyscraper city. Many of his illustrations introduced the forms of the tall buildings of New York during this period in which the architectural forms were influenced by the "setback requirements" that created the stepped profile of the typical metropolitan towers of this period.

His 1929 book, *The Metropolis of Tomorrow*, illustrates his studies of the potential architecture of a skyscraper city. In this case, it may be seen as expressive of the visionary potential of new high-density urban forms. Among the many illustrations of the book are the two below which deal with the potential three-dimensional integration of vehicular traffic and pedestrian circulation within the future city. As we have already seen in Hilberseimer's High-Rise City, and as we will see again in Le Corbusier's urban studies below, the subject of traffic in the metropolis and its physical relationship to the new architecture of the city is to become a major issue of anticipatory design, or *futurism*. Making a statement with respect to the automobile and the vast pressure of anticipated traffic in cities becomes one of the major design issues of what will become the future field of urban design.

In the first of the two illustrations, the study presents a proposal for the three-dimensional separation of pedestrian and vehicular movement. The solution proposed involves the development of an elevated pedestrian street. This street is high enough above the roadway that it can also become the level of pedestrian bridges which cross the roadway. The study is shown as potentially integrated within the architectural structure. The second drawing illustrates a series of multilevel roadways which are shown integrated within the framework of the high-rise building structure.

1.4 Le Corbusier and Streets in the Sky as a Generative Concept in Multistory Urban Housing Blocks

Vertical city applications appear frequently in the early work of Le Corbusier. Circulation systems in the sky have appeared previously in many of Le Corbusier's urban designs. In the Contemporary City (*Ville Contemporaine,* 1922) there are six layers of various kinds of traffic including highways in the air. A similar early example of vertical urbanism existed in the Voisin Plan (*Plan Voisin,* 1925). The Plan for Algiers (Le Corbusier and Pierre Jeanneret, *Plan Obus,* 1930) is a long, linear building, the roof of which is an elevated traffic viaduct.

The impulse to employ circulation ways as the basis for instigating socialization between neighbors as well as the medium for sharing new social and cultural attributes within tall buildings derives from the design of Le Corbusier's Unité d'Habitation, Marseilles, 1947–1952.

This building contributes two significant design mechanisms to high-rise housing. The horizontal circulation ways (an *interior street* in the Unité; these become *exterior streets* in later, new multistory housing structures of the 1950s and 1960s. This is a truly generative design concept of multistory of the period. From the horizontal movement system one can enter an apartment that is two stories high (duplex)—after entering, the remainder of the dwelling is either up or down. The horizontal street is both an access street and a "collector" for a larger number of apartments than might be accessed if they were all on a single floor. The horizontal access is located on a vertical system (the elevator) that is organized as a system of stops and no stops, or skipped floors. Thus, the system of vertical distribution in the Unité is a "skip-skip-stop" system in two directions both up and down. Such collector systems of horizontal circulation in high-rise housing becomes the generative design mechanism of high-density multifamily housing in Europe during the 1950s and 1960s. Together with the integration of multiple amenities (shop, kindergarten, athletic facilities) the design system provides the basis for the new generation of postwar "social housing."

It is primarily in the UK that the concepts of vertical urbanism, and particularly the social and collective idea of streets in the sky, became a dominant theme of postwar housing design. In this sketch by Le Corbusier the street is noted as an "interior street" (*rue interieure*). In the future development of this idea in the UK, the street/corridor is moved to the exte-

Opposite Page Ludwig Hilberseimer, *High-Rise City,* (Vertical City) Project, 1924. Courtesy of Art Institute of Chicago. **Bottom Left** Hugh Ferriss, *The Metropolis of Tomorrow,* 1929. *Pedestrians Over Wheel Traffic,* p. 66–67. **Bottom Right** Hugh Ferriss, *The Metropolis of Tomorrow,* 1929. *Overhead Traffic-Ways,* pp. 64, 65

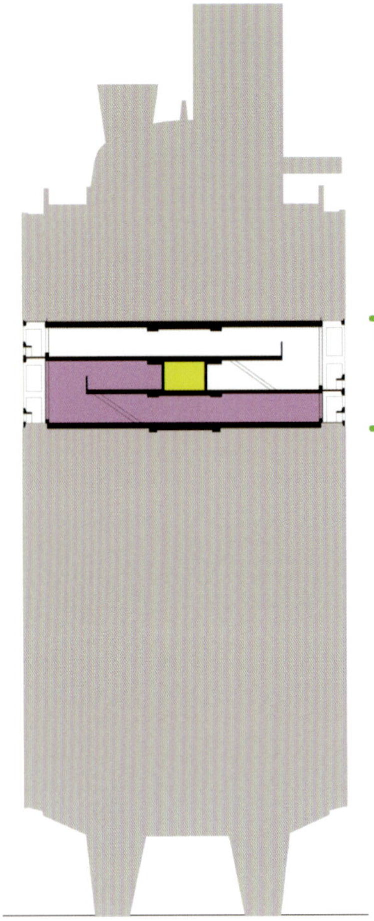

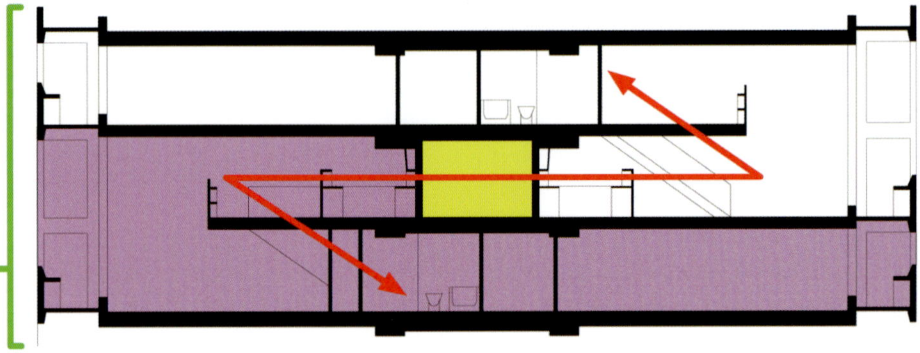

Interlocking Units Section

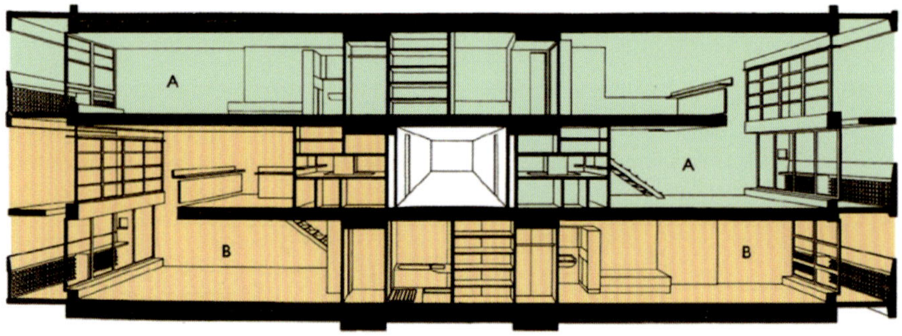

Interlocking Units Section Perspective

Above Le Corbusier, Unité block Marseilles Cross section of interior street and typical duplex Drawing by Gunawan Wibisono. **Right** Le Corbusier, Unité d'Habitation, schematic cross section, 1952.

rior façade of the building, thus providing a view and community space as well as a medium of residential circulation and access. The same up/down movement potential continues to exist. Generally, this is referred to with respect to the elevator stops as a "skip-skip-stop system." As at the Unité d'Habitation, its function is to aggregate traffic in the creation of a street which serves (and potentially creates) a neighborhood community in the sky. This noble and great idea has such theoretical social potential within new forms of high-density vertical urban housing that it becomes a theoretical concept of major influence in postwar European housing design.

The sketch of Le Corbusier illustrates typical multifloor duplex apartments clustered about a "street in the sky." In this sketch the street is noted as an "interior street" (*rue interieure*).

To further socially enliven the Unité, Corbusier introduced various social amenities within the building such as a kindergarten. The latter was located on the roof, which was designed as a roof garden covering the whole of the top floor. The three contributions of the Unité to a novel and conceptual definition of the vertically organized multistory housing structure are:

- The horizontal *collector street* which serves multiple floors through access to private staircases;
- The *roof terrace* as a major public open space and functional amenity for the total structure;
- The potential *distribution of public services*, e.g., gym, shop, restaurant opens the potential for the future integration of collective functions within the social system of the building.

The idea of an enhanced social system is thus comprised of the aggregation of a collective population on the access corridors, their design treatment as a place of community, and the integration elsewhere in the building of communal public amenities. This totality was the *Unity of Housing*.

1.5 The Revival of Streets in the Sky

The concept of turning horizontal circulation ways into "social collectors" rather than mere corridors creates the potential for meeting and social integration. This returns to the design of multistory housing the concept of the potential social importance of "the doorstep as the locus of meeting." Furthermore, it becomes a powerful creative generator for a great variety of sectional organizational possibilities in multistory housing. It is perhaps one of the dominant structural-organizational concepts of multistory vertical housing design of the postwar period of urban reconstruction. The elevator stops not at each level, but only at the level of the "street." In most of the subsequent buildings, in the UK as well as elsewhere in Europe, the street becomes external rather than internal, while still maintaining the

principle of the street becoming a generative element within a structural scheme of flexible organization.

The historical progeny of this body of ideas was amazingly rich and varied. The creative prototype coming as it did in the postwar period of the 1950s and 1960s was truly a germinating body of design ideas. Prominent among these ideas is the potential for treating the vertical and horizontal circulation systems of a building as a generating medium for the organization of multiple functions. So, the system of circulation can be treated as a scaffolding, an *infrastructure*, within which a variety of dwelling types can be inserted. Furthermore, this treatment of the circulation system as infrastructure theoretically enhances the potential for the integration of multiple functions, thus potentially creating *hybrid structures*, integrating functions such as living (housing) with other functions. The momentum for the exploitation of this body of generative concepts to create new forms of urban environments employing high-rise slab organized structures can be observed very clearly in much of the European architecture of the period, particularly in Great Britain.

In the following two British buildings we can clearly see the form of this organizational principle in which the elevator stops on every third floor, in other words, a skip-skip-stop. This organizational order is clearly expressed on the exterior of the building.

Above Balfron Tower, London. Erno Goldfinger, 1967. Streets in the air as a formative structuring concept. **Bottom Left** Trellick Tower, London. Erno Goldfinger, 1972.

Opposite Page Golden Lane Competition submission of Alison and Peter Smithson, 1952 Sketch plan. **Bottom Right** Golden Lane Competition submission of Alison and Peter Smithson, 1952. Street in the sky, perspective collage.

Streets in the sky became one of the most enduring utopian concepts of modern architecture. In its most direct meaning, the term implies the possibility that streets as conveyors of pedestrian traffic might be able to exist aboveground, within, and bridging between buildings. While references to "streets in the air" exist in much of the visionary architecture of the 1950s and 1960s, such as in the work of the Japanese Metabolists and European visionary urbanists, it is in the multifamily housing designs of British architects such as Alison and Peter Smithson that the concept is employed in reference to the potential of external corridors to function as a medium for meeting and social exchange. More than simply as a way to one's apartment, the corridor was broadened in order that it might encourage communal interaction in high-density housing developments by acting as a public space.

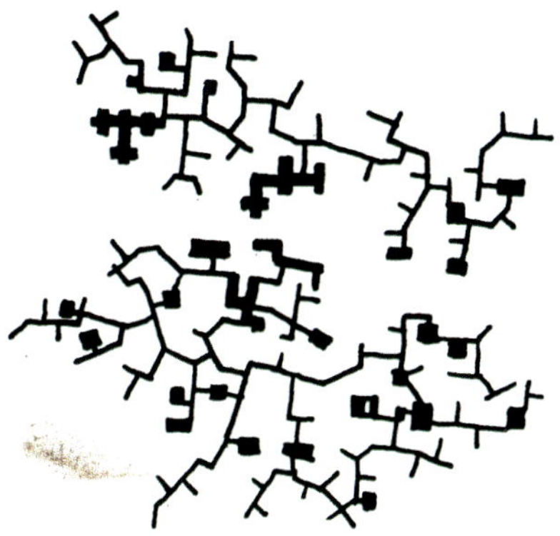

The concept of streets in the sky was promoted by Alison and Peter Smithson. It was employed by them first in their submission to the Golden Lane competition project of 1952. Later it was actually incorporated into the design and construction of their project for Robin Hood Gardens, London, 1972. This was one of the earliest and most outstanding examples of the conceptual form in British social housing. Robin Hood Gardens designed by the Smithsons was built for the Greater London Council. The project consisted of two parallel slab buildings, one of ten stories and the second of seven stories. Similar to many of these British high-density housing structures of the second half of the twentieth century, the project was constructed and finished in reinforced concrete. The employment of raw concrete, or *beton brût* in French, was highly unusual in conventional British housing. This usage became a leading phenomenon in British architecture of the period that was referred to by the British historian and critic Reyner Banham as the *New Brutalism*. Brutalist architecture became a significant theoretical and stylistic phenomenon of the sixties and seventies throughout the world. The streets in the sky provided no additional social function, except for entering and exiting the apartments. With no exterior furnishings, and being open to the climate, they invited little spontaneous activity.

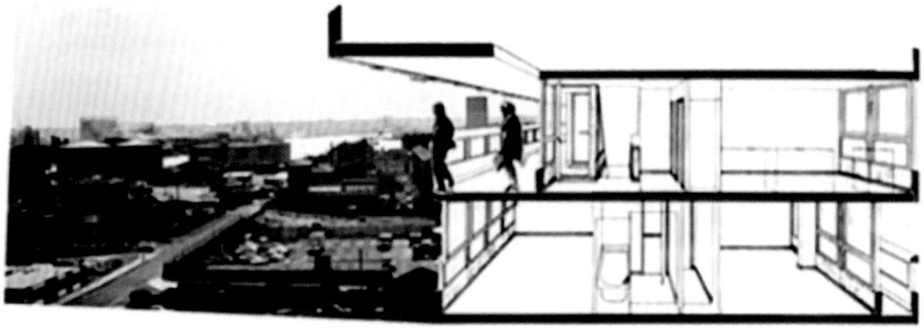

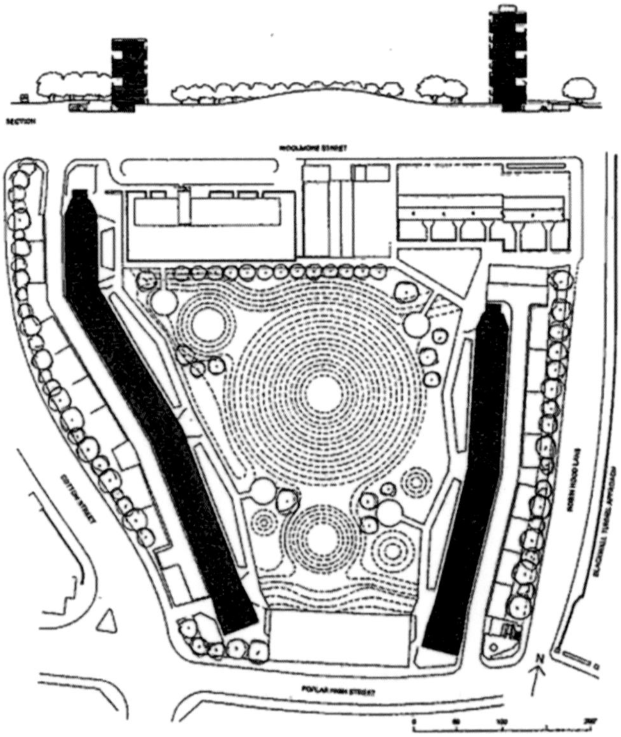

Above Robin Hood Gardens, Alison and Peter Smithson, apartment and deck section.
Bottom Robin Hood Gardens, Alison and Peter Smithson, 1972. Site plan and site section.

Opposite Page Robin Hood Gardens, Alison and Peter Smithson, view of façade.
Photo by John Levett.

However, we must return to the social motivation of the design principle: to create *streets in the sky*. In the case of Robin Hood Gardens and similar buildings of the period, the corridors were broad spaces with exterior exposure. In most cases of British high-rise dwelling design, the projects were relatively limited in size and did not enable connective construction of the streets in the sky. There were various exceptions to such design limitations of the street as an urban amenity to stimulate spontaneous social interaction. One of the most notable exceptions was The Park Hill development in Sheffield, England.

The Park Hill Housing project (1957–1961) was designed by Ivor Smith and Jack Lynn, who had been students of the Smithsons' at the Architectural Association in London during the mid-1950s. They worked under the direction of J. L. Womersley, who was the Sheffield Council City Architect. Park Hill in Sheffield was the first built example of the streets in the sky concept that had been strongly promoted as an idea in the 1952 Golden Lane competition entry by Alison and Peter Smithson. Soon after their graduation, Ivor Smith and Jack Lynn were selected as the architects of Park Hill. Among the historical conceptual sources which they referenced in addition to the Smithsons were Le Corbusier's continuous blocks of housing in the Ville Contemporaine (Contemporary City) of 1922, and Ville Radieuse (Radiant City) of 1935, as well as the Unité d'Habitation of 1936 to 1952. The architects also noted the influence of ideas of Hilberseimer's Vertical City of 1927.

Park Hill was a long, continuous series of twenty interconnected housing slabs on a large sloping site in Sheffield. The buildings are built and finished in reinforced concrete and contain 995 apartments. The streets in the sky circulation system provided the potential for uninterrupted pedestrian circulation over the totality of the large site. In all of these projects and others in the UK, the public pathway was intended to enhance the formation of hoped-for social groupings within the high-density, high-rise dwelling construction.

Above Park Hill, Sheffield, England, Lynn and Smith with Womersley, site plan, 1961.

Opposite Page Park Hill, Sheffield, England, 1961.
Bottom Park Hill, Sheffield, street in the air, 1961.

The project on a triangular site contained twenty linked housing blocks connected by streets in the air, and thus theoretically providing the possibility to move about the site within the public streets of the housing corridors.

The concept of streets in the air never succeeded to prove its viability as a vital social collector. There have been many explanations for the lack of success of this aspect of the projects, including the lack of attractiveness of the material quality of the buildings and spaces, and the lack of suitably inviting street furniture. Another significant deficiency was the lack of appropriate design of the adjacent dwelling façades as an operative interface between community and privacy.

Valid as some of this critique may be, it causes us to miss the more valid question of what are the architectural and urban qualities that have historically proven the ability to achieve the attraction and stimulation of spontaneous social interaction.

Such an analysis is obviously dependent upon the detailed empirical study of actual conditions. However, there are certain generalizations we can postulate regarding what might constitute motivating characteristics for spontaneous social interaction in tall buildings. Considering Le Corbusier's Unité, we can say that the roof terrace, with its variety of functions—particularly for children—is such an attractor. Might we generalize that this is a clearly attractive public space, or zone? The need for a clear transition to a public realm, particularly with respect to scale, suggests some valid potential for the creation of a vertical urbanism. Scale is frequently a medium for the transition from private realm to public realm. Recognized public amenities act as attractors and generators of social interaction.

Above "Notopia: The Fall of Streets in the Sky" (*Architectural Review*, June 9, 2016)

1.6 The Failure of Streets in the Sky and the Disappearance of the 3-D City

To what can the failures of the street in the sky concept as the seed of community formation be attributed? The various descriptions of the problems relate first of all to physical deterioration as well as crime. With respect to crime, it is interesting to note that at Park Hill there are no apartment windows that provide a view of what is happening on the street/corridor. In addition, there was no control of limited entry to the street system; that is, there existed free entry and multiple exits that enhanced, rather than prevented, criminal activity.

If we stop to consider a comparison with other European multifamily housing developments of this period such as those in the Netherlands, there emerge certain contrasting sociological and design principles which are neglected in the British developments. The first is the planning of neighborhoods with a mix and density of building types that guarantee a mix of socioeconomic classes. Wherever the mixed class principle becomes a mixed building type principle, there tends to exist the basic conditions for neighborhoods to emerge successfully. Whenever this principle is ignored, even in the Netherlands, and the scale of individual apartment structures becomes exaggerated in scale, incidents of crime also begin to flourish within low-income housing groups. Such was the case at the 1975 Bijlmermeer project near Amsterdam, which had been influenced by Park Hill. This was, similar to the British projects, a case of exaggerated, monotonic, and excessive building scale. That is, a case in which the Dutch had ignored, or forgotten, their own urban principles of the mixture of building types and scales in the creation of the conditions of neighborhood evolution.[2]

Streets in the sky was an important and promising concept of postwar theory and development. Does its demise indicate that the three-dimensional city of vertical urbanism disappeared forever? It sought the potential for introducing the scale and function of the public realm within the infrastructure and infill relationships of tall buildings. Among the missing ingredients of stimulative high-rise environments was the provision of a socially stimulating series of spatial transitions including changes of scale. Suitable environments must also provide a series of transitions between the public and private realms. Vertical urbanism still seeks the subtle and prudent interrelationship of the public and the private realm.

This intellectual conceptual separation between infrastructure and infill (Corbusier's hand inserting apartment in frame) led to completely new directions and ultimately to the pioneering design of Moshe Safdie's Habitat project at Expo 1967. So is it still possible to achieve a new vertical urbanism within the framework of conventional urban planning practices?

In the following section we present a new multifunctional building typology which has emerged in the past several decades. We have referred to this typology as the tower cluster. Simply defined, this is a tight clustering of multiple towers with a public base and the vertical integration of urban amenities within the various horizontal strata of the towers. We propose that it is such an urban building type that can potentially enhance the spontaneous development of vertical social phenomena at an urban scale.

Ultimately, we shall learn that it is *the integration of publicly accessible urban amenities within the tower cluster* which grants it the potential of becoming a truly generative urban prototype. The addition of linking skybridges between tower clusters can move contemporary urbanism closer to a new metropolis of vertical urbanism.

PART II

Prototypes of the Tower Cluster Typology

2.1 What Is a Tower Cluster? What Isn't a Tower Cluster?

The World Trade Center (WTC) was a complex of two twin towers located in the financial district of lower Manhattan in New York City. At the time of construction, they were the tallest buildings in the world at approximately 400 meters, or 1360 feet high. As we can see from the plan diagram, the site also contained five additional lower buildings, including a hotel. Certain amenities such as a viewing platform and several restaurants were incorporated within the structures, mainly at the upper levels.

The architect for the project was Minoru Yamasaki, who was appointed lead architect in 1962 with Emery Roth and Sons appointed as associate ar-

Left World Trade Center, New York City, Minoru Yamasaki, 1973.

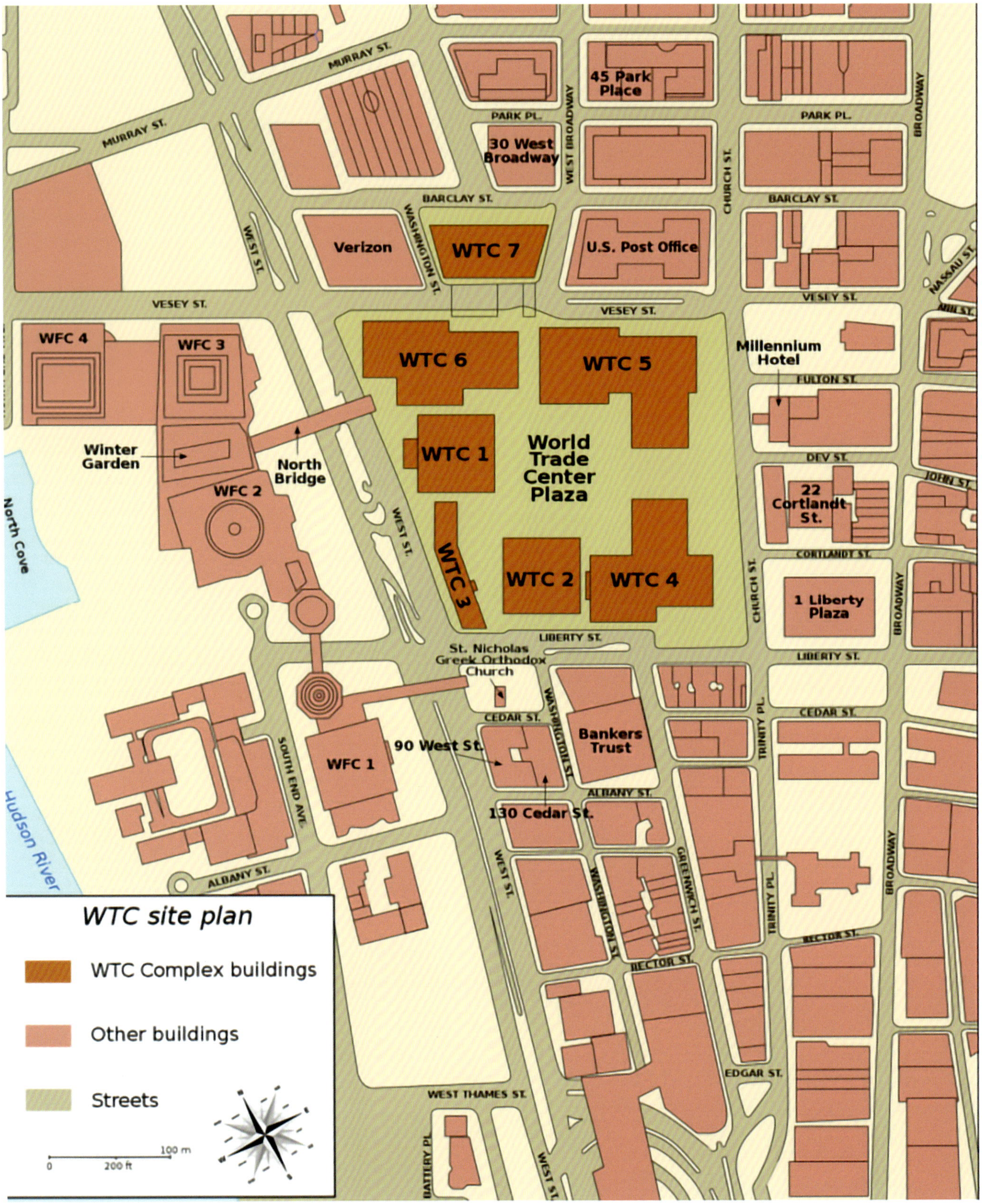

Above World Trade Center, New York City, site map, Minoru Yamasaki, 1973.

chitect. The first plans were completed by 1964 and the major construction took place between 1966 and 1975.

With respect to the site plan, the towers and ancillary buildings are arranged on the site around a square open space. Other than sharing this space, the elements of the total composition appear to be unrelated. This isolation of the towers and the rather simplistic urban landscape treatment appears surprising considering that the urban design statement of Rockefeller Center's core development had already been completed by 1939. Thus, there were numerous precedents for the intrinsic value and richness of the integration of significant urban developments within large urban architectural projects. It was by now known that the future metropolis thrives only with a generative interaction of the architectural and the urban. The true tower cluster, as we are attempting to define this new typology, is characterized by the compactness and structured form of its base elements and their integration with urban and urban landscape content.

During this same period, the Regional Plan Association was preparing its second regional plan for the future development of New York City. Lead consultants on the plan were Rai Y. Okamoto and Frank E. Williams as urban design consultants. The study was eventually published by the Viking Press in 1969 under the title *Urban Design Manhattan*.

Among the many interesting proposals, there is a suggestion regarding a cluster of towers in the historically and theoretically remarkable chapter 3 of the plan, entitled *Urban Design Principles and Prototypes*. This is a proposal for a series of ten office tower blocks organized as a matrix of elements ordered about a complex three-dimensional circulation infrastructure. There are multiple continuous horizontal levels of pedestrian movement. The matrix of these circulation flows creates the 4-D spatial order of the blocks. This movement system is also integrated with the existing underground public transportation system.

This spatial matrix of movements is proposed to be carried up within the infrastructure with a series of "skywalks" recurring throughout the structure at approximately ten-floor intervals. There is also a series of commercial levels proposed within the matrix and this is notably present as a multilevel base for the system. This movement system acts as a strong basis for horizontal movements that are potentially independent of the level of vehicular traffic movements.

There is here an ingenious preliminary proposal for the three-dimensional multilevel city which was more or less simultaneous with the rise of "streets in the sky" in the UK. The concept of the generative potential of tower clusters planted upon a matrix of movements will become an idea of great future potential. It further suggests to us certain axiomatic principles as we attempt to define the typological content of a new urban type based upon the potential of multiple towers, multifunctional complexes as components of a new urbanism—an urbanism of generative continuities.

It is clear that in contrast to a finite building as a *closed developmental system*, a tower cluster is an *open organizational system* of architectural and urban elements. It is possible to define the general characteristics of such

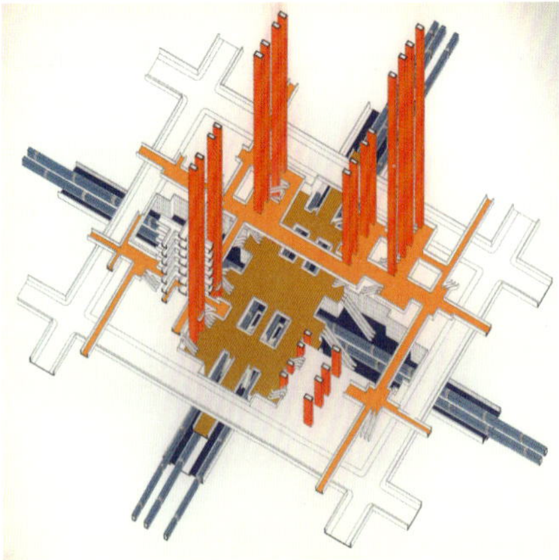

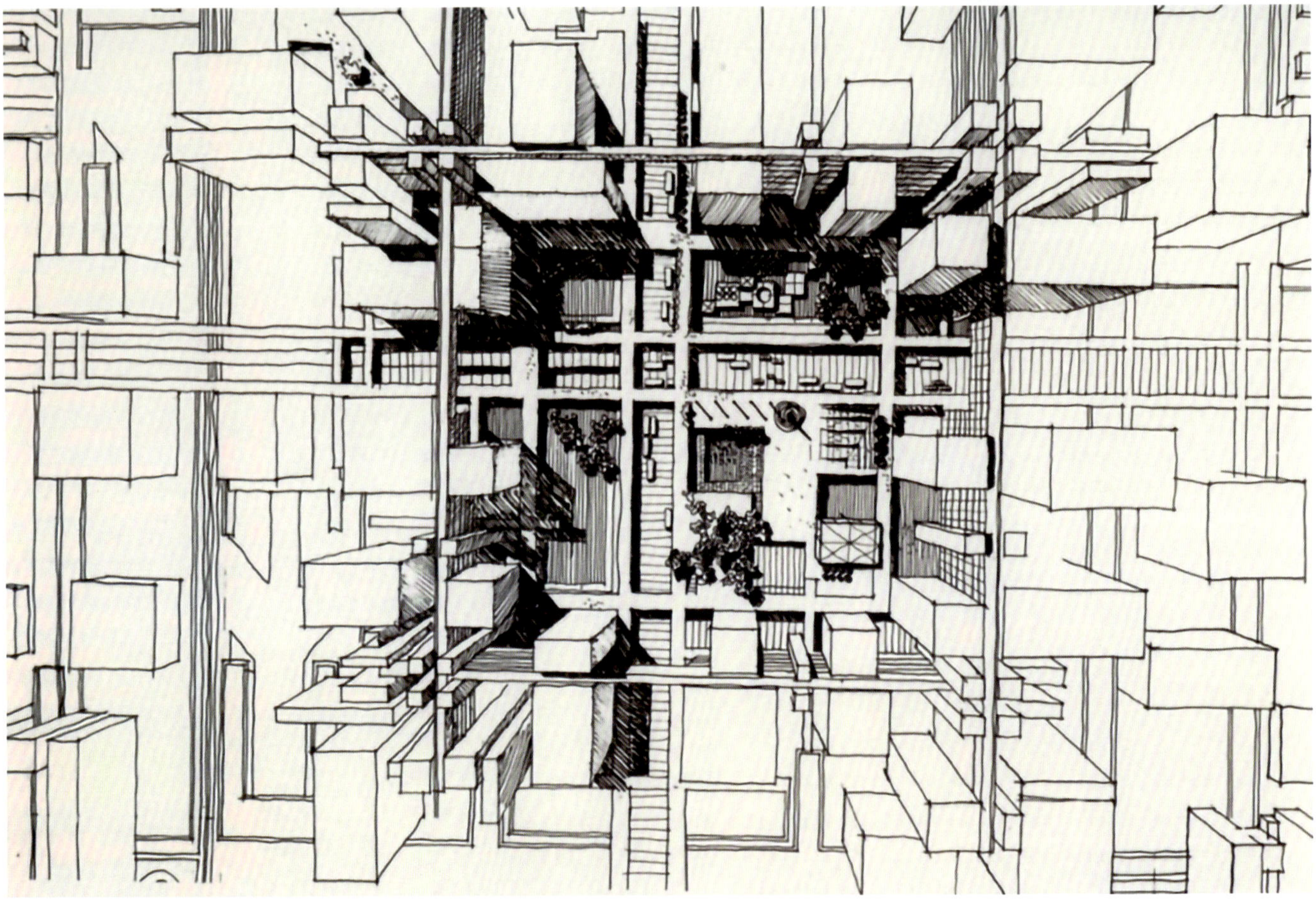

Above Left *Urban Design Manhattan*, Regional Plan Association, 1969. Courtesy of Regional Plan Association. **Above Middle** *Urban Design Manhattan*, the concept of the tower cluster access tree, 1969. Courtesy of Regional Plan Association. **Above Right** *Urban Design Manhattan*, the tower cluster, model, 1969. Courtesy of Regional Plan Association. **Bottom** *Urban Design Manhattan*, the tower cluster, 1969. Courtesy of Regional Plan Association.

a system of elements which includes both architectural and urban characteristics. It is significant to note that this is an integrated system in which the relationship of the architectural program, architectural characteristics, size, and interior circulation systems (both vertical and horizontal) are integrated with the urban framework of spatial and circulation elements.

We can now attempt to redefine and expand upon our initial statement regarding the basic characteristics and the essential components defining the tower cluster:

- **A Related Grouping of Interconnected Towers**
  The tower cluster is a related grouping of multiple vertical high-rises, or towers, between which there is created an articulated connectivity of circulation linking the towers. As we shall see below in section 2.5 in which we identify prototypes of the tower cluster, the number of towers in the cluster is an open design variable. Generally, the scale of vertical elements in a cluster ranges from two to an open upper limit. However, the towers are part of an integrated system of building elements, and it is always legible as a formally and functionally integrated system.

- **A Formal Ensemble of Vertical and Horizontal Elements**
  The elements of the tower cluster are therefore always related by an integrated formal system. This formal language of the cluster is generally consistent in all of the elements including tower form and connector elements which are legible as a system. However, in other cases, the towers and connecting elements may constitute a formal duality.

- **A Multifunctional Program**
  The functional program of the cluster is generally multifunctional. Some elements of this multifunctional order are private functions such as housing units, or hotel rooms, and others are public functions such as commercial malls.

- **A Series of Distributed Common Amenities**
  Within the organizational system of the tower cluster there are distributed a variety of communal amenities. As well as being open to inhabitants/users, these may also be accessible by visitors. Such amenities can include a variety of programmatic elements from spatial elements such as courts, plazas, and gardens to commercial elements such as restaurants/cafes, sports facilities, shopping areas, educational facilities, etc.

- **A Connecting Plinth Element and Potential Aboveground or Upper-Level Bridge Connectors between Towers**
  The tower cluster shares a common base element which provides a strong statement of unification. From a functional and circulation point of view this strengthens the functional as well as the formal integration of the elements of the cluster into a totality. In addition, upper-level bridge (skybridge) connectors frequently exist to link the towers at the highest of the base levels, or at upper levels.

- **Urbanistic Integration**
  The cluster grouping may contain large-scale public urban spaces integrated within the complex of towers at various levels throughout the complex.

- **The Potential for Vertical Urbanism**
  Frequently these urban spatial elements of squares, plazas, and malls are located aboveground, as part of a cluster subsystem of vertical urbanism. In addition, continuous horizontal circulation systems may be above, and/or below grade. In many cases, urban spatial elements such as plazas and parks may be located above grade, including at roof level.

- **The Potential for Intercluster Urban Connectivity**
  This provides the possibility of urban connectivity via streets in the sky between the public spaces of tower clusters which might serve to achieve socializing the sky, or the foundation of a new multilevel metropolis of vertical urbanism.

While we shall observe from the case studies that it is possible to identify the emergence of a new typology from the presence and diversity of these interrelated systems elements, we shall also observe certain formal nuances, hiatuses, or missing ingredients that create questions regarding the particular case study and its legitimacy of membership in the definition of the tower cluster.

This then leads us to the question of what is a *sine qua non* for the tower cluster? When is the absence of one element the cause for the lack of typological consistency?

What Isn't a Tower Cluster?

Peabody Terrace, Harvard University. Sert, Jackson and Gourley, 1964

Peabody Terrace, the facility for married student housing of Harvard University, was designed by Sert, Jackson and Gourley, the firm of Josep Lluís Sert, who was at the time the dean of the Harvard Graduate School of Design. The neighborhood is located along the banks of the Charles River in Cambridge. The project contains approximately 1,500 apartments in both high- and low-rise housing.

As we can observe from the photograph below, to vehicular traffic along the main thoroughfare, the towers in fact appear to be a cluster of towers. However, at ground level, the design is characterized by the physical continuity of the linear organization of its low-rise elements. The towers lack a continuous base element, and there is no articulated connection between the towers, such as connecting bridges. The site is organized around a series of connected courtyards reminiscent of the pedestrian spaces of the Harvard campus.

Above Peabody Terrace, Harvard University. Sert, Jackson and Gourley, 1964. **Middle** Peabody Terrace, Harvard University. Sert, Jackson and Gourley, 1964.

Opposite Page Peabody Terrace, Harvard University, site plan. Sert, Jackson and Gourley, 1964.

The typology of the tower cluster requires some form of physical unification usually achieved by an articulated base and/or bridge links. When I was a student at the Graduate School of Design, Sert told me in speaking about the project that three was a "very good massing" number. Meaning that the visual interaction between the tower elements was highly dynamic to the moving observer. But this consistency and integration is visual rather than physical or programmatic. Peabody Terrace lacks the compactness of the tower cluster. Thus, we cannot consider this important project of large-scale urban community housing a true tower cluster in the sense of the proposed new typology.

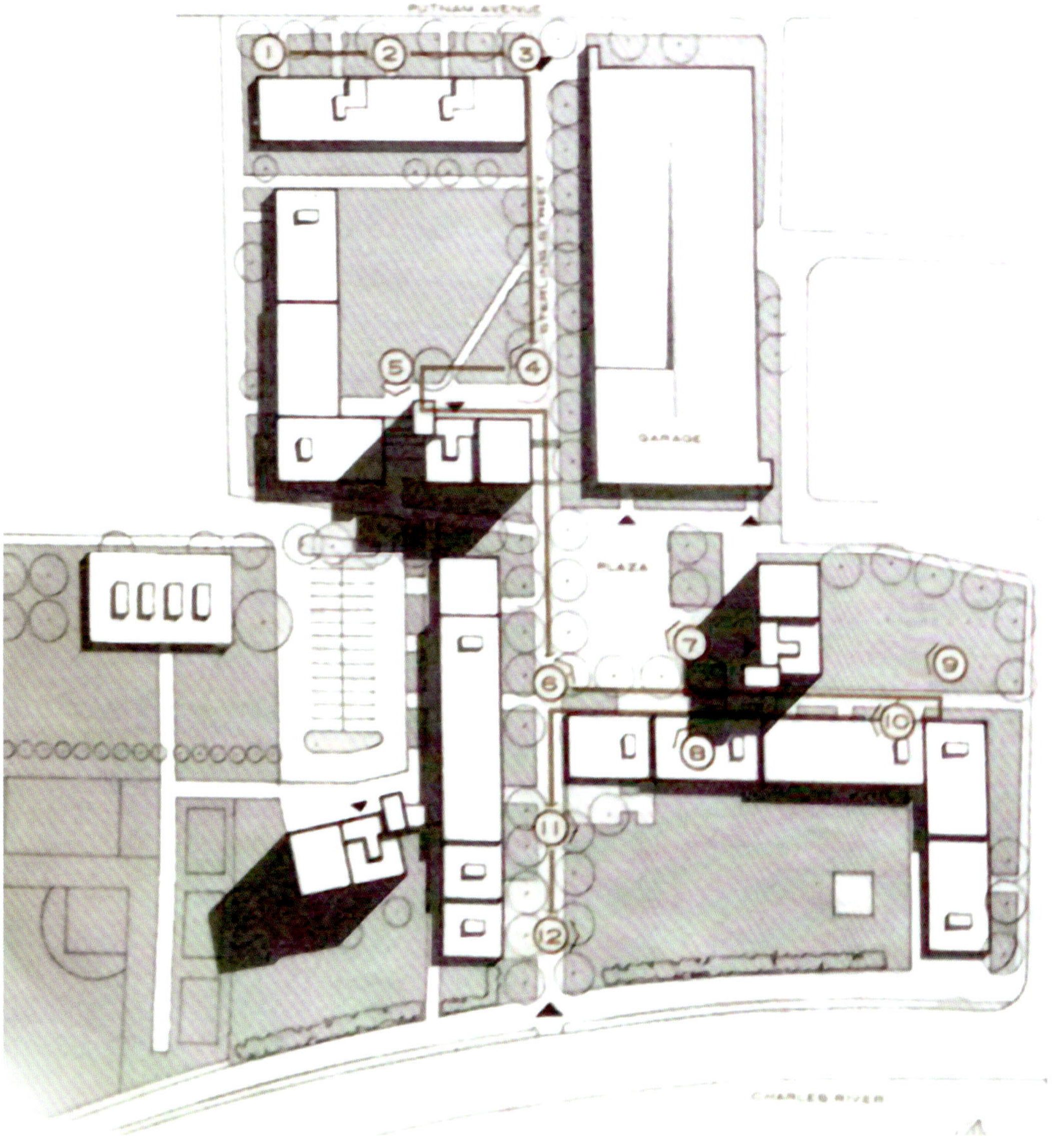

The Linked Hybrid, Beijing, China. Steven Holl, 2009
Linked Bridges and Functions

The Linked Hybrid, a much more recent project, begins to approach the new typology with the linked contiguity of its *amenity function bridges*. It is a 222,000-square-meter complex containing 644 apartment units, commercial areas, hotel, cinema, and schools. Its base creates a closed public urban space primarily for the use of the resident community.

The Linked Hybrid consists of eight towers of differing heights and mass configurations in a mixed-use residential complex. It contains two levels of interconnected multifunctional circulation; one level at the ground plane and one at the level of the sky loop (skybridge multifunctional connectors). In addition to these two major distributors of public facilities and pedestrian circulation, there is a series of public roof gardens at an intermediate level.

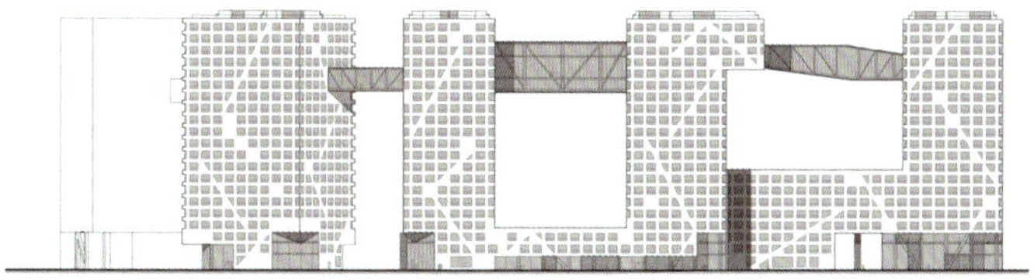

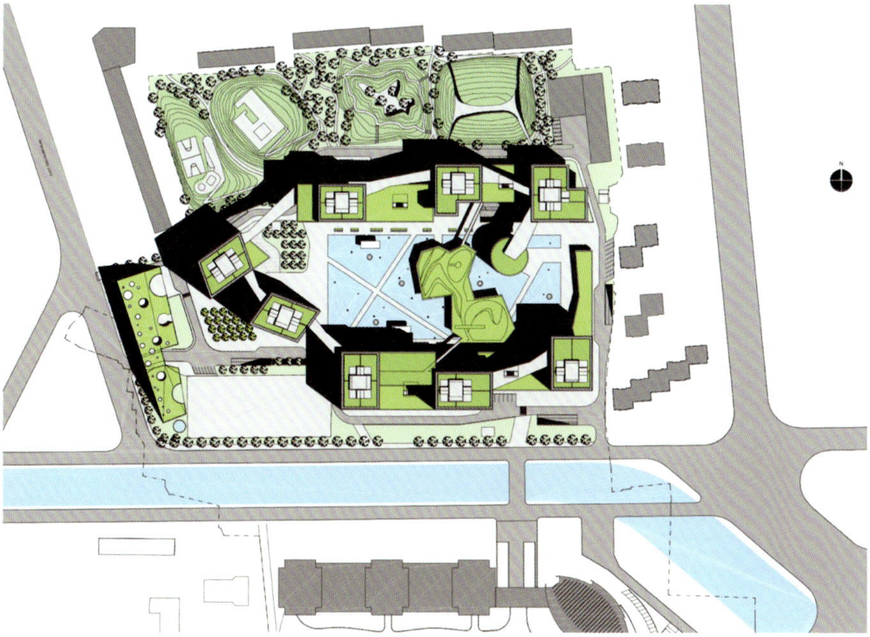

Opposite Page Linked Hybrid, Beijing, China. Steven Holl Architects, 2009. Photo courtesy of Shu He.

Above Linked Hybrid, Beijing, China. Steven Holl Architects, 2009. Elevation courtesy of Steven Holl Architects. **Bottom** Linked Hybrid, Beijing, China. Steven Holl Architects, 2009. Site plan courtesy of Steven Holl Architects.

The public functions at ground level include a hotel, restaurant, kindergarten, cinema, and Montessori school. On the 18th floor there is a series of multifunctional skybridges including a swimming pool, fitness areas, meeting rooms, cafés, gallery, auditorium, museums, etc. The sky loop is intended to function as a social impetus for new social meetings and interaction. Both the base loop and sky loop work together and are considered nonlinear loops, akin to a semi-lattice of movement.

Among its other distinctions, the project has been recognized and received numerous awards for the sophisticated operations of its environmental systems.

With respect to its definition as a tower cluster, its skybridge system is a very clear and significant component of the typological definition of the tower cluster. Here again, the informal distribution of the tower elements and the lack of clarity of the formal definition of the communal base element create a certain degree of ambiguity with respect to typological membership. However, despite these considerations, Linked Hybrid is very close to the emerging definition of the tower cluster.

2.2 The Emergence of the Tower Cluster

La Grande Arche de la Défense, Paris. Von Spreckelsen and Andreu, 1982

La Grande Arche de la Défense, or La Grande Arche, was the subject of an architectural/urban competition initiated by the then president of France, François Mitterrand, in order to extend the historic axis (Axe Historique) of Paris to the new business and financial center of La Défense.

The winning entry was by the Danish architect Johan Otto von Spreckelsen, whose architectural conception was to create an abstract modern version, in the form of a building, of the Arc de Triomphe. This new structure was to be the terminus of the historical axis in the La Défense district.

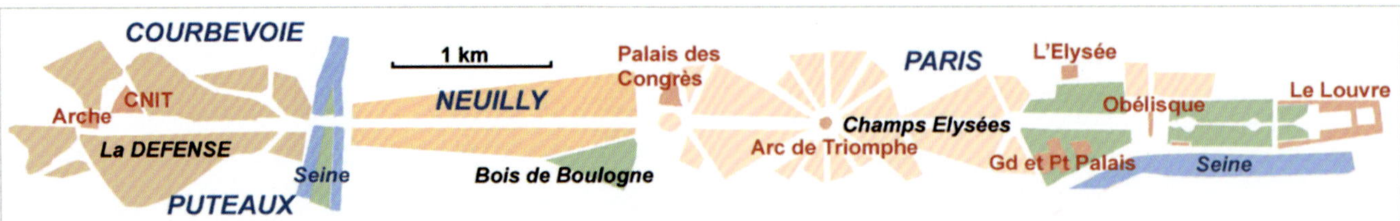

As illustrated in the diagram above, this axis begins at the Louvre and continues through the Arc de Triomphe until it reaches La Défense.

Von Spreckelsen's design was a building in the form of a rectangular arch-shaped structure creating a 110-meter cube (360 feet). The two side walls that form the open interior space of the arch contain various government offices. The upper floor that covers the arch space contains a conference center, an exhibition space, a museum, and a restaurant. There is also an outlook open area on this upper floor/ceiling. There is an open glass elevator running through the open space of the arch as can be seen in the section. The monumental arch-shaped office building is created by two parallel office structures of approximately 100m x 100m, upon which is located the roof of the arch containing the skybridge of public facilities. This skybridge element and the three-story base of the open court are the connecting spaces of the cluster.

The two identical slab-shaped office towers rise to thirty-five stories. They are connected by a public skybridge element containing a diverse program of public facilities. In addition, they are also connected by the large base element. With respect to the definition of the typological constituents of the tower cluster, the Grande Arche constitutes a prototypical case of the emerging typology.

As we further develop this typology, we shall observe the design significance of "typological variables." Among such variables are "tower form" and "building geometry." In the case of the Grande Arche, the tower forms are identical and the geometry is that of a regular rectangle. As we examine further examples of the typology, we shall observe the significance of the design variables within the evolving typology.

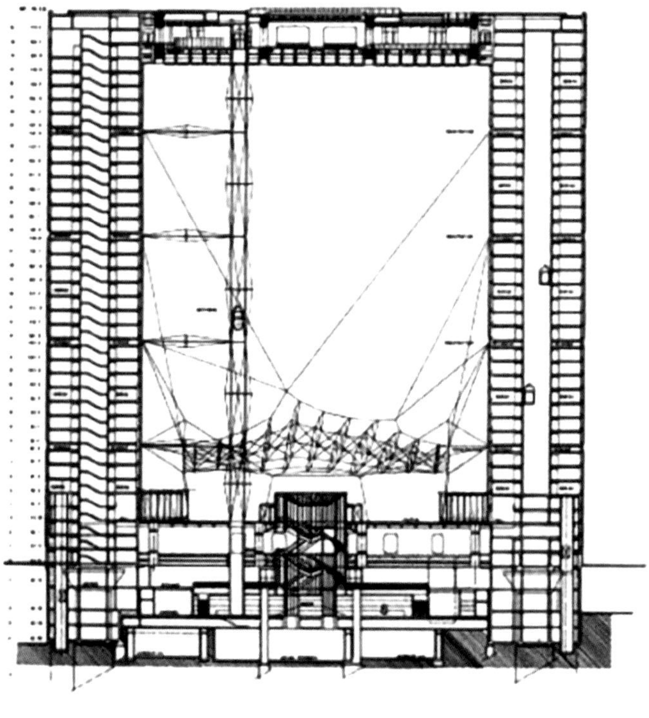

Opposite Page La Grande Arche de la Défense. Von Spreckelsen and Andreu, 1982–1989 100-meter cube. **Bottom** Map of Axe Historique, Paris. Courtesy of Wikipedia.

Left La Grande Arche de la Défense, section. Von Spreckelsen, Andreu and Rice, 1982–1989.

Columbus Center, Manhattan. Moshe Safdie Architects, 1985–1987

With Habitat 1967, his first architectural work, Moshe Safdie demonstrated that he was capable of producing perhaps the highest level of architectural creativity—typological innovation. In that noted project, Safdie demonstrated that the infrastructural form of high-level, high-density housing was capable of supporting certain of the attributes of low-density housing. Village qualities, personal space, and design flexibility might also be achieved at high density. With the unbuilt project for Columbus Center in New York, he again demonstrated the achievement of typological innovation in the creation of what can be identified as one of the first tower clusters. Without considering the critical controversy associated with Columbus Center at that time, we will briefly present the project and introduce the importance of this typological contribution.

Columbus Center was a high-rise, high-density project located at Columbus Circle in New York City. The towers are sixty-two and sixty-nine stories high and are connected by a skybridge at the 39th floor. At the base

there is a four-story-high atrium connecting the towers. At the street entrance side there is a large public galleria/commercial mall which follows the geometry of the circle. The components of the tower cluster are a duo of towers, connected by a skybridge, and at ground level, the base responds to the urban condition with a multilevel mall providing an interior alternate movement system to the street. The Center project thus includes *a strong interface with the urban content of the site*, a condition which must be considered one of the important potential attributes of each tower cluster.

The crescent element of the base also has a sky garden located on its roof. The provision of such urban amenities to the city are possible because of the high density of the urban complex. The connection with, and contribution to, the development of the urban context is one of the important potential attributes of the tower cluster. Each tower cluster always makes a potential contribution to the strengthening and further development of the urban context. Furthermore, in Columbus Center's main entrance, Safdie demonstrates that the individual components of the tower cluster are independently adaptable to diverse urban contextual conditions and geometries.

Both of these early examples of the emergence of the tower cluster are notable for their contributions (the first actual; the second as design concept) to the urban structure of the cities of Paris and New York. It is the scale, density, and typical multifunctional program of the tower cluster that justifies and encourages the interaction between private architectural functions and public users, between private architectural spaces and functions. This leads us to the conclusion that in any future city the tower cluster typology can potentially make an important contribution to the ideal of urban connectivity.

Opposite Page Columbus Center, New York City, model photograph. Safdie Architects, 1985–1987 Courtesy of Safdie Architects.

Above Left Columbus Center, New York City, photomontage. Safdie Architects, 1985–1987. Courtesy of Safdie Architectsz.
Above Right Columbus Center, New York City, interior view of galleria. Safdie Architects, 1985–1987. Colored pencil rendering courtesy of Safdie Architects

Petronas Twin Towers, Kuala Lumpur, Malaysia. César Pelli, 1998

Petronas Twin Towers is a double tower grouping with a prominent two-story skybridge functioning mainly as an observation deck. There is a public base element common to the two towers and composed of a relatively simple geometry. The towers are used as office buildings. They are the tallest twin towers in the world.[3]

The identical towers were designed with the intention of producing a symbol of the emerging importance of Malaysia as an eastern nation-state. The design attempts to exploit Islamic symbolism in the formation of the shape of the towers' periphery and silhouette. The project was started in 1992 and completed in 1998. The towers contain eighty-eight stories above grade and five stories below grade.

The skybridge on floors 41 and 42 provides a linkage between the large half-floor sky lobbies existing in each tower. Thus the 41st floor of both towers is in the form of a dumbbell. It provides a public amenity of significant scale, the existence of which does not interrupt the repetitive quality of the building elevation. Level 41 is considered the "podium" for accessing the upper levels of the cluster. The skybridge with its two inclined supporting braces creates a prominent archlike symbol of the tower cluster. There is another sky lobby on the 86th floor of tower 2. There are conference areas and a lounge on floors 85 and 86, and a lounge and observatory deck on the 83rd floor.

The large, symmetrically organized base beneath the towers contains five stories of public facilities. These include a large multilevel shopping mall and a philharmonic hall. There is also a public gallery, an aquarium, and a science center. In addition to these facilities in the base, there is also a seventeen-acre park.

Left Petronas: A canonic tower cluster.

Opposite Page Petronas Twin Towers, Kuala Lumpur, Malaysia. César Pelli Architect, 1998.

Azrieli Center, Tel Aviv, Israel. 1996–1999

The developer of this innovative tower cluster, built in Tel Aviv in the last decade of the twentieth century, was the remarkable businessman, designer, and architect David Azrieli. Born in Poland, he wandered through various lands to avoid the Nazis during World War II, eventually arriving in Israel. Between 1943 and 1946 he studied architecture at the Technion-Israel Institute of Technology. In 1948 he fought and was wounded in Israel's War of Independence. In 1954 he emigrated to Canada, where he began a business as a real estate developer. Beginning with housing, first low-rise and then high-rise, he eventually began to develop enclosed shopping centers in Canada.

In the early 1980s, Azrieli brought his developmental and design expertise back to his homeland. In 1985 he opened Israel's first enclosed shopping mall, the Ayalon Mall in the city of Ramat Gan, not far from Tel Aviv. He began to develop other malls throughout the country, which created a revolution in retailing there. In the 1990s he changed Tel Aviv's skyline and urban image with the development of a true tower cluster prototype—Azrieli Center, which was to become the iconic image of the city.

The Azrieli Center is composed of a tight cluster of three towers—a circle, a square, and a triangular tower. The tallest of the three is a circular tower forty-nine stories high. At the time of its construction, it was the tallest building in Tel Aviv and the second-tallest in Israel. It is 187 meters tall, or 614 feet. The top floor has an indoor observation deck and an exclusive restaurant with views of the city. The triangular tower is 169 meters in height, or 554 feet. It has forty-six floors and was completed in 1999. The square tower was the last completed component of the cluster in 2007. It has forty-two floors and is 145 meters high. In addition to office space, the square tower also includes a hotel which occupies the lower thirteen floors.

The uniformity of the window wall system of the towers creates a remarkable level of visual and formal consistency to the complex. This attribute of an internalized sense of formal consistency will become a leading attribute of the typology. Another important characteristic is the integration with the urban transportation system. There a prominent station of

Above Azrieli Center, Tel Aviv. Eli Attia Architects and Moore Yaski Sivan Architects, 1996–1999. **Right** Tower plans as part of the symbol of the Azrieli Foundation.

Opposite Page Azrieli Center Spiral Tower, Tel Aviv. KPF and Moshe Zur Architects, 2018–2025. View of scrolling tower with existing towers, perspective by KPF. **Bottom** Azrieli Center Spiral Tower, Tel Aviv. KPF and Moshe Zur Architects, 2018–2025. View of area, perspective by KPF.

Pages 52-53 Azrieli Center Spiral Tower, Tel Aviv. KPF and Moshe Zur Architects, 2018–2025. Entrance to new shopping area, perspective by KPF.

Fondation
Azrieli
Foundation

the public transportation system at the center with a bridge leading into its base. The adjacency to a major highway also provides a convenient and direct entrance to the large parking base of the center. The base's most prominent occupant is one of the largest enclosed multilevel urban shopping centers in Israel.

The Azrieli Center's New Centerpiece

The iconic Azrieli Center, the third tower of which was completed in 2007, is currently in the process of being expanded, with the addition of a fourth tower. The design architect of the addition is KPF—Kohn Pedersen Fox—whose main office is in New York City. The Israeli architect for coordination, construction implementation, and supervision is MTA—Moshe Tzur Architect of Tel Aviv. The fourth tower, which is elliptical in plan form and spiral in overall shape, will be 340 meters high when completed in 2025. It will have ninety-one stories.[4]

Functional Contents

This is a mixed-use development (MUD). The upper levels of smaller floor plates as the spiral scroll closes are devoted to residential and a hotel. The tower is designed to accommodate 65,000 square meters of office space, 17,000 square meters of residential space, 15,000 square meters of hotel, and 15,000 square meters of commercial space. The peak of the spiral is designed to accommodate a dramatic outlook space providing a 360-degree view. At the pinnacle it will also provide public spaces for gathering and entertainment. The notable urban precinct with its concentration of high-density functions is also well served by excellent and immediate connections to stations of public transit lines.

AZRIELI CENTER

Design Strategy

The exterior wall surface of the scroll is a screenlike pattern that resembles the grid window pattern of the three towers of the existing center. This screen/scroll is the formal element that begins by wrapping the base of the existing center and then continues to scroll upward, creating a decreasing circumference for the new tower and its floor plates. This formal element of the continuous wrapping screen, as seen in the photograph below, is the medium of visual unification of the expanded Azrieli center into a newly unified whole. This symbolism of the dynamic scroll is also intended to convey a sense of the extended center as an epicenter of activity in Tel Aviv.

There are numerous other examples similar to tower clusters that share some, but not all, of the characteristics of the tower structure. For example, Rappongi Hills Complex in Tokyo, containing the fifty-four-story Mori tower, high-rise residential towers, a shopping center, observatory, and art museum, has been referred to as a "self-contained micro-city," and is such an example. However, its lack of the formal and spatial integration of the diverse tower elements and base elements is missing certain essential and defining characteristics.

2.3 Typological Innovation and the Creation of a Prototype

What is creativity in architecture? This is a question of great complexity due to the variety of diverse attributes that are usually associated with architecture. This variety of attributes can range from the iconic quality attributed to the work of architecture (the Guggenheim Museum, Bilbao, by Frank Gehry), the historical importance of the work (the Unité of Le Corbusier, or the Seagram Building, New York, by Mies van der Rohe), the uniquely outstanding formal beauty of the design or designs (Vitra Campus Architecture, Germany, by Zaha Hadid, Frank Gehry, and others), the genius of structural integration as a significant component of architectural design (Santiago Calatrava's Oculus at the World Trade Center in New York), the powerful symbolic quality and monumental power of the design (Peter Eisenman's Monument for the Six Million in Berlin, or Daniel Libeskind's Jewish Museum, also in Berlin), and so forth. The question is very complex, and the list of potential attributes signifying greatness of historically outstanding quality is extensive.

How disciplinary knowledge can be defined in architecture is also, surprisingly, a problematic question. Among the large number of root qualities of creativity in architecture, typological innovation can be proposed as a unique attribute of architecture's disciplinary knowledge. The understanding of the knowledge associated with the various typologies of building types is undoubtedly a powerful class of disciplinary knowledge in architecture. While other subjects, such as structural design, are considered important parts of the knowledge galaxy of architecture, it is typological knowledge—the knowledge and understanding of a variety of central

Opposite Page Peter Eisenman, Monument to the Murdered Jews of Europe, Berlin, Germany, 2005.

building types—that links architectural knowledge and theories to the process of design. This is one of the universal fundamentals of architectural education throughout the world: the theoretical bonding linkage between the classroom and the so-called design studio. Despite the fact that few students understand this central truth while they are in the process of studying architecture, this connection between theoretical knowledge and the design process is the foundation of architectural education.

If typological knowledge—the knowledge and understanding of building types—is a central class of architectural knowledge, what constitutes typological innovation? How can a new typology be defined? In the previous chapter we identified the concept of the building section combined with the specific duplex apartment section in Le Corbusier's Unité building in Marseilles, France as a pivotal design concept that inspired a younger generation of European architects to pursue the implication of that concept in the realization of streets in the sky in multifamily housing. This emerged as both social as well as urban content in what became a new scale of the architectural typology of high-rise multifamily housing structures. We also recall that the Unité had other communal functions such as a public roof terrace, kindergarten, and shops, which were intended to strengthen the collective social content of the new typology. So the building typology contains more than classes of organization of typical programmatic spaces. Typological innovation contains organizational, functional, structural, and formal change. Typological innovation is a high level of a unique combination of significant typological content.

In order to continue to establish what constitutes the achievement of typological invention as one of the highest forms of architectural creativity, we have so far determined that a high level of change within or between the constituents of the typology must be achieved. The scales of change may be defined as: typological variation; typological adaptation; typological transformation; and typological invention, or innovation. These levels, or scales, of typological change may be defined as follows:

Typological Variation

The application of a minor variation in one of the design variables of the typology without changing the definition and/or relationship of the constituent elements of the typology. For example, the modification of the apartment form or layout of the apartment in a multifamily, high-rise housing block such as the Unité, while still maintaining the sectional principle and the general form of the dwelling section as a duplex.

Typological Adaptation

The typological modification of one of the constituent elements of the typology, such as the circulation system, while maintaining all other elements and basic relationships of the typology. For example, modification of corridor location at the building exterior instead of the interior (as in the precedent work of Le Corbusier, the Unité), and change of corridor width, as at Alison and Peter Smithson's Robin Hood Gardens project in London. Rather than creating a conventional corridor, or "interior street," as noted in Le Corbusier's sketch of the building section, it aspires to become a movement system possessed of the views, spatial width and appropriate relationships capable of fostering community-like social relationships characteristic of a public street.

Typological Transformation

One of the important characteristic spatial/functional elements of the typology is significantly modified in form, characteristic location, and also, possibly, functional contents.

For example, the modification by addition or subtraction of a significant functional component of the typology. A notable example of typological transformation is Moisei Ginzburg's Narkomfin Building of 1932. This building was acknowledged as a precedent for many of the key concepts of Le Corbusier's Unité d'Habitation of 1952. Narkomfin has five inhabited floors, an intermediate two of which are accessed by staircases rather than by elevator stops. The building has "strip windows" (i.e., no structural interruptions in the plane of the continuous horizontal windows), and there was planned to be a penthouse designed as a communal recreation area. Most significantly, it has an attached separate wing for public collective dining and other public communal functions.

Typological Invention

A major scale of organizational and/or functional change of the typology that in fact establishes a new typology. For example, the major modification of the dwelling types and organizational system of high-rise buildings while maintaining the conventional circulation system. Moshe Safdie is distinguished as a brilliant typological innovator, as we have already observed above in his project for Columbus Circle, New York City. His first work as an architect, when he was only some few months out of school, was the Habitat 67 building at the international Expo of 1967 in Montreal.

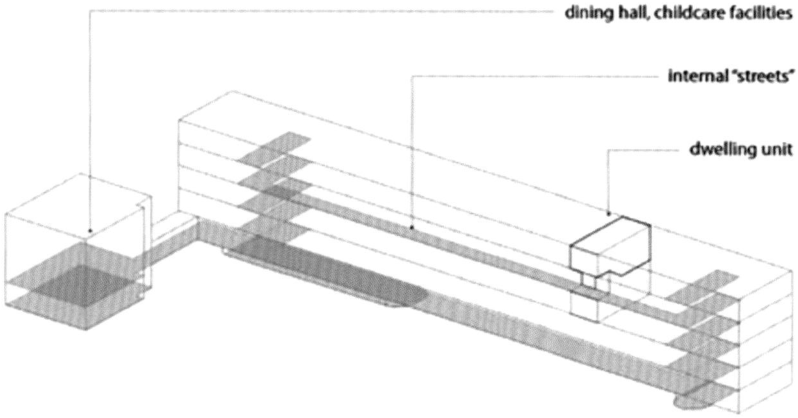

Above Narkomfin Building, Moscow, diagram. Moisei Ginzburg, 1932. **Bottom** Narkomfin Building, Moscow, perspective. Moisei Ginzburg, 1932.

In this building, Safdie employed the concept of housing as being composed of an infrastructural model of a structural and circulation system plus a housing organizational system. In the Habitat neighborhood at the Expo site in Montreal, Safdie employed a characteristic infrastructure with a skip-stop circulation system. However, the housing organizational system is transformed from the compact packing of a characteristic housing block to an open spatial organization of independent, three-dimensional housing modules.

We must recall that the post-Corbusian British housing designs were contemporaneous: Smithson's Golden Lane project in London is from 1952, Park Hill in Sheffield is from 1961, and the Smithsons' Robin Hood Gardens is from 1972. This was during the height of the theoretical and disciplinary importance of Team X, and among Safdie's teachers during his thesis project was Blanche Lemco van Ginkel, who was an active member of Team X. This closes the circle of precedent generative design concepts.

This work was also designed during a period of high professional interest in prefabrication. The combination of influential concepts contributed to a creative leap of great magnitude: the streets in the air model becomes the supporting infrastructure for what is, effectively, *a village in the sky*.

In the case of Habitat as a case of typological innovation, one may question the validity of the attribution of typological innovation in a situation in which the original project was followed by a succession of typologically related projects based upon the typology, though few, if any, were actually realized.[5]

Above Habitat 67, Montreal Expo, Canada. Moshe Safdie Architect, 1967. Photo by James Brittain.

Opposite Page Van Ginkel with Le Corbusier at the Unité in Marseilles, France, 1959.

We have observed above that Safdie's typological transformational creativity continued in the case of, for example, the unbuilt project for Columbus Center, 1985–1987. This project for a cluster of two towers on the prominent Manhattan site at Columbus Circle contained a complex base structure, internal interconnection between the towers, and other components of the tower cluster typology, including multifunctionality.

2.4 The Destruction and Reconstruction of the World Trade Center

The terrorist attack on the World Trade Center on September 11, 2001 was an attempt to symbolically shatter the image of American world dominance and geographical presence, as well as its image as the leading international commercial power. The destruction of the towers was an attempt to destroy what had emerged as a powerful symbol of that economic and technological leadership—the skyscraper. The process of reconstruction had, among others, two important objectives. Firstly, there was a pressing national motivation to memorialize the loss of life and the symbolic presence of place at the site. Secondly, there existed a need to use the symbolic power of the vertically unlimited reach of the tall building to prove that the United States was still powerfully and creatively present. Thus, these symbolic motivations for the reconstruction of the site were present throughout this historic process.

From the point of view of typological innovations in skyscraper form, this long, complex, arduous, and controversial process has certain pivotal developments, as well as seminal design agents. We shall only concentrate on those incidents in the long process that are seminal for our theoretical search for typological developments.

The slow job of clearing and repairing the site required full-time work for eight months. In August, 2002 there began a design study for the future development of the site by a diverse group of invited design firms. Ultimately, seven architectural firms were invited to compete to become master plan architect for the new World Trade Center:

- Foster + Partners
- Studio Daniel Libeskind
- Peter Eisenman, Richard Meier, Charles Gwathmey, and Steven Holl
- Peterson Littenberg
- Skidmore, Owings & Merrill (SOM)
- Shigeru Ban, Frederic Schwartz, Ken Smith, and Rafael Viñoly (Think team)
- United Architects

Among the seven entries there were several proposals for linked towers. Both the Foster proposal and the Think team proposal were designs for sky-bridge-linked pairs of towers that dominate the site. The SOM proposal was distinctive in being a large, tight cluster of multiple bent towers.

The Eisenman, Meier, Gwathmey, and Holl team proposal was also typologically exceptional in its attempt to achieve a formally integrated cluster appearing as a vertical grid with the vertical elements dominant and the horizontal bridge links unifying the design into two clusters of vertical elements.

From this process, two finalists, the Think team and Studio Daniel Libeskind, were selected. On February 27, 2003, Studio Daniel Libeskind won the competition to become the master planner for the redesign of the WTC site.

Of all the seven proposals for the reconstruction of the site, the Libeskind proposal has five tower elements surrounding the prominent subsite given over to the memorial and museum for the destroyed tower sites.

Opposite Page The Twin Towers of the World Trade Center under attack, 09/11/2001.

Left World Trade Center master plan design of Studio Daniel Libeskind. Model photo by Jock Pottle courtesy of Studio Daniel Libeskind.

While WTC 1 is given the vertical prominence, the footprints of the destroyed twin towers are given a prominent landscape presence. In the Libeskind scheme, it is the meaningful memorial significance of this proposal that perhaps makes it a most suitable as well as developmentally flexible solution for the whole site. That is, the multiple towers are each physically independent. This enables the final form and expression of the towers to be determined as required. Ultimately, each of the towers was designed by a different architect with Libeskind's role limited to that of master planner.

In retrospect, this tragic historic event ultimately provided an opportunity for New York to develop a major urban spatial composition for the city as well as an important memorial site. The process of reconstruction established a unique opportunity for the theoretical rethinking of skyscraper design as well as its urban spatial and formal connections. Libeskind's selection as master planner was conservative from a typological point of view, and perhaps among all of the proposals of the competition it proved to be highly manageable and flexible in the complex decision-making context of the situation.

Of all the designs in the competition, it was the Eisenman, Meier, Gwathmey, Holl proposal that attempted to grasp this historic opportunity in order to find a new typology for the skyscraper—in this case as two connected clusters—thus achieving in 2002 the phenomenon of closely grouped and connected towers, a typology which we have referred to as the tower cluster.

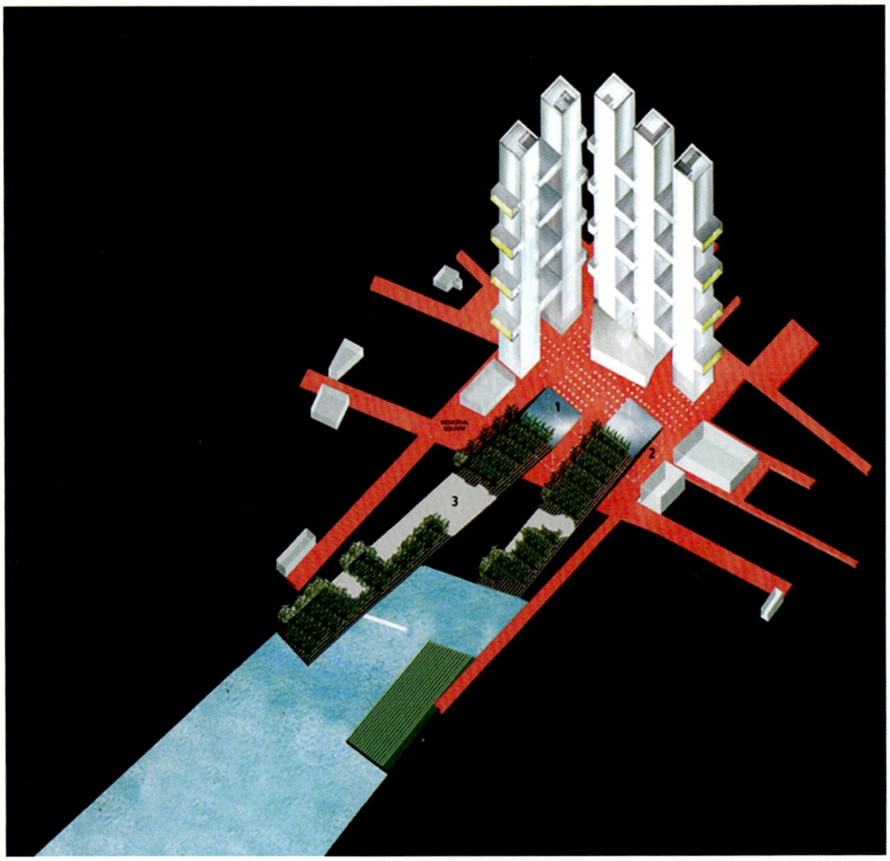

Opposite Page World Trade Center design by Eisenman, Meier, Gwathmey, and Holl. Model photo by Eisenman Architects. **Bottom** Memorial Square at WTC. Eisenman, Meier, Gwathmey, and Holl. Illustration by Eisenman Architects.

Above Reconstruction of the WTC Site with Towers by David Childs of SOM (1),Richard Rogers (3), Maki (4). A proposal for a fifth tower (2) was designed by BIG. Construction of WTC 1, also called the Freedom Tower, was 2006 to 2014. Photo courtesy of DBOXC.

2.5 The Crystallization of the Morphology of the Tower Cluster

The morphology of the tower cluster has a clearly achieved definition by the end of the twentieth century. We can postulate that at this point there were two opposing morphological subtypes: the *geometric model* and the *numerical model.*

The Geometric Model

The tower, or slab, high-rise elements are connected by a public element of large scale and a base element to create a geometrically pure architectural volumetric form. For example, the Grande Arche in Paris is an open-ended cube in which two slabs of office space on the sides are connected above by a roof element containing public spaces and functions, and below by basement spaces and additional functions.

The Numerical Model

This is a simple and direct expression of the numerical components of the towers. For example, the Petronas Towers in Kuala Lumpur, Malaysia clearly represents a statement of the duo of two identical towers superimposed on a common public base and joined by a skybridge. We shall observe from the case studies that it is possible for the numerical model also to have a superimposed major horizontal element such as a sky plaza (see 2.5.5 Marina Bay Sands below). It is possible to consider such cases as a third major subtype of the tower cluster.

The prototypical expression of the two subtype models has evolved dramatically over the period of evolution of the tower cluster during the past two decades. These mutations each explore the potential for development within the basic format of the definition of the typology. Before beginning the presentation and analysis of recent outstanding cases of the tower cluster it is important to clarify certain points regarding the architectural content of the typology.

In an important recent research study published by the CTBUH and written by Wood, Du and Safarik (2020), the presence of skybridges is considered one of the key elements in the architecture of the tower cluster as well as a key to the potential future contribution of tower clusters to the achievement of urban connectivity. Given that skybridges have been demonstrated to be structurally problematic elements due to the swaying of tall towers (see, for example, the structural design of the Petronas Towers skybridge), we have chosen to present skybridges as potential elements of the tower cluster rather than essential components. The tower cluster requires horizontal connectivity, though not necessarily by means of an upper-level skybridge as compared to the horizontal extension of part of the base structure. It should also be clear from the case study of Steven Holl's Linked Hybrid project that the presence of a skybridge does not necessarily constitute a tower cluster. Tower clusters without skybridges, for example in the Azrieli Center in Tel Aviv, possess and continue to demonstrate their potential for horizontal connectivity.

The components of the morphology as already presented include the vertical elements of towers, slabs, and other vertical elements such as stepped, inclined organization; the above-grade common base elements of multiple levels; some form of bridging medium, be it a skybridge or the roof structure, or other structure, of the base element; the cluster amenities such as sky plazas, sky pools, etc. The invention and elaboration of what we have referred to as tower cluster amenities will become an important class of contribution in the case studies below. A detailed presentation of two pioneering prototypes of the typology is given early in the presentation of case studies: these are the integrated resort Marina Bay Sands, which was completed in 2010 in Singapore; and Raffles City, the mixed-use, high-density urban center in Chongqing, China, which was completed in 2020. Other recent examples of tower clusters will be presented and analyzed. We also outline the method, objectives, and expected applications for the development of a typology of the tower cluster as an important emerging urban form.

It is with the beginning of the second decade of the twenty-first century that we can say that there is a true crystallization of the tower cluster as a unique typological and programmatic phenomenon of architecture and urbanism. Over the second decade it becomes rapidly clear that among certain of architecture's prominent and more experimental firms there is emerging a unique interest in this promising typology. As a reflection of the growing interest in this new medium of architecture and urbanism, we have selected fifteen prominent examples of the investigative blooming of this new typology. This presentation of tower cluster prototypes also introduces us to an important contribution to what might be termed the *Far Eastern architectural/urban renaissance*.

List of Prominent Tower Clusters since 2010

Building types constitute a fundamental class of architectural knowledge. Yet all knowledge is an unstable proposition, open to interpretation, modification, and innovation. This challenge to replicate, to reinterpret, and to invent always exists in the intellectual realm of typology. The underlying questions of form and meaning are also always present and seeking consideration, though rarely explicit in the architectural program.

The tower cluster is an emergent architectural/urban morphological typology rather than merely a building type. However, it is experimental building typologies that are the counter-form of functional building types. To invent a typological class is a form of conceptual invention, which is, in turn, a form of knowledge creation. It is these high-level processes of knowledge invention and formulation that we can observe in the following recent prominent projects for tower clusters.

Case Studies: Prominent Tower Clusters since 2010

OMA

CCTV Headquarters, Beijing, China, 2002–2012
Continuous 3-D Geometric Model

De Rotterdam, Rotterdam, Netherlands, 1997–2013
Linear Trio Tower Cluster with Linked Base

CMG Qianhai Global Trade Center, Shenzhen, China, from 2016
Integration of Tower Structure, Sky Structure, Urban Structure

VDMA Van der Meulen-Ansemsterrein, Eindhoven, Netherlands, from 2020
The Microforest as a Multi-Element Tower Structure

Safdie Architects

Marina Bay Sands, Singapore, 2010
Horizontally Continuous Sky Structure and Base Structure

Sky Habitat, Singapore, 2016
Sky Pool and Public Exterior Garden Elements as Skybridges

Raffles City, Chongqing, China, 2020
Horizontally Continuous Enclosed Sky Structure

ORCA Toronto, Canada, from 2021
Multifunctional Continuous Development through Major Urban Park

Zaha Hadid

Galaxy Soho, Beijing, China, 2009–2012
Tower Cluster with Four Linked Dome-Shaped Towers

Wangjing Soho, Beijing, China, 2009–2014
Tower Cluster with Linked Base

Nanjing International Youth Cultural Center, Nanjing, China, 2011–2018
Tower Cluster with Linked Base

OPPO Headquarters, Shenzen, China, from 2020
Tower Cluster with Linked Base and Amplified Envelope

Tower C at Shenzen Bay Super Headquarters, Shenzen, China, from 2021
Tower Cluster open heart public spaces are integrated with urban landscape

Ole Scheeren

Duo Twin Towers, Singapore, 2021
Tower Cluster as Medium of Urban Reconstruction

FOSTER + PARTNERS ARCHITECTS
DJI Headquarters, Shenzhen, China, 2022
Tower Cluster as High-Tech Office Headquarters with R+D Units

2.5.1 CCTV Headquarters, Beijing, China, 2002–2012, OMA[7]

Introduction: The Outdated Typology of the Skyscraper

Where might the *theoretical origins* of a new typology of the skyscraper as a high-rise, high-density urban structure be found, and what new formal and functional characteristics, or constituent parts, or constructive urban elements might it contain? The answer is, perhaps, best found in an insightful critique of the skyscraper as a typology for which the true contemporary utility value has long since evaporated. Where, when, and by whom can such meaningful typological critique be identified?

So, historically the question became: How do we transcend the dominant model of the skyscraper? An answer emerged from the writings of one of the leading theoretical voices of the period, Rem Koolhaas of OMA/AMO. His critique and new theory of the skyscraper is explicated by Ingrid Böck in her incisive and analytical 2015 book on Koolhaas, *Six Canonical Projects by Rem Koolhaas: Essays on the History of Ideas*. The chapter entitled "The Outdated Typology of the Skyscraper" lays out Koolhaas's long history of theoretical writings concerning the concepts and the means of achieving a new approach to the skyscraper; first, as a critique of the limitations of the *endless vertical tower* tradition of the existing skyscraper, and then, related to this definition of the outdatedness of the typology, the effort to create a new typology.

According to Böck's presentation of Koolhaas's writings, "he fundamentally questions the typology of the free-standing, or autarkic, tower." In *Content* (Koolhaas, 2004), he refers to the constant repetitive reuse of this view of the stagnated skyscraper form as "repetitive banality." Beyond simply a critique of traditional skyscraper form, he points toward the general necessity to question and to transcend the continued validity of normative architectural form.

What then are the possible new directions of the skyscraper? What is proposed by Koolhaas is an arrangement of multiple, mutually supportive towers. The ensuing ensemble of towers should also provide a system of *vertical and horizontal connections* that creates fluid circulation inside the whole arrangement. He has referred to such a new typological system as "Hypertowers."

Among the many significant attributes of the definitions towards defining this newly emerging typological designation of the urban tall building is that new urban complexes such as the CCTV building complex can also form a *new urban icon* for the city in an important district of emerging new urbanism in Beijing. The proposed formal organization also functions to provide a significant urban symbolic role in this emerging business district.

In CCTV, the proposed new formal species of urban ensemble building incorporates all of the highly diverse functions of a national media center in a single unified form. This highly multifunctional tall building form includes manufacturing, technical development, recording, display, and administration—that is, a highly vertically integrated synthesis of elements. This systems characteristic is also present in much of the rapidly developing technological sector as represented in many of the following case studies.

Far beyond the race for simply "taller and taller" skyscrapers, Koolhaas also questions the limited vision of the current undeveloped urban role or cultural contribution of the conventional skyscraper. If in his view the skyscraper is the ultimate typology of the city, in what ways can a new typology of the skyscraper contribute to what he sees as the requirement for new forms of provision of adaptive urban spaces in the city?

This vision may be satisfied by what he refers to as the *skyscraper loop*, or the *bent skyscraper*. Such characteristics in a new typological form may be what he sought to suggest in the Hyper building for Bangkok project of 1996 (see below) as "seeking a self-contained metropolis within a single building."

At last, in this generative typological process, we can ultimately identify the genetic formulae of a great period of urban typological inventiveness. Beyond the case of this emerging typology, Koolhaas's theoretical contributions also represent an example of an intellectual means to the potential fulfillment of a major contemporary necessity of the professional culture of urbanism/architecture: the rethinking of the intellectual foundations of the discipline.

These concepts for a new genesis of constructive urban form are part of the conceptually important modernization of Chinese, as well as Asian, urban/architectural space. We shall observe this throughout the case studies as one of the major contributions of the emerging new typology of tall building urban form. To some extent, most of the case studies all share this impetus towards typological creativity. To a great extent, this impetus is also a component in the tale of what might be termed *the Chinese Renaissance*.

After the emergence of various exploratory formal statements of linked towers in the last two decades of the twentieth century, there now begin to emerge three main prototypes of a new skyscraper typology in the first two decades of the new millennium:

- Linked Towers
- Linked Towers capped by a dominant horizontal element(s)
- Linked Towers in a holistic, regular, geometric statement

In the first two decades of the new millennium, this experimentation is frequent and begins to evolve as a new architectural high-density, high-rise urban form. As has been stated, this developing typology is of both architectural and urban significance. This current work is a research-based attempt to trace the history and define the new typology which has been achieved within the culture of international architecture by what was found to be a small group of inventively distinguished architectural firms.

Opposite Page CCTV Headquarters, Beijing, China. Design 2002–2004. Construction 2004–2012. OMA Architects. Photo courtesy of Freepik.com

Secondly, this research results in the definition of the typology, its multiple typical subsystems, its diverse formal and functional components, and its major subtypes.

We have named the new typology the tower cluster, and it is herewith identified in its historical evolution, its emergence, and its formal and typological crystallization. This crystallization, as previously defined in detail, essentially consists of the following integrated group of essential components which together contribute to a new typology:

- A common *typological structure;*
- A *vertical campus* of vertically distributed urban scale sites within the structure;
- An *amenities revolution* of the vertical distribution of programmatic functional amenities for various important urban functional types such as residential or office structures;
- The definition of the tower cluster as the emerging major high-density urban building type of the twenty-first century;
- An explication of *typological knowledge* of the new building type as essential knowledge for the creative realization of important *emerging subtypes* of the tower cluster. Without a typological knowledge definition such as is created by this book, emerging examples may be formally interesting, but lacking in any meaningful contribution to the creative evolution of the typology.

a. Geometric Cubical Order/Double Tower Cluster: Introduction

The design of the building for the Chinese national television (China Central Television) headquarters was an attempt by OMA to redesign the form of the skyscraper as a building type. We have previously defined the two primary models of the tower cluster type as *classical* or *numerical* (defined by tower number) and *geometrical* (defined by geometric form). CCTV is an attempt to employ the latter model in order to achieve a significantly unique approach to skyscraper form. Geometrically, it is a skeletal cubical form in which the connection between base form and the elaborated top levels are the supportive elements of the twin towers. CCTV was one of the first of the many new towers to rise in the Beijing CBD. In 2013, the CCTV Headquarters building won the award for the Best Tall Building of the year from the CTBUH, Council on Tall Buildings and Urban Habitat.

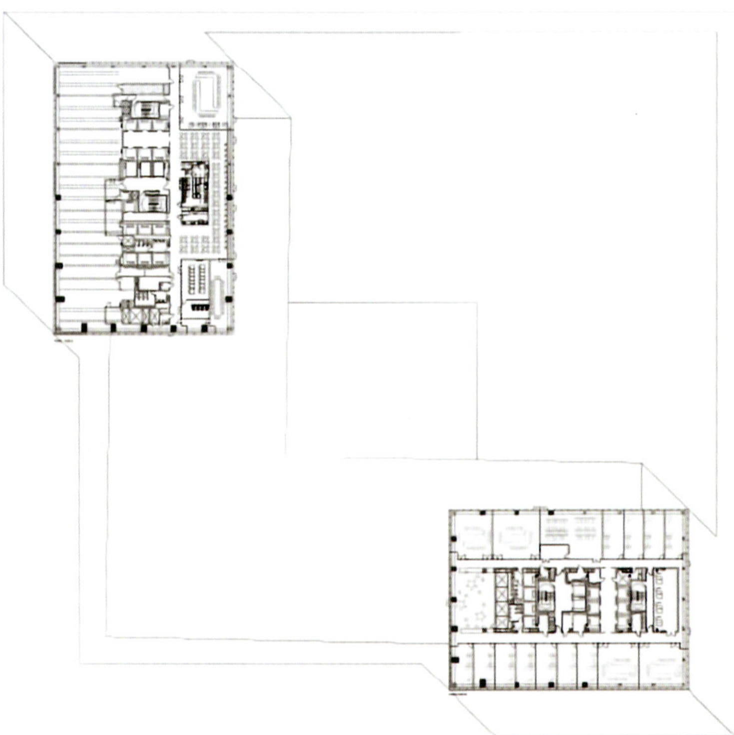

Above CCTV Headquarters, Beijing, China. OMA, 2002–2012. Photo courtesy of Phillippe Ruault.
Right CCTV Headquarters, Beijing, China, floor plan level 25. OMA, 2002–2012. Courtesy of OMA.

Opposite Page CCTV Headquarters, Beijing, China. OMA, 2002–2012. Photo courtesy of Gili Merin.

The use of this unusual architectural form creates a "loop," or continuity, of the diverse functions of the headquarters building. We have seen above that La Grande Arche de la Défense is also a continuous loop tower cluster.

b. Geometric Cubical Order for the Double Tower: Program

The design of the building for the Chinese national television headquarters is a consolidation in one building of the diverse functional components that were previously located in various sites in Beijing. Its 473,000 square meters of functional space includes not only administration and offices, but also studios, program production facilities and services, broadcasting, and theater facilities. The tower is 234 meters high (768 feet), and has fifty-one stories.

The building serves approximately ten thousand staff members. The major production facilities are in the base, a part of which is underground. In general, one tower functions as space for services, research, and education, while the other provides broadcasting facilities. The upper horizontal cantilevered layer serves management and provides public access spaces. In general, the building is a secure facility. However, there is a special pathway for public access that provides insights into the processes involved in TV production as well as access to large audience studios. The upper levels also offer spectacular views over the city.

The two fifty-story legs function primarily as office space and production studios. The northwest tower has both offices and production, while the southeast tower is mainly office space. Escalators from the underground station lead to the main lobby. Below the lobby space is an exhibition area. Above and overlooking the lobby is a VIP lounge. On the roof of the base section is an exterior garden for employees. On the upper floors are the director's offices and apartment, VIP dining room and, on the roof, a helipad. The upper bridge element also contains a large public observation area.

c. Siting and Extended Program

The building is located on East Third Road and Guanghua Road in the Central Business District of Beijing. It is adjacent to the new building for the Television Cultural Center, which was also designed by OMA as part of the original contract. This is an adjunct facility for the CCTV and contains a hotel, a theater, and several studios. On the site plan, the TVCC is north of the CCTV.[8] The building has an attached subway stop.

Right CCTV Headquarters, Beijing, China, landscape plan. OMA, 2002–2012. Courtesy of OMA.

d. Tower Cluster Contributions

- **The Tower Cluster as Endless Form**
  The cubic geometry and the dual towers provide a continuous movement system through the interrelated components of the TV production and public delivery system. The formal and spatial character of the building's components reflect this system as a collective productive entity.

- **The Tower Cluster as Symbolic System**
  The unique formal character contributes considerable symbolic power to this important public facility. Here the tower cluster form provides multiple and different possible interpretations. However, no other contemporary building has so strongly come to symbolize Beijing's movement into the future.

- **Amenities in Ancillary Building**
  TVCC is an adjacent building which was a part of the original program. The intention of this adjunct is to provide special facilities for, among others, visitors to CCTV. Among these are a hotel and other functions that do not normally relate to the ongoing functions of the main building.

- **The Tower Cluster as Multiple Privacy Paths**
  The tower cluster can provide a medium of multiple circulation paths throughout the facility. These generally provide differing access for different employee classes.

2.5.2 De Rotterdam, Rotterdam, Netherlands, OMA. Design 1997–1998. Construction 2009–2013.

a. De Rotterdam as a Vertical City: Introduction

De Rotterdam is a linear tower cluster of three adjacent towers. It was designed by the Office for Metropolitan Architecture (OMA) beginning in 1997. Construction was delayed until 2009 for economic reasons. It was completed in 2013. The north elevation of the building is sited along a harbor pier (Wilhelminapier) at a prominent and highly visible location in the city. At the time of its construction, it was the largest building in the Netherlands at approximately 160,000 square meters. The tower cluster is forty-four stories high and reaches a height of 150 meters. The total mass of the three towers reads as a single vibrant body of inflected submasses which imbue the structure with a powerful symbolic urban connotation. It is a waterfront architecture in which the modulated solidity of the total building appears totally appropriate.

b. De Rotterdam as a Vertical City: Program

The theme of the vertical city is founded, in the rationale of OMA, on a series of urban architectural concepts that are characteristic of the tower

Above De Rotterdam, Rotterdam, Netherlands. OMA, 1997–2013.

Opposite Page De Rotterdam, Rotterdam, Netherlands, perspective plan high-rise. OMA, 1997–2013. Courtesy of OMA. **Above Left** De Rotterdam, Rotterdam, Netherlands, program isometry. OMA, 1997–2013. Courtesy of OMA. **Bottom** De Rotterdam, Rotterdam, Netherlands, program section. OMA, 1997–2013. Courtesy of OMA.

cluster. First of all is the attempt to achieve density and functional diversity within the architectural matrix of a compact multistructural entity. This vertical city contains work as well as living; it has a complex usage profile including, among other things, short-term stays, meeting, entertainment, dining, and other functions. Thus, this totality contains apartments, a hotel, office buildings, conference areas, sports facilities, commercial areas, and restaurants and cafes.

All is organized in a series of staggered vertical elements—one hesitates to say modules, since the objective appears to be to achieve a sense of unity within diversity. The section illustrates the profoundly unifying function of the multilevel, horizontally continuous base.

From the historical profile section above, De Rotterdam, designed in 1997/8, is one of the early examples of the emerging tower cluster typology. De Rotterdam is also a pre–skybridge/sky plaza case study, in which the major common and public amenities are to be found in the monumental spatial qualities of the plinth.

c. Major Amenities: Program and Organization

De Rotterdam contains 1.74 million square feet. The functional program contains 240 apartments (blue in the above section), 775,000 square feet of office space (green), and a 278-room hotel in the eastern tower's lower half (red). There is a six-level plinth containing conference facilities, shopping, restaurant and café spaces, and sports facilities. Both below grade and on upper levels within this multifunctional base there is a multilevel parking garage containing 650 spaces. The base also contains separate lobbies for each tower.

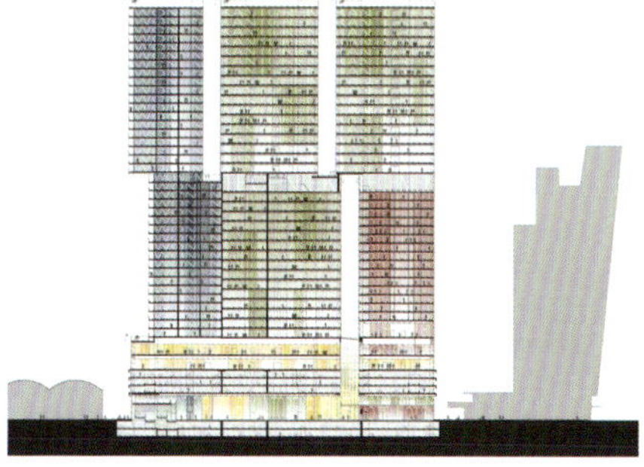

The base level, or plinth, is organized about a seven-story atrium (see model photo below). The horizontal slippage of the masses creates several large terraces for inhabitants at the midlevel of the building.

Above De Rotterdam, Rotterdam, Netherlands, perspective atrium. OMA, 1997–2013. Courtesy of OMA.

Opposite Page CMG Qianhai Global Trade Center, Shenzhen, China, render. OMA, from 2016. Courtesy of OMA.

d. Siting (+ Extended Program)

The Wilhelmina Pier was part of the old port area for oceangoing intercontinental liners. The site area is part of a large urban rehabilitation program. It is adjacent to the new Erasmus Bridge, which together with De Rotterdam forms the cornerstone of the renewal project. Thus, the statement of the multifunctional tower being made to read as one undulating mass with a width of 350 feet and a height of 490 feet acts as the punctuation point after the river crossing and the beginning of the vibrancy of the newly rehabilitated urban area. The power of its formally unified, but vibrant, masses appear as a great creative urban gesture.

e. Tower Cluster Contributions

- **The Tower Cluster as a Vertical City**
  The tower cluster exemplifies both formal and functional diversification represented by a large sampling of high-density urban functions of the modern city. Despite this diversity, there is a formal unanimity achieved through the use of a unifying skin solution for all of the diverse masses.

- **Unity in Diversity**
  This is a dialogue of independent, interactive masses. This same degree of interactive diversity appears in the overlapping multiple circulation systems provided for the diversity of users as well as urban visitors.

- **The Plinth as Collective Public Amenity**
  The multiple functions of the plinth as a multifunctional and multiuser amenity of this collective skyscraper are given expression to seek a complex formal language of intensified diversity in the place of spatial and formal harmony. Again, this is an architecture of challenging sensibility.

- **Beyond the Skyscraper**
  As exemplified by CCTV, above, De Rotterdam is also an experiment in the extension of the conventional definition of the skyscraper beyond merely the aspect of extreme height.

- **Multiple Towers as a Modulated Unity**
  De Rotterdam is a unified totality of indefinite number. It is a single building that reads as several, and a multiplicity that reads as one.

f. Special Amenities Provision: The Functional and Symbolic Role of the Tower Cluster

The structural and formal expression of the exterior skin provides a medium of expression of unity within the sense of volumetric diversity. It also contributes to the impression of the infinite and unlimited verticality of the project.

2.5.3 CMG Qianhai Global Trade Center, Shenzhen, China, OMA, from 2016, Construction 2020.

a. Tower Cluster Duo: Integration of Tower Cluster, Sky Structure, Urban Structure: Introduction

CMG Qianhai Global Trade Center is a two-tower cluster with a skybridge and a unifying plinth. In addition to these three basic elements, there is a cubic volume hovering over one side of the base. The total area of the project is 360,000 square meters. The tower height of the taller tower is fifty-four stories; it is 213.5 meters high, or 700 feet. The second tower is slightly lower at fifty-one stories high.

The tower cluster is located in the Ma Wan neighborhood of Qianhai in Shenzhen. This is a newly developing central business district of Shenzhen. Construction was started in April of 2020. Expected date of completion is 2024.

The major objective of the tower cluster as described by OMA partner Chris van Duijn, is to create a "compressed urban environment"—a Micro-City—"blurring traditional boundaries between building and city." That is, the massing of the cluster—particularly at the base—will be responsive to the high-density urban conditions of this new neighborhood.

b. Tower Cluster Duo: Program

Despite the overall characterization of the tower cluster as a classical duo model, the program contains a high level of functional and formal diversity. The fifty-one-story tower above the shopping base is an office building (blue). The fifty-four-story tower above the base is offices until level 35; from level 35 to level 54 it is a hotel (yellow). The amplified skybridge continues across the entire façade of both buildings.

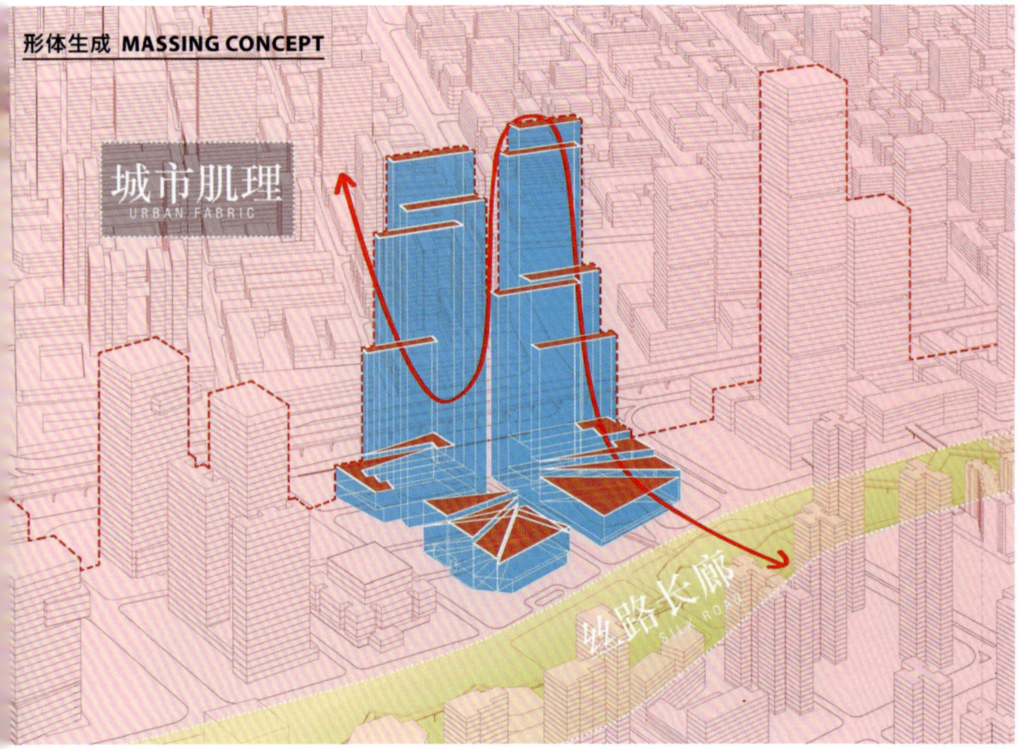

Above CMG Qianhai Global Trade Center, Shenzhen, China, render. OMA, from 2016. Courtesy of OMA. **Left** CMG Qianhai Global Trade Center, Shenzhen, China. OMA from 2016. Project narrative long façade. Image courtesy of OMA.

Opposite Page CMG Qianhai Global Trade Center, Shenzhen, China. OMA. Program courtesy of OMA.

On the top of the base in front of the office building is a cubic-shaped apartment hotel (orange) which is built around an interior courtyard and elevated on columns. Beneath this are one to three levels of office space (blue), beneath which is a multilevel area of commercial space (red). Integrated within the primarily commercial functions (shops and food service areas) of the tower cluster base are cultural functions such as galleries (green and purple) and functions for the hotels such as a swimming pool and banquet hall (yellow). Parking (light green) is located below and beside the shopping/cultural areas. There exist multiple underground entry/egress roads to adjacent urban areas as illustrated in the diagram below.

c. Major Amenities: Program and Organization

Diversity of Multifunctional Plinth

The plinth, or base, of the tower cluster has a high degree of diversity: it is diverse programmatically; it is diverse organizationally, being partially of contextually derived radial organization; and on the opposite side beneath

功能分布 PROGRAM

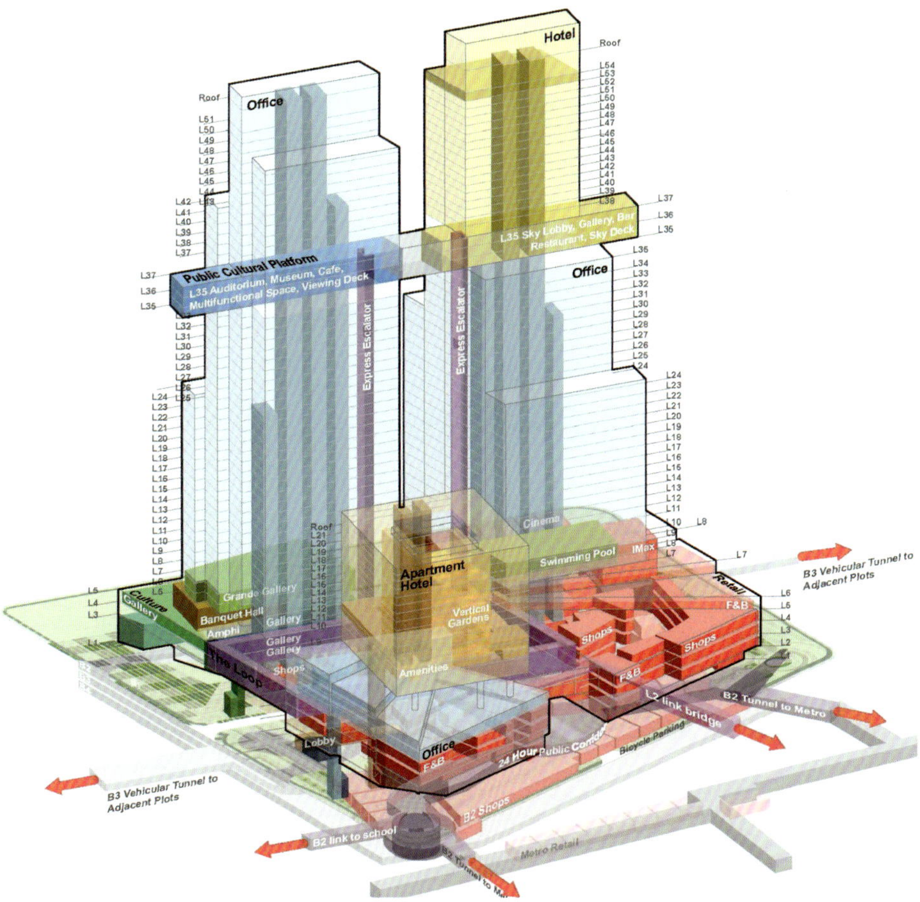

the apartment hotel, the organization is mainly orthogonal. Furthermore, the shopping areas are covered and internal on one side, and on the radially organized side they are open to the sky and organized around internal courtyards.

Skybridge, or Extended Multifunctional Sky Plaza

The skybridge is a two-story element (from L35 to L37). Functionally, it is divided internally into two sectors. The first half, on the side of the office building, is a public cultural platform containing an auditorium, a museum, café, multifunctional spaces, and viewing deck. The second half, on the side of the hotel, contains the sky lobby of the hotel, a gallery, bar, restaurant, and sky deck.

Loop

The loop is the major public horizontal circulation distributor. It is located on level 4. It provides access to the major vertical elevator and express escalator lobbies and cores. See program axonometric projection above and circulation diagram below.

Twenty-Four-Hour Public Corridor

The corridor provides twenty-four-hour public access to the shopping and cultural areas in a major public space.

d. Siting

The site is located in the rapidly developing high-rise neighborhood of Ma Wan in the region of the Qianhai Bay area of Shenzhen. The building has been designed to integrate its circulation matrices (pedestrian and vehicular) with two main roads, three metro public transit lines, and a bus terminal. Thus, the new tower cluster will be a transit-oriented development. The tower cluster is close to the Silk Road Corridor and a major public park. The tower cluster has been designed with a major orientation to the bay and the mountains.

e. Tower Cluster Contributions

- **The Urban Crafting of the Organizational Structure of the Base**
  *Base contextual interaction*s, in this case by geometric and organizational response to access vectors, is a major typological contribution of this case study. The commercial, cultural, and special office program of the base is designed to integrate with contextual connections and orientations. The base structure is treated as a flexible organizational and geometric model free of the dominant potential influence of the tower forms and their geometries.

- **The Interlocking Duo as Classical Tower Structure Circulation Model**
  The *interlocking duo with major extended skybridge* appears to be emerging as one significant classical typological model of tower cluster typologies.

Opposite Page CMG Qianhai Global Trade Center, Shenzhen, China, circulation diagram. OMA. Image courtesy of OMA. **Bottom** VDMA, Eindhoven, Netherlands, project, model in urban context. OMA, 2020. Image by Frans Parthesius courtesy of OMA.

The interlocking of vertical and horizontal loops of circulation also appears to be emerging as a characteristic form of circulation model in this tower cluster subtype.

- **Separation of the Two-Loop Circulation System from the Contextual Complexity of the Base Structure**
  The interlocking vertical and horizontal circulation loops are geometrically regular and independent from the geometrical complexity of the base elements.

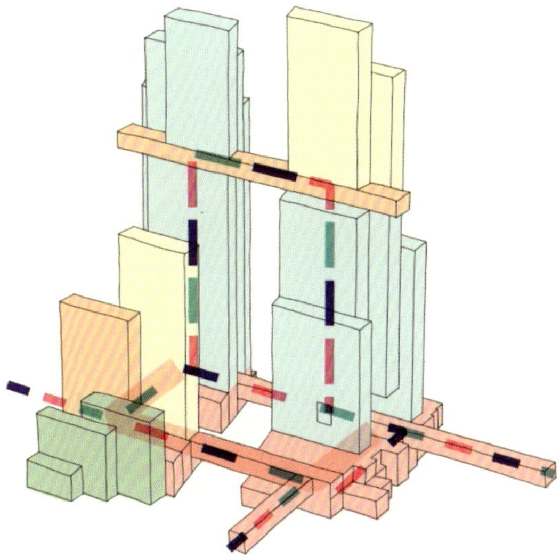

2.5.4 VDMA Van der Meulen-Ansemsterrein, Eindhoven, Netherlands, Project, OMA, 2020

a. Functionally Integrated Quartet: Introduction

This tower cluster quartet on a site near the mercantile town center of Eindhoven, the Netherlands, has several unique characteristics. The most outstanding of these is that instead of the frequent Dutch preference for the construction of new housing with minimal or no integration of additional functions, in VDMA there is a very high level of multifunctional integration. Secondly, in addition to the main residential quartet grouping, there is a large linear site of trees and other vegetation, called a *microforest*, around which has been located a large WeWork-like site for individual and group offices devoted to new technological development. The first of these multifunctional residential developments appears to be a significant urban design development with future potential. The second, the integration of a working environment (the technological development center) within the integrated housing complex, appears to be an important precedent for future "live-work" developments in the Netherlands. A third unique charac-

teristic of the VDMA development is the restoration and repurposing of two existing historical buildings on the site.

The credits for the design are OMA as main design architect together with diederen-dirrix, FABRICations, landscape architect DELVA, and design collective NUL ZES.

b. Functionally Integrated Quartet: Program

The major program elements are led by the new residential buildings, which are located in two major towers and two minor towers. The program of housing includes social housing, rental properties, private houses, and a community home. This diversity of housing program is expressed architecturally by the vertical stratification, or layered differentiation, of a series of stacked volumes. The volumes are to be treated differently on the exterior with some having technically refined glass external walls, while others have sustainable features such as "green walls" and photovoltaic panels to produce and store solar energy during the daylight hours. This tactic of the layered moving of housing masses will also generate spaces for communal terraces at various levels.

The new center for coworking on various aspects of technological development will provide space for start-ups, which will occupy a five-story volume with large floor plates that follows the linear outline of the microforest. The microforest itself is linear in organization and occupies a third of the site.

It is too early in the design process to anticipate in detail how this project will turn out. However, even at this stage there is an admirable emphasis on architecture as a social and cultural medium. This is beyond the statement of architecture as formal innovation as certain of our architects would have us believe. Here, for example, the concept of the integration of a multifunctional program, the combination of work and residential, and finally—above all—the closely related interaction of living environments of diverse socioeconomic classes appears not only to create meaningful precedents for a new urbanism, but also to achieve a positive statement of architecture's ability to enhance social and democratic objectives. Here is a new expression of what might become a truly aesthetic environment. As stated by the architect: "The redeveloped VDMA site will offer the city a platform for the engagement with the most innovative ideas in technology and culture."

c. Major Amenity: Program and Organization

Offices, cultural functions, and commercial space are located in masses which link the various towers. In addition to spaces for internal cultural and community activities, roofscapes will be developed for community use as appropriate.

d. Site and Extended Program

The site was a former industrial area, and the current design includes the renovation and repurposing of two historical buildings. A nineteenth-century factory will be restored to provide for cultural, educational, and retail programs. A garage will be redesigned into a flexible public space for exhibitions, events and theater performances. These buildings are within the U-shaped space created by the four towers.

A continuous public circulation way exists (see red line in the model photos below) to the cultural, retail, and outdoor open spaces of the project.

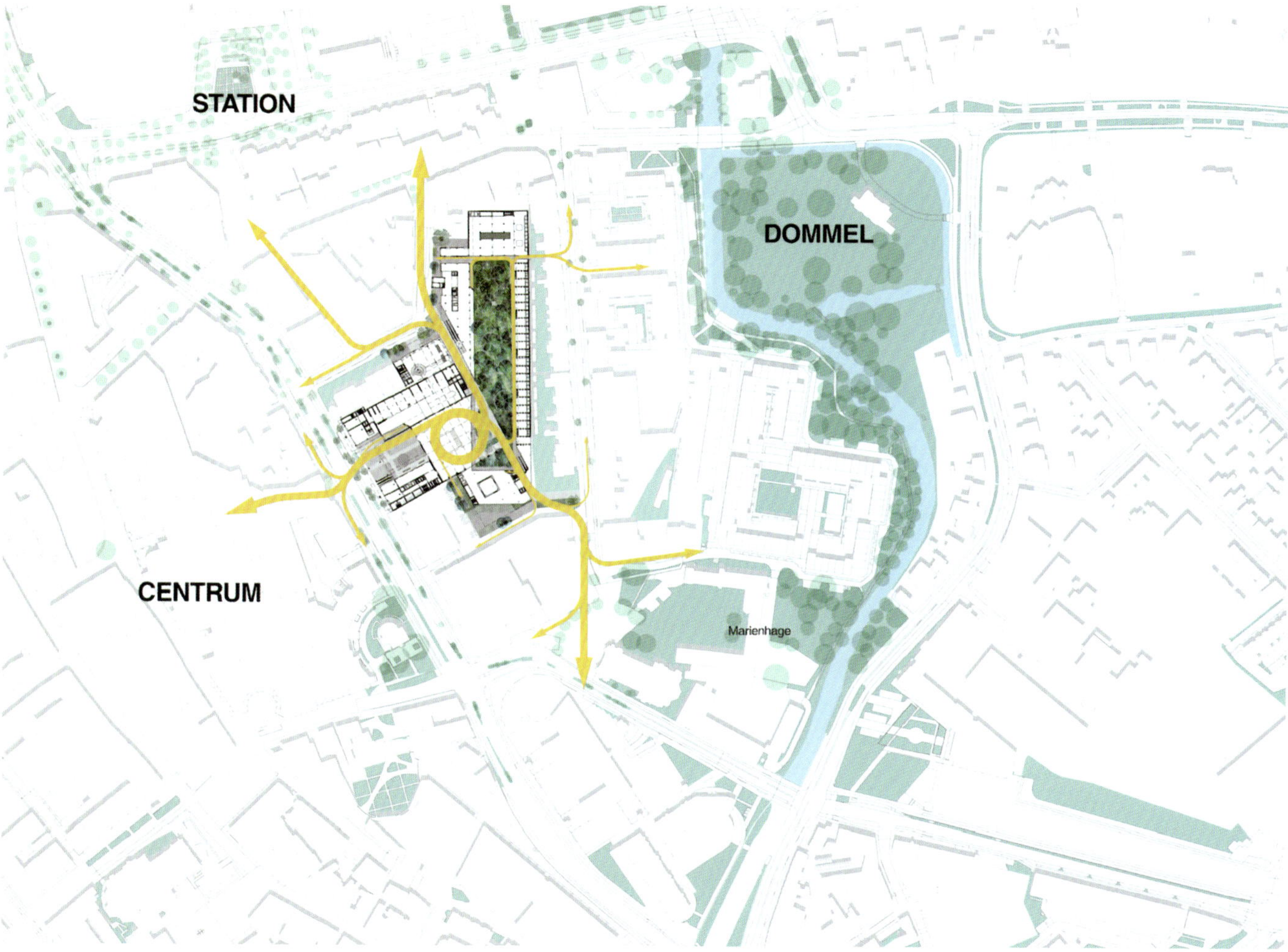

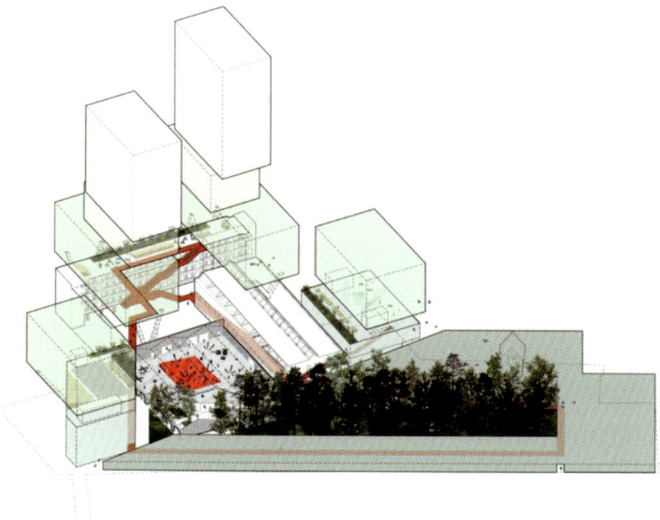

Above Van der Meulen-Ansemsterrein, Eindhoven, Netherlands, project. OMA, 2020. Site plan courtesy of OMA. **Left** VDMA, Eindhoven, Netherlands, axonometric of project. OMA, 2020. Courtesy of OMA.

Above VDMA, Eindhoven, Netherlands, project. OMA, 2020. Courtesy of Proloog. **Right** VDMA, Eindhoven, Netherlands, project, view of base of tall towers. OMA, 2020. Courtesy of Proloog.

Opposite Page VDMA, Eindhoven, Netherlands, project, view with future planned towers. OMA, 2020. Photo by Frans Parthesius. Courtesy of OMA.

e. Tower Cluster Contributions

- **Tower Cluster as a Compound Medium of Urban Renewal**
  In VDMA the typology provides a highly flexible medium for urban renewal in an urban situation with multiple diverse historic and programmatic conditions.

- **Tower Cluster as a Medium in the Construction of Social Democracy**
  The towers integrate solutions for various socioeconomic groups, and the tower cluster provides common community amenities.

- **Tower Cluster Integrates Work-Live Environment**
  A novel WeWork-like environment is integrated as a significant component within the cluster.

- **Stratified Differentiation of the Tower Program**
  Diverse program functions are implemented within the stratified modularity of the architectural solution of the towers.

f. Future Tower Expansion in Vicinity of Project

Above Marina Bay Sands, Singapore. Safdie Architects, 2010.

Opposite Page Wolkenbügel (Cloud Hanger), El Lissitzky and Mart Stam, 1924. Lissitzky, *Cloud Iron*, courtesy of Van Abbemuseum, Netherlands.

2.5.5 Marina Bay Sands, Singapore, Safdie Architects, 2010

a. Introduction: Tower Cluster Order as Generator of Project Structure and Form

In the tower cluster, it is the significance of the cluster elements as an integrated design whole that motivates the designation of elements, the order and relationships, the overall organization, as well as the particular expression of the individual elements. Among other things such as site characteristics and functional program, the individual tower elements and their aesthetic expression are also functions of the design order and organization of the cluster. It is at the Marina Bay Sands that Moshe Safdie celebrates with boldness and illuminating clarity the expression of the emergence of a new urban architectural typology.[6]

This section begins with a significant documentation of Marina Bay Sands as a pioneering contemporary case study of the tower cluster and its contribution to the concepts of tower structures and to the potential of the tower cluster for achieving vertical urbanism. It is here that Safdie demonstrates the creative and morphologically generative potential of the typology. It is here that he, again, also demonstrates his outstanding capability as a true architectural typological innovator. This achievement, in effect, constitutes not only a high level of building design along with important urbanistic implications, but also, ultimately, an enlargement of the disciplinary knowledge base.

Marina Bay Sands introduces an element of importance to the tower cluster typology that we have previously seen in indistinct form in the geometric model of La Grande Arche de la Défense. We may denote this novel programmatic element of the tower cluster with the generic title of the *sky plaza,* or in Safdie's usage, the *sky park.* Morphologically, we have seen two forms of this large horizontal capping structure in the tower forms of the tower cluster: the reversed-U tower form of la Défense, as opposed to the multiple-T form of Marina Bay Sands. In future case studies we shall continue to see both of these morphologies.

The T morphology of a capped tower is unique in modern architectural history. The closest we have found for a historical precedent is the Cloud Hanger proposal of El Lissitzky and Mart Stam of 1924.

This experimental project was for the development of an architecture to be integrated into the existing urban form, transportation systems, and circulation patterns of Moscow. Most of the works involved horizontal office buildings raised on vertical piers and elevator cores. One of the most notable characteristics of the structural conditions is the existence of large cantilevers. The other condition assumed as a design principle is the integration of the proposed structures with existing transportation systems at ground level. Both the image and programs are visionary, but they provide a visionary urbanistic aesthetic which also characterizes Safdie's strikingly iconic statement regarding the existence of monumental urban amenities in an elevated horizontal structure within the emerging typology of the tower structure. Vertical urbanism heretofore becomes an integral component part of the new urban morphology.

Marina Bay Sands is what is termed an *integrated resort development.* That is, it is basically a very large resort hotel integrated with other programmatic components, both commercial and cultural. The hotel's form and organizational structure constitute the basis for the organization of the tower structure. This structural modulization is further projected throughout the project and its diagrammatic circulation system. We shall begin with a schematic description of the project as a whole, and then focus upon the tower structure and its innovative contributions.

b. Marina Bay Sands Tower Cluster: Linear Trio

The Marina Bay Sands tower cluster is composed of three fifty-seven-story slab-form towers which function as the hotel. The hotel in total contains 2,600 rooms with each tower containing approximately 865 rooms. The towers are splayed at their base to create space for a grand, linear multistory lobby.

In addition to the hotel, there is a 340-meter-long (1,120 feet) sky park which connects the three towers at their upper level. Beyond the hotel cluster, in the direction of Marina Bay, there are five large-scale public elements. The first of these is the casino, which is designed in an atrium space with four levels. This facility is among the world's largest casinos and is

a major component of the multifunctional integrated resort. Adjacent to the casino, in a linear arrangement parallel to the length of the hotel, are also located the Sands exhibition and convention center of 110,000 square meters (1,200,000 square feet) and a theater. Running along the bayside edge of these three elements is a large linear mall, the Shoppes at Marina Bay Sands, containing three hundred stores. The linear mall contains an internal waterway along which it is possible to travel by small boat. On the outer water-side edge of the mall is a large outdoor space for public events. Finally, on a promontory at the north end of the linear elements, there is an art/science museum of 19,000 square meters (200,000 square feet) which has the shape of a lotus. Throughout the complex there are also multiple chef restaurants.

There are two commercial pavilions built in the bay adjacent to the land-side edge of the integrated resort. A fourth tower containing one thousand luxury suites is planned for construction. It is to be accompanied by a 15,000-seat arena. (See final illustration at completion of MBS presentation).

c. Sky Park: Program and Structure

The sky park is a multifunctional private park for hotel use. Its total area is approximately three acres, or one hectare. Prominent among its functions is a 150-meter-long (490 feet) infinity swimming pool. The pool, which looks out over downtown Singapore, is 191 meters (627 feet) above ground level. Also included are a garden area, jogging paths, and several rooftop nightclubs. The sky park's northern end is devoted to a viewing platform which projects over the edge of the northern hotel building by a 66.5-meter (218 feet) cantilever, the longest public overhang in the world.

Opposite Page Marina Bay Sands, Singapore, base structure between splayed hotel slabs. Safdie Architects, 2010.

Above Marina Bay Sands, Singapore, viewing platform at sky park. Safdie Architects, 2010.
Bottom Marina Bay Sands, Singapore, plan of sky park. Safdie Architects, 2010. Courtesy of Safdie Architects.

Above Marina Bay Sands, Singapore, render. Safdie Architects, 2010. Courtesy of Safdie Architects.

d. Marina Bay Sands Complex: Siting and Extended Resort Program and Organization

The total site area of Marina Bay Sands is twenty hectares. On this bayside site, the Singapore Planning Office requested that the tallest elements of the hotel be sited furthest away from the shoreline of the bay. This site planning principle created a situation in which the four layers of the program (the tower cluster hotel, the linear arrangement of three large-scale volumes, the shopping mall, and the exterior public event space) are arranged in a sequence from low to high beginning at the shore of the bay.

The circulation is generated by the modularization of the hotel with the major circulation way between the four different height level functional groups generated by the hiatus between each pair of hotel towers. Thus, the intricate geometry of the total order of the integrated complex is established by the modular order of the hotel tower structure.

e. Tower Cluster Contributions

The tower cluster of MBS establishes a unique set of contributions to the morphological definition of the typology from 2010 onward. These include the following eight attributes of design of the typology.

- **Creation of a New Urban Sector of the City**
  The MBS complex establishes a new urban area opposite from the central city location. The concept of the new urban medium as a vehicle of urban development becomes a significant ingredient contributing to its international success in the second decade, and we believe, in the future. The tower cluster here in Singapore becomes a tool of large-scale urban design.

- **Major Precedent for the Establishment of the Typology**
  The intricate formal, functional, and organizational integration exemplified by MBS becomes a model for future tower cluster developments. It creates the *linear trio* subtype of the typology.

- **Establishes the Sky Park and the Linear Atrium as Prominent Urban Amenities**
  The uniqueness and formal/functional/spatial significance of the monumental connective base element and the unique program and form for the multifunctional sky park are early precedents for the tower cluster's newly emerging compositional definition. This definition establishes the typology as including the multiple elements of *towers plus urban attributes*.

- **Interconnectedness at Ground Level and Upper Level (Sky Park)**
  The tower cluster is an urban design medium for the creation, or enhancement, of urban interconnectivity. This interconnectivity occurs both within the tower cluster, between the tower cluster and its extended program, and between the towers, the complex, and the city. This urban interconnection can occur at various levels and by various design media

such as continuous multifloor base or sky structures, e.g., the sky plaza or skybridges. These design principles of urban interconnectivity will be extended and further developed later in the decade, as we will see below.

- **Circulation System Designed for Extension of Tower Cluster Programs**
  Marina Bay Sands's internal circulation system is expandable for the future addition of major new architectural/urban programs. See, for example, the 2019 hotel complex extension below.

- **Connection to Mass Transit and Bus Transport**
  MBS is connected to both bus and rapid transit public transportation.

- **Connection of Outdoor and Indoor Spaces**
  Throughout the complex there are multiple opportunities for connection with exterior spaces and functions.

- **Tower Cluster as the *Architecture of Amenities***
  The architecture and the organization of the tower structure provides for an *architecture of amenities*. The distribution of the amenities within the organization of the tower cluster becomes a strong statement of the conceptual basis of the tower structure. This is another important contribution of Marina Bay Sands as a precedent. From this project, we have also learned how the pattern of circulation can become the basis for the extension of additional programmatic elements added beyond the tower structure.

- **Tower Cluster as the *Architecture of Integration***
  The typology of the tower cluster, in general, and MBS, in particular, is distinguished by a complex integration of elements: functional, formal, constructive, spatial, and urbanistic. Ideally, this characterizes all architecture. However, at MBS we have observed how complex and intricate this can be to achieve. At MBS the orchestration of spatial and experiential integration is an extraordinary experience. One can sense the potential richness of the experience of clustering. By definition, therefore, the successful design of the tower cluster constitutes a high level of architectural/urban achievement.

f. Tower Cluster Expansion

The proposed expansion contains a fourth hotel tower of 1,000 luxury suites to be added to the existing 2,561 rooms and suites, a 15,000-seat entertainment arena, and related functions.

2.5.6 Sky Habitat, Singapore, Safdie Architects, 2016

a. Introduction: Linked Duo with Community Amenity Skybridges

Sky Habitat is a duo, or two-tower cluster, which was completed in Sin-

gapore in 2016. It is a project for high-density living which attempts to optimize the design potential of the tower cluster typology by two means. First, as at Habitat 67 in Montreal, there is an attempt to provide a formal emphasis on the expression of the physical independence of each dwelling. Secondly, three skybridges are employed to achieve a sense of community in the situation of high-density living by creating outdoor and indoor community functions and spaces. Thus, these facilities are intended to promote both physical and social linkage through the media and programmatic amenities that are uniquely characteristic of the tower cluster. Contrary to the compressed mass of conventional high-density housing, Sky Habitat's spatial organization is open to allow penetration of light and air, while providing private terraces for each dwelling. In addition, the organization of the towers exploits typical assets of the typology among which are the in-between connectivity of the tower cluster and its vocabulary of urban amenities to provide a medium for the interweaving of communal space, gardens, and pools skyward as amenities of community.

The tower cluster contains two residential towers of thirty-eight stories in height. There is a total of 509 residential units. There is a total project area of 130,000 square feet (12,077 square meters). The towers are interconnected by three skybridges. At each of the skybridge floors there are also enclosed interior spaces for communal functions and activities.

The three-dimensional matrix of towers and stepped forms with rich landscaped areas recalls in high-rise form the texture of ancient hillside

Above Sky Habitat, Singapore. Safdie Architects, 2016. Photo by Edward Hendricks.

Opposite Page Sky Habitat, Singapore, axonometric diagram. Safdie Architects, 2016. Three skybridges and plans of adjacent communal indoor facilities. Courtesy of Safdie Architects.
Right Sky Habitat, Singapore. Safdie Architects, 2016. Photo by Edward Hendricks.

communities. The project creates a sense of a boldly new architectural system somehow also founded upon ancient cultural principles of habitation.

b. Sky Habitat of Gardens in the Sky creates the Shape of Community

The design system of the tower cluster is a flexible matrix of vertical and horizontal movement. All communal functions and activity spaces, both indoor and outdoor, are located on this matrix. Such structures of amenity matrices can be programmed and designed to fit the differing situations of place, climate, and user needs.

This grid of vertical and horizontal movements is the shape of community. It is a socially formative medium that can create social formation, and thus it demonstrates the achievement of the general social objective of socializing of the sky.

c. Social Function of Skybridges

The skybridges on three levels function as public garden and sports spaces. Particularly in this tropical climate such spaces fulfill an important social role as well as a climatic function.

d. Site and Site Development: Tower Cluster in a Park

The generative theme of this tower cluster is that of combining the concept of the tower cluster in a park with that of a duo with gardens as social linkage.

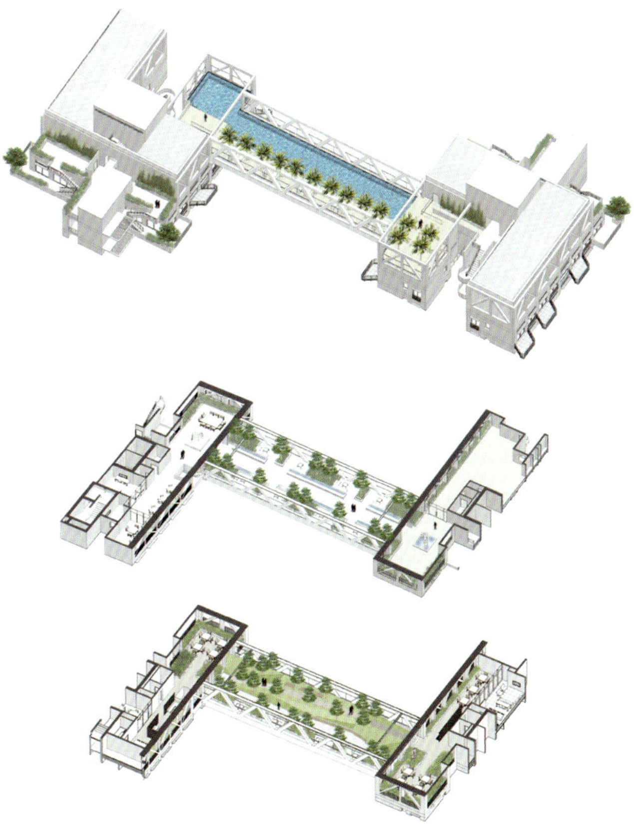

e. Tower Cluster Contributions

- **System of Streets in the Air**
  Interconnection through skybridges provides access for all units to all amenities and communal functions.

- **Stepped Towers Create Special Units**
  The duo subtype supports diverse tower accommodations. The geometry of the towers—in this case through stepping—creates the potential for the accommodation of special dwelling shapes and functionality. For example, in the case of Sky Habitat, larger units are created with multiple orientations, which is an advantage for solar and breeze orientations.

- **Stepped Organization Creates Tall Atrium at Ground Level**
  The stepped section of the lower housing group of the lead tower creates a covered atrium-like space at ground level.

- **Gardens in the Sky: Multiple Skybridges for Socializing the Sky**
  The skybridges are used to provide a new kind of public realm for the inhabitants. On two of the three skybridges, this is used to create public gardens in the sky.

A GATE GUARD
B ENTRY COURT
C LILY PONDS
D WATER WALL
E POOL ISLAND
F PERGOLA
G BOSQUE TENNIS VIEWING GARDEN
H SOCIAL AREAS / BBQ
I PLAY AREA
J REFLECTION GARDENS
K TENNIS COURT
L LEISURE POOL
M KIDS POOL
N LAP POOL
O CONTEMPLATIVE GARDENS
P OUTDOOR FITNESS
Q BUS SHELTER

- **For Every Man a Garden**
  The stepped units (one-third of the total) have large terraces and potentially large private gardens.

- **Special Amenities Provisions**
  At the meeting of the three skybridges with the floors of the towers, the spaces are devoted to a wide range of public functions, including sports, a gym, tennis court, function rooms, etc.

- **Tower Cluster in a Park**
  The tower cluster is sited in a private park situation which creates the possibility for the establishment of a large selection of private amenities for the inhabitants.

Opposite Page Sky Habitat, Singapore, ground-floor amenities in the park setting. Safdie Architects, 2016. Photo by Edward Hendricks.
Bottom Sky Habitat, Singapore, site plan. Safdie Architects, 2016. Courtesy of Safdie Architects.

Left Sky Habitat, Singapore, first skybridge. Safdie Architects, 2016. Photo by Edward Hendricks.

2.5.7 Raffles City Chongqing, China, 2019

Safdie Architects Design Architect
Chongqing Architecture and Design Institute Architect of Record
P&T Group Architect of Record

a. Introduction: Tower Cluster of Eight Linked Towers

Raffles City Chongqing is located at the intersection of the Jialing and Yangtze Rivers. It is sited on a 9.2-hectare triangular property. At the head of the project is the historic urban site of Chaotianmen Square. The property has a sloping site and thus the base of the complex lies at various urban levels. The base of public access has an external movement system through the complex and into the urban site of the square. Connecting the whole of the project on multiple levels is a multifunctional commercial base facility. Thus, the development of the project located on a prominent historic site is motivated by its urban importance and the need to integrate the functional components of the program around this major urban design project. The project is also noted for its innovative humanistic approach to the design of high-density housing, which integrates social motivators within the organization of the urban and architectural systems.

b. Raffles City Chongqing: Octet Tower Cluster as Core of Urban Complex and Responsive Medium of Urban Design

The program contains four residential towers, one serviced residential tower, a hotel, and three office towers (two of which are half towers also occupied by other functions—the hotel and a private club). A five-story retail galleria is the element of continuity at the base of all eight towers. A major skybridge called The Crystal contains 15,000 square meters of facilities. It connects four of the towers, and by two additional skybridges, The Crys-

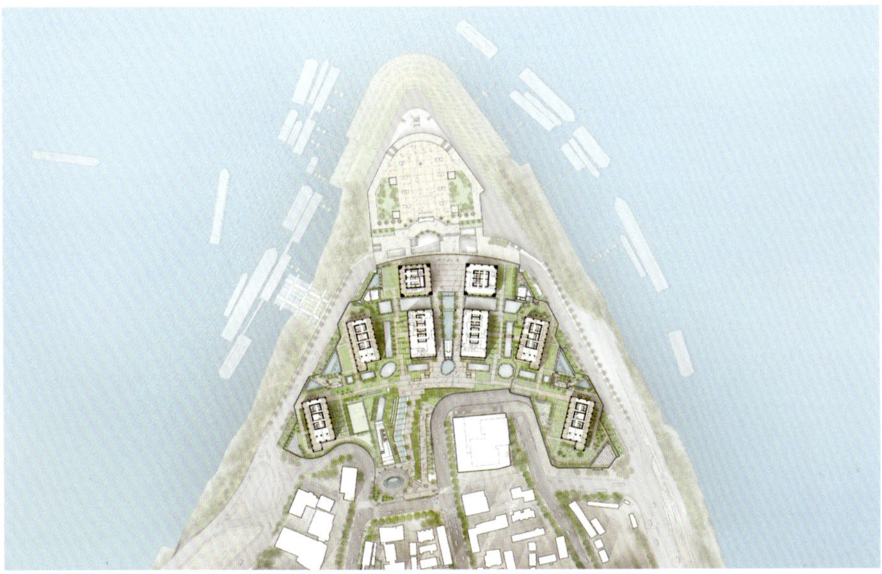

Above Raffles City Chongqing, Chongqing, China. Safdie Architects, 2019. Rendering of The Crystal courtesy of Safdie Architects. **Right** Raffles City Chongqing, Chongqing, China, site plan. Safdie Architects, 2019. Courtesy of Safdie Architects.

Opposite Page Raffles City Chongqing, Chongqing, China. Safdie Architects, 2019. Photograph by Elay, courtesy of Safdie Architects.

tal is also connected to the two tall towers adjacent to the historical urban square which is located at ground level. The layout of the towers canalizes the urban movement system between the city and the historic urban square.

The total development is 1,200,000 square feet (110,000 square meters). This includes, among other functions, 1,400 residential units, a 450-room hotel, 200 luxury serviced apartments, and a landscaped park area that contains approximately 45,500 square meters of public and private landscaped open space.

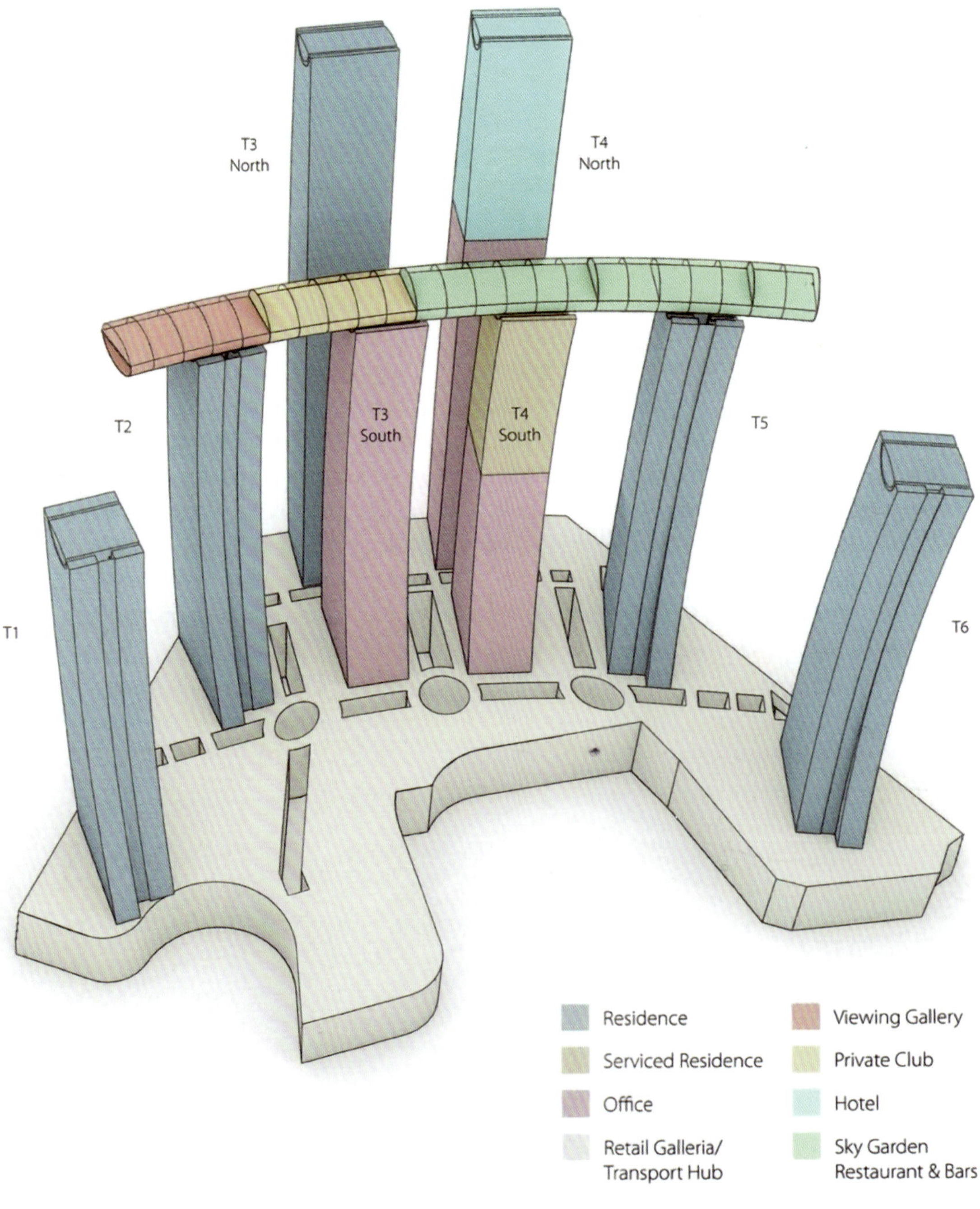

c. Major Amenities: Program and Structure

The base element contains the five-story galleria which provides a major commercial facility as well as major urban circulation systems for urban purposes (see site section). The roof level of the galleria provides a major public park of approximately 45,000 square meters of green spaces including areas for public functions.

The skybridge, called The Crystal, contains (from right to left) an observation deck, a conservatory of trees, a clubhouse with gym and swimming pool, a plaza with a connection to a skybridge containing the hotel lobby, restaurants and lounges, an additional observatory, and an exterior observatory.

The program of amenities thus includes the diverse functions of The Crystal and the major base of six levels of public and commercial functions of the galleria. Public transportation and urban movements are integrated within the organizational structure of the tower cluster. This total integration of a multifunctional tower cluster with a major urban amenity of the city as well as its own generation of urban circulation constitutes an important contribution to the assets of the tower cluster as a typology.

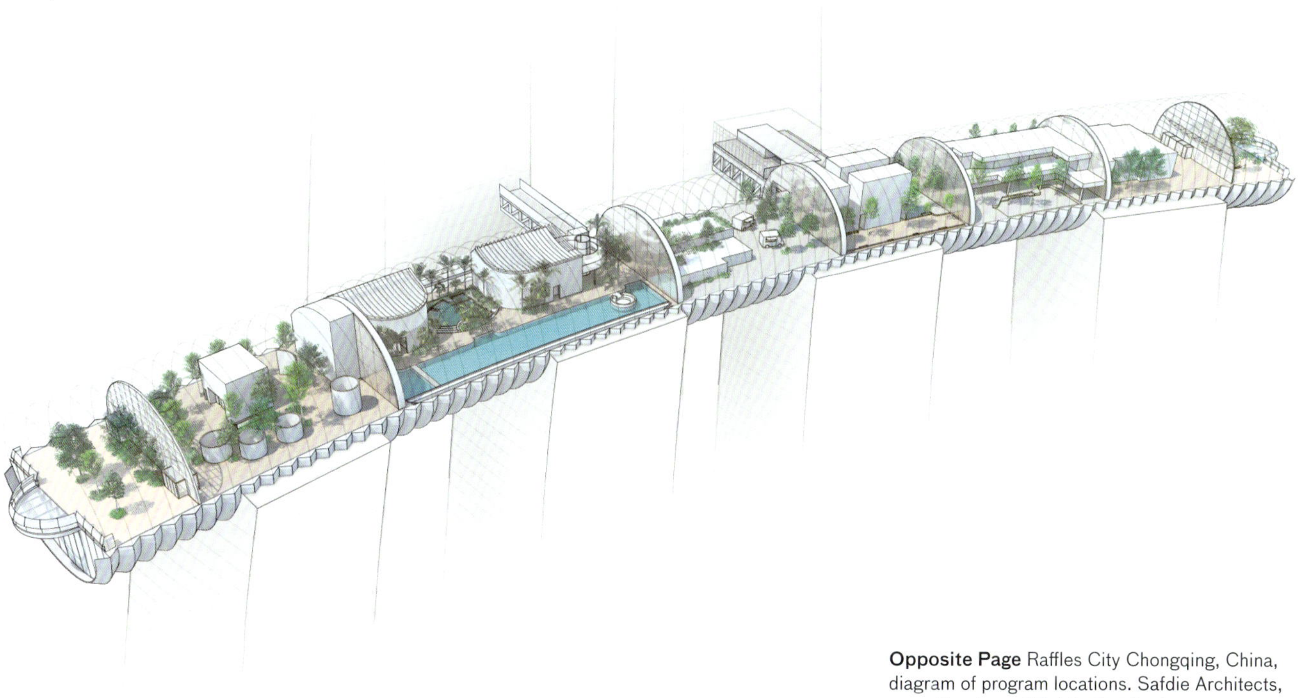

Opposite Page Raffles City Chongqing, China, diagram of program locations. Safdie Architects, 2019. Courtesy of Safdie Architects.

Above Raffles City Chongqing, China. Safdie Architects, 2019. End view of enclosed sky park The Crystal. Photo by Shao-Feng Hsu. **Bottom** Raffles City Chongqing, China. Safdie Architects, 2019. Rendering of enclosed sky park The Crystal Courtesy of Safdie Architects.

d. Siting and Extended Program

The major vehicular circulation system is based on the existing circumferential road layout of the promontory site. The major public plaza at the roof level of the galleria provides areas for public event space as well as panoramic views of the central city. The site has been transformed into a dual-functional medium. On the one hand, the tower structure design provides a new and humanistic approach to dense multifunctional development; on the other hand, it provides a monumental structure for the new and extended urban design experience of the city.

e. Tower Cluster Contributions

- **The Symbolic and Civic Role of the Tower Cluster**
  The structure and form of the tower cluster elements form a monumental symbolic gateway for pedestrian movements through the site towards the square. Viewed from the main section of the city, the slightly bowed shape of the towers suggests a group of sails upon the waters of the two rivers.

- **The Tower Cluster as Three-Dimensional Urban Design**
  The structured form of the tower cluster organization canalizes the pedestrian movement system through the galleria and down to the square.

- **Socializing the Sky by a Major Community Function Skybridge**
  The Crystal skybridge becomes a major sky-based location of community amenities and social interaction.

Left Raffles City Chongqing, China. Safdie Architects, 2019.

Opposite Page ORCA Toronto, Canada, project. Safdie Architects, 2021. Rendering courtesy of Safdie Architects.

f. Special Amenities Provision: The Functional and Symbolic Role of the Tower Cluster

The Crystal skybridge contains a variety of recreational and commercial functions. It is designed within a tube-shaped structure approximately 300 meters in length providing approximately 15,000 square meters of functional area. The skybridge superimposed on four of the towers creates a gigantic gateway to the historic square at the promontory.

2.5.8 ORCA Toronto, Canada, Project, Safdie Architects, 2021

a. Introduction: A Park-Oriented Double Tower Cluster

ORCA is a large urban design and architectural project that is to be built over the air right-of-way above the underground railroad lines of the major rail corridor entering Toronto. It is a multifunctional project containing six residential towers and an office tower in the first tower cluster. The residential towers are linked by skybridges. There is also a commercial connective base that runs under the residential towers. The second tower cluster to the

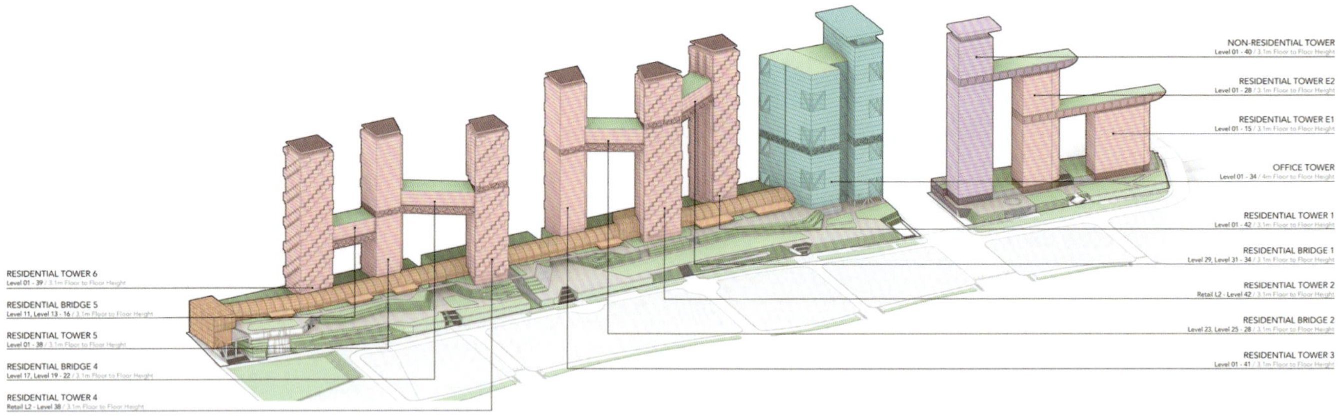

Above ORCA Toronto, Canada, project. Safdie Architects, 2021. Program diagram looking north. Courtesy of Safdie Architects. **Bottom** ORCA Toronto, Canada, project. Safdie Architects, 2021. Residential tower cluster and skybridges/gardens. Rendering courtesy of Safdie Architects.

Opposite Page ORCA Toronto, Canada, project. Safdie Architects, 2021. Three-tower cluster at east end. Rendering courtesy of Safdie Architects.

east contains three towers descending in height towards the east connected by skybridges. The first and tallest of the three towers is nonresidential, while the remaining two are residential.

An important feature of the urban design program is that the project is to be accompanied for its full length by an urban park which is to be a multilevel park integrated with the multilevel commercial base beneath the residential tower cluster complex.

b. Double Tower Cluster: Program

ORCA contains ten towers that are assembled into a duo, or pair, of tower clusters. In the case of this project, the two tower clusters as well as the linear park are separated by a major north-south road crossing. The program includes 3,500 dwelling units with 207,000 square meters of dwelling space; 78,400 square meters of office space; 38,000 square meters of retail space; 1,700 square meters of day care facilities; and 10,300 square meters of gallery space. There are also 44,400 square meters of open space. As well as opening to a grand interior arcade space, the stepped retail facility faces outward along the southern park side of the site. The interior arcaded space in the commercial area is openable in good weather. Total development built will be 474,000 square meters (5,100,000 square feet) including a new 11-acre park.

The tower clusters are forty-three and forty-six stories. The skybridges are each five stories in height. They occur at various levels and are designed to be surmounted by roof gardens. The office tower is planned to be thirty-six stories high.

The eastern tower cluster's tallest building is a nonresidential structure. It is forty-three stories high and planned to be used for a hotel, office space, and retail. The two remaining towers are both for residential usage; one is thirty-three stories high and the other is twenty-two stories high. The three eastern towers are linked by skybridges containing public functions as well as residential space.

There are underground parking facilities of one and two stories under the development which provide approximately nine hundred internal parking spaces.

c. Siting and Extended Program

The site is an active rail corridor. It is currently crossed by certain active traffic streets which must be maintained in the design of the development. Therefore, providing for optimal spatial and circulation connectivity despite the large scale and multifunctional diversity of the program was a significant design challenge. The typology of the tower cluster with its attributes of multilevel connectivity through skybridges and other characteristic urban media of the tower cluster exhibits the potential design flexibility of the type as well as its capability to flexibly accommodate complex urban programs.

d. Tower Cluster Contributions

- **From Identity Park to Identity Mall**
  The base structure is a multilevel commercial mall that is integrated by landscape design with the linear park. Exterior space connects by axes in the north-south direction with the interior mall, which is planned to be a linear atrium space covered by a transparent, operable vault.

- **Tower Clusters as Connective Urban Tissue**
  Due to the multilevel integration of park-mall-circulation and transportation in ORCA, the project illuminates the function of tower clusters as an effective urban design medium of connectivity.

- **Inhabited Skybridges**
  In addition to providing shared collective space for communal services and activities, at ORCA we observe the multiple potential uses of the skybridges. In this case they are used for residential space in addition to providing interior space for communal uses.

- **The Connected Community**
  As compared to the "streets in the sky" corridor medium for enhancing social interaction, the tower cluster provides for enhancing community at a higher scalar level of the community, or the subcommunity of multiple floors in multiple buildings. Tower clusters are the tools of urban community. In this case, tower clusters are employed to create an urban park–oriented social community.

- **The Cultural Orientation of New Urban Communities**
  The cluster community is culturally integrated with multiple functions of society, work, commerce, and cultural functions. This is a new unique form of cultural interaction which may also become a new model of urbanism.

Above ORCA Toronto, Canada, project. Safdie Architects, 2021. Cross section of multilevel park. Rendering courtesy of Safdie Architects.
Right ORCA Toronto, Canada, project. Safdie Architects, 2021. Site section at bridges showing relation to railway and multilevel park. Courtesy of Safdie Architects.

Opposite Page Galaxy Soho, Beijing, China. Zaha Hadid Architects, 2009–2012. Courtesy of Chikara Inamura.

2.5.9 Galaxy Soho, Beijing, China, Zaha Hadid Architects, 2009–2012

a. The Linkage of the Quartet: Introduction

The origin of the conceptual development of Galaxy Soho is stated to have been the attempt to realize a major courtyard development reminiscent of the historical significance of that element in traditional Chinese architecture. In the case of this project, that ordering element is transposed to urban scale in order to achieve a new and contemporary scale of urban order. Furthermore, a circular and curvilinear formal system has been developed to create a dynamic ordering of space into and within the complex. The flowing architecture of movement through a sequence of atria creates a uniquely dynamic continuous architecture of the tower cluster.

Four eighteen-story asymmetrical circular towers are organized about the main courtyard. Each of the towers is organized around an atrium topped and enclosed by a skylit transparent dome. The base entry floor has continuous circulation within the main court and into each of the four subcourts.

The same degree of flowing circulation exists at the fourth level of the cluster, which is the base level of office circulation between the four towers. Thus, level 4 contains multiple skybridges that enhance business circulation between the various offices in the different towers.

b. The Linkage of the Quartet: Program and Organization

The towers are fifteen stories high. The tower cluster is stratified into three vertical program sectors. The base element is three stories high and contains commercial and entertainment functions. These are readily accessible by moving though the main courtyard and into the four tower atrium spaces. The retail floors have an area of 90,000 square meters. Below the base is a parking area of 1,275 spaces and the connection to the city's public transit system.

The second zone is that of the office functions generally for firms dealing with technical development. Both the fourth and fifth floors have skybridge connections. See the plan of the fourth floor below, which shows a typical office floor linking two tower areas.

Finally, the third zone at the top of the towers contains restaurants, bars, and viewing areas. Three of these four penthouse areas are connected by skybridges.

The major public access amenities are, therefore, in the first and third zones. These are the commercial and entertainment stratum of the base levels, and the penthouse level on the top floor. The total project area is 332,857 square meters.

c. Site

Soho is a company that provides tech offices in Beijing and other major cities. The Soho Galaxy tower cluster is located in the southwest corner of the Chaoyangmen Bridge area in the Second Ring Road of Beijing. The site area is 46,965 square meters.

d. Tower Cluster Contributions

- **The Tower Cluster as a Spatial Continuum**
  Through the organization of spatial elements and the design of circulation and building geometry, the tower cluster has been transformed into the experience of movement through space as a continuum. Furthermore, this continuum is flexible (i.e., it can be modified over time) and discretionary (i.e., the user can select various potential continuous paths).

- **A Double Duo**
  The four core atria can be organized as a double duo, or continuous space containing two core areas. There is further possible flexibility of core space organization (e.g., at the penthouse level).

Opposite Page Galaxy Soho, Beijing, China. Zaha Hadid Architects, 2009–2012. Courtesy of Hufton and Crow.

- **Spatial Organization / Circulation as a Flexible Matrix/Optimizing the System of Connectivity**
  There exist multiple possibilities for the organization and experience of the core sequence.

- One Base Space: the major atrium
- Double Bridge Connectors: the office stratum at plan 4
- Three Spaces Linked: by penthouse restaurants and bars
- Four Linked Spaces: by the route of the tower atria
- Five Linked Spaces: the commercial/entertainment continuum

- **The Base Aligned Skybridge**
  The major skybridge connections exist at the upper levels, or just above the highest floor of the main base layer. In the case of Galaxy Soho, this constitutes one of the levels of intersection between mainly public and mainly private circulation. We shall see in the later chapters on the skybridge and the potential for urban continuity that this location also constitutes a potential level for *intercluster urban connectivity*.

- **A Colony of Atria/Linked Atria/Multiple Core Spaces**
  In Galaxy Soho each of the towers contains an atrium. The main public route for the connection between atria is on the main entry floor. On the fourth floor and the penthouse floor there again exist multiple routes for the connection of atria.

- **Multiple Interrelated Skybridge System**
  There exist multiple routes at level 1 and multiple skybridge access points at levels 4 and 15 for alternate routes of connection between the towers.

- **Tower Cluster Linkage**
  The flexibility that is achieved by planned redundancy in the connection system provides for the strengthening of the linkages between specific units. Thus, this contributes a medium for the enhancement of connections for interaction or, in the case of the commercial areas, attraction. This case thus introduces the concept of, and media for, planning of connectivity between multiple towers, or between other parts of the tower cluster.

- **Special Amenities Zones**
  Vertical zoning creates the potential for vertical amenities zones in the tower cluster. In addition to the atria and special amenity zones of the base and upper levels, there also exist many outdoor plateau spaces throughout the building.

e. The Functional and Symbolic Role of the Tower Cluster

Galaxy Soho is the first of two tower clusters designed for the Soho company. The second is Wangjing Soho, which is also in Beijing. In both clusters there is an attempt to create an expression of continuous flow and formally continuous differentiation. This is perhaps symbolic of the spatial expression of parametric support for continuous differentiation and variation. In addition, the structural and material expression of the architecture creates a

poetic symbolization of the technological creativity that is housed in Soho's flowing, clustered environments. The scale is monumental, as is appropriate for Beijing's monumental and symbolic architecture and urbanism.

2.5.10 Wangjing Soho, Beijing, China, Zaha Hadid Architects, 2009–2014

a. Clustered Trio: Introduction

Wangjing Soho is a tower cluster grouping of three towers of diverse heights. The tower forms are non-orthogonal and naturalistic in form, and they taper as they rise. As a result of their individual forms and their placement relative to one another, there is a sense of spatial flow as one moves into and through the central court space. The vertical tapering, the curved plan forms, and the twisted rather than orthogonal locations enhance this sense of spatial movement as one moves through the cluster.

The tallest tower has fifteen floors above ground including twelve office floors and three floors of retail space. In 2014, Wangjing Soho won the Emporis Skyscraper Award.

Opposite Page Galaxy Soho, Beijing, China, central court. Zaha Hadid Architects, 2009–2012. Courtesy of Iwan Baan. **Bottom Left** Galaxy Soho, Beijing, China. Zaha Hadid Architects, 2009–2012. Rendering courtesy of Zaha Hadid Architects. **Bottom Right** Galaxy Soho, Beijing, China, fourth-floor plan. Zaha Hadid Architects, 2009–2012. Courtesy of Zaha Hadid Architects.

Above Galaxy Soho, Beijing, China. Zaha Hadid Architects, 2009–2012. Courtesy of Iwan Baan.

Pages 112-113 Wangjing Soho, Beijing, China. Zaha Hadid Architects, 2009–2014. Courtesy of Jerry Yin.

SOHO

b. Clustered Trio: Program

The program includes three office towers of varying heights: 200, 127, and 118 meters high. The office floors and layouts are designed as flexible, open-plan office space to provide for the maximum possible flexibility in order to accommodate offices of a range of sizes. In addition, there is a significant requirement to provide for some degree of flexibility with respect to providing the potential for expansion over time.

c. Major Amenity: Program and Organization

The major building amenity is the commercial center, which is located primarily at the ground level with one additional level above and one below. This is to provide for shopping, restaurants, and cafes for the center's employees as well as for the public. The building entrances are arranged in such a manner that there is generally a multilevel entry system which provides the option to choose the appropriate entry level. Each of the three towers has an individual lobby space.

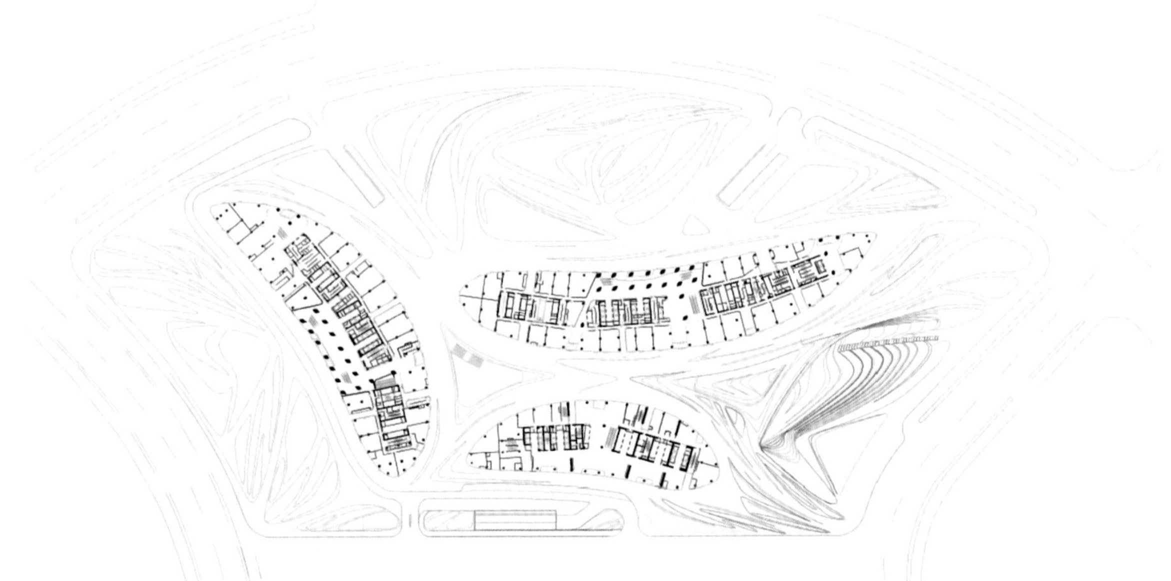

Above Wangjing Soho, Beijing, China. Zaha Hadid Architects, 2009–2014. Plan courtesy of Zaha Hadid Architects

Opposite Page Wangjing Soho, Beijing, China. Zaha Hadid Architects, 2009–2014. Courtesy of Zaha Hadid Architects. **Middle** Wangjing Soho, Beijing, China, outlying functional structures. Zaha Hadid Architects, 2009–2014.

There are multilevel entries at the main entrances. These provide the possibility to enter directly into the lower retail area or, alternatively, to enter the plaza level and tower entrances. At these entrances, there are sky-bridges at the plaza level. See the photo below entitled, "multilevel entrance to court."

In addition, at various locations around the exterior there exist a series of low-level ancillary structures that provide opportunities to feature special brand-name commercial companies. These additional structures are designed in relationship to the formal system of the towers. There are three underground floors of parking. There are also 8,256 spaces for bicycle parking and spaces for showers for cyclists.

The total size of the complex is approximately 521,265 square meters. The inter-tower space provides a central plaza. Each office building has a unique lobby space. The exterior space on the site provides landscaped gardens and a park.

d. Siting

Wangjing Soho is a major office and retail hub located in northeast Beijing between the airport and the city center. The area is rapidly developing as a center for high-tech and IT sector offices and industries. There are gardens and a park in the area of the site.

The area of the site is 115,393 square meters. Within the site development of the tower cluster there is a major internal plaza and a series of adjacent garden areas. The ancillary structures shown in the photo above also provide a reduction of scale at the intersection with the neighboring buildings.

The site is located close to the major public transportation links. The orientation of the towers is intended to direct the tower users and visitors to rapid transportation stations.

e. Tower Cluster Contributions

- **Major/Minor Tower Cluster Elements through Ancillary Structures**
  Ancillary structures have been built which employ geometric and formal characteristics similar to the major tower structures. In the case of Wangjing Soho, this tower cluster subsystem is used to provide for the expansion of the base-located commercial space in order to accommodate major brand-name clients.

- **Major/Minor Theme**
  The major/minor tower cluster theme can be applied to a variety of potential tower cluster subsystems, such as providing space for alternative program functions. They can also be applied as media for expansion.

- **Scale Transition Methods**
  The addition of elements of moderate scale at the periphery of the tower cluster can be employed as a means of reducing the large-scale impact of the dense cluster towers on neighboring developments.

2.5.11 Nanjing International Youth Cultural Center, Nanjing, China, Zaha Hadid Architects, 2011–2018

a. Tower Cluster Linked Duo: Introduction

The tower cluster was originally built for the 2014 Youth Olympic Games. Currently the towers house two hotels which are joined in the tower cluster with the Jumeirah Nanjing. This is a cultural center that contains conference facilities, an auditorium, mixed-use areas, and office space. The hotel towers are directly linked to the center through an urban plaza space on the ground level, and through the continuous space of the second-floor plan (see below). The tower cluster is also integrated with the landscape elements of the site, such as the Yangtze River shoreline, with a highly developed landscape plan. Among other cultural and social functions, the center and hotel are used for Jiangsu Province's annual conference.

Above Nanjing International Youth Cultural Center, Nanjing, China. Zaha Hadid Architects, 2018. Photo by Hufton and Crow.

Opposite Page Nanjing International Youth Cultural Center, Nanjing, China. Zaha Hadid Architects, 2018. SWA landscape master plan.

b. Tower Cluster Duo: Program

The four components of the Nanjing International Youth Cultural Center are freestanding elements around an urban court on the ground floor of the tower cluster. The conference center contains 106,500 square meters. The two towers contain 258,500 square meters. In addition, the lobbies of the two hotel towers are located opposite one another (see plan above). On the second floor of the cluster, the complex is functionally integrated in a unified spatial and circulation system (see plans below). The facilities of the five stories of the cultural center serve the hotel as well as visitors.

The lower, or western, tower contains the conference hotel and serviced apartments. The taller, or eastern, tower contains a five-star hotel and exclusive office space. Between the two hotels on the ground floor there is a hotel atrium plaza.

c. Major Amenity: Program and Organization

On the first level, there is the following organization of facilities. The cultural center (see plans below) consists of a conference hall of 2,200 seats and contains its own lounges and service spaces. It is located on the northwest side of the plan. Adjacent to the conference hall in the northeast corner of the plan is the VIP lounge and gallery. It has its own lounge as well as a press facility. On the east center of the plan is the auditorium and multifunctional hall. Opposite the auditorium on the west side of the plan is located a retail facility with showrooms. On the south side are located the two hotels. On the east side is the five-star hotel and high-end office tower. On the west side is located the conference hotel and serviced-apartment tower. Each of the towers has its own entrance lobby; there is also a special lobby for the office tower area. On the ground level, these six elements are organized around a central sunken court. All of the five major elements have external access ways between them.

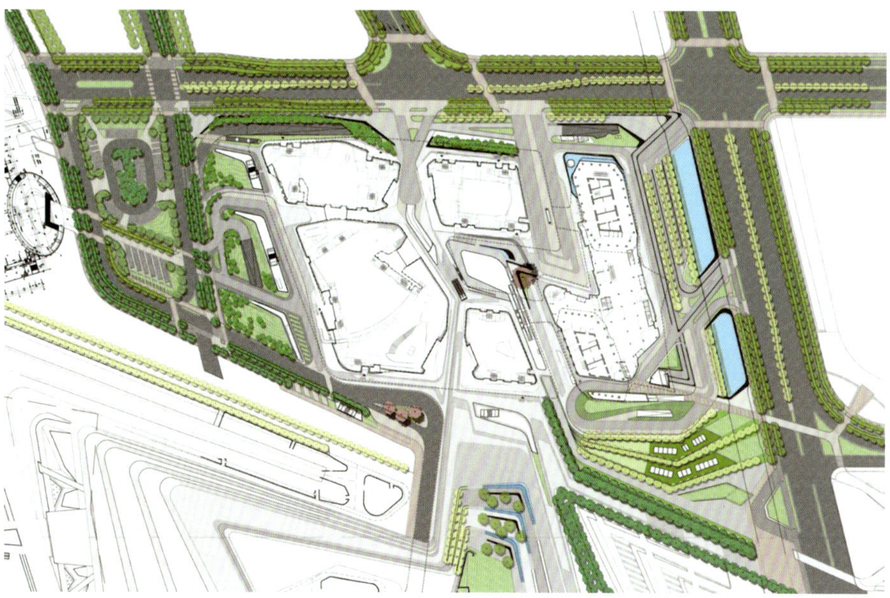

The second floor of the amenity area has a continuous spatial and circulation organization. There are three multifunctional halls: A, B, and C. There are various common spaces such as atria, lounges, terrace spaces, and a riverside lounge.

d. Siting (+ Extended Program)

The site area is located in the new central business district of Nanjing in the Hexi New Town area. It is adjacent to the river. The total site area is 5.2 hectares. The total construction area of the project is 465,000 square meters of floor space.

The site has been designed to provide outdoor event spaces and large public outdoor areas. These include a riverside park, a plaza of events, the boulevard of lights, and a waterscape plaza.

e. Tower Cluster Contributions

- **Plaza-Oriented Integration of the Tower Cluster and Its Amenities**
  The tower cluster is integrated with, and serves to provide various facilities for, a cultural center.

- **Special Amenities Provisions**
  In the case of Nanjing Cultural Center, the tower cluster is, in effect, in partnership with a more or less independent series of functions that constitute the cultural center. Many of the tower cluster functions, such as serviced apartments and the five-star hotel, are independent.

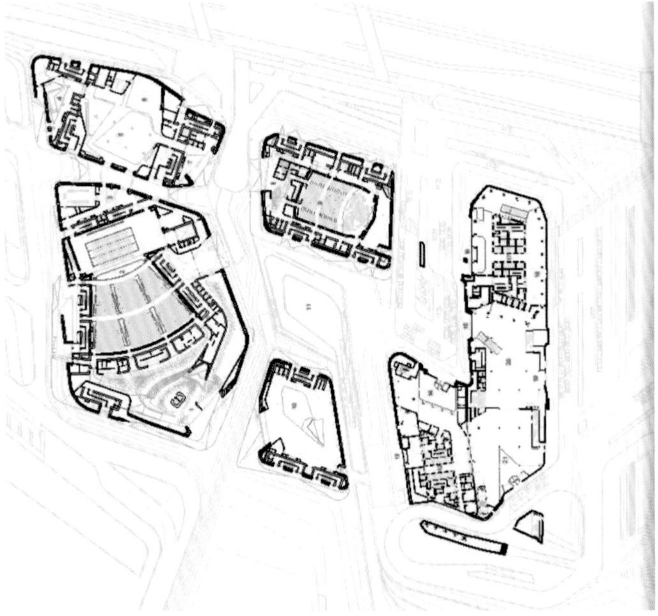

Right Nanjing International Youth Cultural Center, Nanjing, China. Zaha Hadid Architects, 2018. Plan of first level. Courtesy of Zaha Hadid Architects.

2.5.12 OPPO Headquarters, Shenzhen, China, Project, Zaha Hadid Architects, from 2020

a. Linked Quartet: Introduction

The tower cluster is the new headquarters of Oppo Telecommunications, a leading manufacturer of smartphones. It is a cluster of four interconnected towers located in one enveloping glass skin. Two of the towers are exclusively devoted to open-plan office space. The towers are linked by a twenty-story lobby; in addition to this grand lobby there will also be multiple large atrium spaces. All of this sense of openness is designed to enhance visual and functional interaction in order to encourage collaboration between employees and departments.

b. Linked Quartet: Program

The main office tower will be 200 meters tall (656 feet), and the main two towers will provide the basic open-plan work environment. These towers will provide a diversity of functional work environments as well as a variety of routes to circulate through the buildings. The remaining two towers will provide service and functional cores. This frees the two office towers from visual obstructions, with the intention of fostering maximal interaction between diverse departments.

The multilevel base of the building will provide a commercial area of shops, an art gallery, and restaurants. There will be a large, open landscaped plaza with multiple terraces. These spaces are intended to offer new civic spaces for the growing city's population. There will also be direct access to the city's subway system.

On the tenth floor there will be a sky plaza with publicly accessible facilities for restaurants, leisure activities, and entertainment. The dome-shaped upper levels, called the Sky Lab, will contain restaurants, bars, and spaces for enjoying the view. The built area of the tower cluster is expected to be approximately 185,000 square meters.

c. Major Amenities: Civic Program and Open Organization

The major amenities, as have been described above, are structured in three unique *amenity nodes*, which provide the structural order of the amenities. The first node of spaces is located in the public access mound which constitutes a base for the tower cluster. As can be observed in the perspective, this platform is pierced by a monumental entrance path which cuts the platform diagonally. The intention of the design of this mound area is that it will provide not only public access to the amenities of the base floors, but that it will also create an urban garden plaza for Shenzhen's population as well as for the building's employees. This civic motivation attempts to give symbolic form to the new urbanism of a dynamic city.

The second node of amenities is again open to the public. It engages the public visually, and to some extent, also physically within the creative order of the building's interior office floors. Thus, on the tenth floor there is a cluster of dining, leisure, and entertainment facilities known as the Sky Plaza.

The third node of amenities is at the apogee of the towers. In the context of the open-plan platforms sitting freely within the glass enclosure, the rooftop Sky Lab is to be a series of public spaces for meeting, dining, and bars. It is arranged in a series of levels organized as a pyramidal order of successive platforms. The Sky Lab will offer spectacular views of the city, the developing technological precinct, and the bay area. As can be observed from the perspectives, there appears to be current planning for multiple sky labs.

Opposite Page OPPO Headquarters, Shenzhen, China. Zaha Hadid Architects, from 2020. Render by Zaha Hadid Architects.

Bottom OPPO Headquarters, Shenzhen, China. Zaha Hadid Architects, from 2020. Ramped major access path into and between the towers. Render by Zaha Hadid Architects.

d. Siting: A Constructed Site within a Constructed Spatial Order

This tower cluster has a unique form of spatial organization in which one continuous glass envelope contains four towers within. The glass volume is, in effect, the building's spatial site. We may perhaps consider this the creation of a spatial omniverse within which the inner spatial order is freely created with respect to the outer shell. The skeletal structure is loosely inserted with the outer glass structure.

The objective is to create the sense of an internally integrated series of spaces floating freely within the transparent and polished environmental skin. In the envelope, two office towers are arranged within this enclosing glass site as a skeletal structure of curvilinear, scalloped-edged structural platforms (see interior perspectives below). The two additional towers are also within the glass skin and contain vertical cores of circulation and mechanical services.

e. Tower Cluster Contributions

- **Tower Cluster of Multiple Towers in Single Envelope**
  The glass envelope is continuous over four towers without interruption. The conventional definition of a tower cluster is of multiple joined, independent towers.

- **Tower Cluster as Symbol of Advanced Technology**
  The smooth geometry and minimalist effect of the glass envelope, which without interruption wraps the four towers, creates a symbolic impression of an object of high technology.

- **Multifloor Open-Plan System to Encourage Interaction**
  Visual interaction within and between open-plan floors is optimized by withdrawing the slab ends from its periphery being closed off at the curtain wall. The geometry of plan form also enables some degree of visual interaction between successive floors (see perspective below).

- **Uninterrupted Visual Contact by Displacement of Cores**
  There is a physical subdivision between servant and served space. Vertical services and vertical circulation are located in separate towers in order to not impede visual contact and interaction.

- **Reduction of Plan Size at Base Increases Size of Public Exterior Space**
  This is achieved by the arching inward of the curtain wall towards the base of the cluster (see perspectives above).

Above Left OPPO Headquarters, Shenzen, China. Zaha Hadid Architects, from 2020. View of interior open-plan floor space. Render by Zaha Hadid Architects. **Above Right** OPPO Headquarters, Shenzen, China. Zaha Hadid Architects, from 2020. View of interior open-plan floor space and common space. Render by Zaha Hadid Architects. **Bottom** OPPO Headquarters, Shenzen, China. Zaha Hadid Architects, from 2020. View of upper floor Sky Lab. Render by Zaha Hadid Architects.

2.5.13 Tower C at Shenzhen Bay Super Headquarters, Mixed-Use Complex, Shenzhen, China, Zaha Hadid Architects, from 2021

a. Name Tower Cluster: Linked Duo: Introduction

Tower C is actually a pair of independent towers joined both by a multilevel base as well as by a series of bridging levels above the base. As in other contemporary high-rise buildings of Hadid Architects, there is an ambiguous formal situation between individual buildings founded upon paired elements or the motif of joined dual elements. Here we clearly have two towers rather than one tower internally subdivided (see section 3.1 below). From the point of view of the tower cluster typology, this project is remarkable for the manner in which the amenity spaces of the base coalesce into a podium condition at the center core terraced upwards between the towers. The public, multilevel core being located on the city's urban green public axis can potentially propagate the concept of the green urban core to other urban complexes along the axis.

b. Name Tower Cluster: Linked Duo: Program

The tower cluster is intended to become a part of a vertical city development combining high density, tall building, work, and living environments with public access cultural and commercial amenities. It is also a part of the city's metro transportation network.

The highest of the two towers reaches nearly 400 meters in height. Tower C1 is 394 meters (1,293 feet) with seventy-eight floors of hotel and office space; Tower C2 is 356 meters (1,167 feet) with sixty-eight floors of office space. The towers accommodate office space, a hotel, a convention center and provide public amenities such as cultural facilities, exhibition galleries, shopping, entertainment, and dining facilities. Cultural, entertainment, and leisure functions are located primarily in the core spaces of the base and in the skybridges that join the towers. There is a public transportation interchange below ground level which is naturally lighted from above.

c. Siting (+ Extended Program)

Shenzhen Bay Super Headquarters Base is an important business and financial center, and a technological hub, in the bay area of Guangdong, Hong Kong, and Macau. The area is expected to eventually house approximately three hundred thousand workers in a group of corporate office buildings. This specific building site is integrated with the city's north-south green axis and its east-west urban corridor. It is directly connected with an adjacent park and urban plazas, and is a part of the transit-oriented development of Shenzhen's spine. This direct connection of building complexes to the spine is intended to create a "super-scape." The base design of the cluster connects to the park through the design medium of a series of terraced plazas to create a multistoried podium that opens the core space of the cluster to the public. Visitors arriving by bicycle will have extensive bicycle storage facilities available.

d. Tower Cluster Contributions

- **"The Multidimensional Vertical City"**
  The term is that of the architect. Here, in combination with the following two typological contributions, the tower cluster becomes a vertical nexus among a collective of urban clusters each of which is integrated with the movement paths, public transportation system, green axes, and spatial systems of the city.

- **The Open Heart**
  The spatial core of the cluster is open to the public, which is invited to use its spaces and facilities. The medium of spatial integration is a series of green terraces that invite the public to enter the core and participate in its spaces. Each vertically developed core can thus become part of a continuous urban spatial system.

- **Events on the City's Green Axis: Unification of the Urban Landscape**
  The design system of terraced green cluster spaces is functionally and formally integrated physically within the city's green space system. It is designed to be part of a public urban spatial continuum.

- **Skybridging Internal Functions Creates Sky Plazas and Sky Gardens**
  The internal functional system of collective commercial, entertainment, and dining functions is roofed by plazas and green terraces. Public facilities perform the function of bridging between the twin towers.

- **Precedent Making and the Power of Connectivity**
  Create an idea that can become a precedent for other tower clusters of various numbers. Such an idea is the concept of the *open heart* in the core of the tower cluster, and the development of the open heart and the further use of that core as a medium for public-accessed landscape terraces. These terrace clusters can potentially be connected from one cluster to another, thus creating a system in which the landscape becomes a medium of urban connectivity.

e. Special Amenities Provision: The Potential for Linked Tower Clusters with Public Access to the Open Heart

The Shenzhen green spine is linked to the transit-oriented development (TOD), which in Tower C is also linked to the public access core spaces of the tower cluster. Given the potential for further development of high-density complexes on the spine offering the potential for public access, this, in effect, will create what is described by the planners as a "super-scape."

Opposite Page Above Left Tower C at Shenzhen Bay Super Headquarters. Zaha Hadid Architects, from 2021. Render by Brick Visual courtesy of Zaha Hadid Architects. **Above Right** Tower C Shenzhen Bay Super Headquarters. Zaha Hadid Architects, from 2021. Render by Brick Visual courtesy of Zaha Hadid Architects. **Center Left** Tower C Shenzhen Bay Super Headquarters. Zaha Hadid Architects, from 2021. Render by Brick Visual courtesy of Zaha Hadid Architects. **Bottom Left** Tower C Shenzhen Bay Super Headquarters. Zaha Hadid Architects, from 2021. Stepped garden terraces. Render by Brick Visual courtesy of Zaha Hadid Architects. **Bottom Right** Tower C Shenzhen Bay Super Headquarters, night view. Zaha Hadid Architects, from 2021. Render by Brick Visual courtesy of Zaha Hadid Architects.

2.5.14 Duo Twin Towers, Singapore, Büro Ole Scheeren, 2018

a. Tower Cluster Duo: Introduction

Duo is a tower cluster of two towers which makes a uniquely significant contribution to the analysis of tower cluster contributions in our selected case studies. Duo is a multifunctional tower cluster that has been designed to transform an existing condition lacking a distinct urban form into a unique urban order of a well-ordered sequence of urban spaces and forms. This has been termed by the architects as "an act of urban reconciliation."

Here, the consideration of the language of urban form has been the motivating determinant of the overall design. The reordering of urban space is achieved through the form of the tower cluster and its elements, such as the base of terraced gardens and plazas. An axial order of curvilinear forms has been the guiding principle of the design, and this curvilinear spatial order has also been a design motif applied to the architecture of the towers. In this example, architecture follows urbanism, or perhaps more accurately, the two orders of scale are integrated.

The architect has created a Sitte-like urban order, particularly with respect to imposing an irregularity of form on the two towers within what is actually a symmetrical order. The objective of these strategies has been to create an environment of usable public spaces for pedestrians.

b. Tower Cluster Duo: Program

The two towers of the Duo have diverse functions. The residential tower (see foreground tower in photo above) contains 660 residences, while the second tower with the cantilevered extension contains a five-star hotel and office space. The residential tower is 192.8 meters high and contains forty-nine floors. The hotel/office tower is 185.35 meters high and contains thirty-nine floors. The multifloor base of the towers contains various public commercial facilities.

The resulting newly developed urban environment has created within the physical context of a dense urban order a new spatial environment for work, living, entertainment, leisure, shopping, and socializing in a lushly landscaped multilevel pedestrian area within tropical gardens.

c. Major Amenity: Program and Organization

The major amenity of the project has been the provision of a new and unique urban nexus of integrated spaces, pathways, gardens, plazas, and terraced commercial and entertainment zones within the context of a high-density environment for living, working, and visiting. This is available to the public on a twenty-four-hour basis. There is also a public connection to the MRT transportation hub.

At a finer degree of detail, the commercial multilevel area at the base of the Duo's twin towers provides facilities for shops, dining, and entertainment. In the hotel tower at the level of the cantilevered mass, there is a large public-access sky plaza with the hotel's swimming pool and outdoor leisure facilities. Within the towers there are a series of public-access roofscapes and viewing areas, the largest of which is 180 meters above the ground plane.

d. Site (+ Extended Program)

The site is located on the main road from the airport to the city. It is adjacent to both the known Kampong Glam district and the commercial area of Bugis Junction.

The design of the tower cluster has created a twenty-four-hour accessible series of gardens and public plazas. The larger urban area has been designed to create a series of circular urban spaces (see diagram below). This also creates a series of amenities such as walkways, parks, cafés, and dining facilities. The introduction of a duo of towers, commercial/entertainment facilities, and lush landscape development within the urban fabric of an existing neglected urban area has created a new urban center that welcomes visitors in a lively social environment.

- **Tower Cluster Design as a Medium for Urban Renewal**
  The transformation of an existing neglected urban environment has been achieved by the uniquely instrumental design of the Duo tower cluster.

Opposite Page Duo, Singapore, perspective. Ole Scheeren @ Büro OS, 2018. Courtesy of Ole Scheeren @ Büro OS.

Above Duo, Singapore, urban figure and context. Ole Scheeren @ Büro OS, 2018. Photo courtesy of Iwan Baan. **Middle** Duo, Singapore, permeable public landscape. Ole Scheeren @ Büro OS, 2018. Photo courtesy of Iwan Baan.

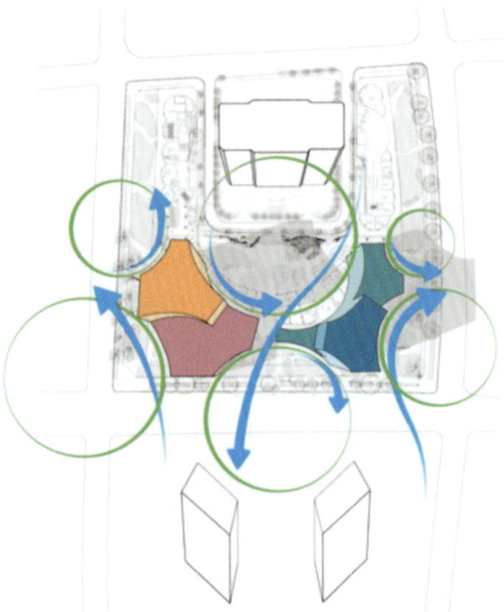

CARVED URBAN SPACES

- **The Potential for Urban Space Design**
  The design of the physical dimensions and geometry can influence and/or transform the spatial quality and character of the urban environment of the tower cluster's site.

- **The Creation of an Urban Space System for Pedestrian Use**
  The design of landscaping amenities such as gardens and plazas *within the site area* of the tower cluster has been a motivating factor of several of our prior case studies. In the case of Duo, this has been extended to the design and creation of such landscape amenities in the larger total urban spatial context of the site.

2.5.15 DJI Headquarters, Nanshan District, Shenzhen, China, Foster + Partners, 2016–2023

a. Tower Cluster Duo: Introduction

The bridge-linked twin tower cluster is the new headquarters building for DJI, which is one of the world's leading robotics companies and particularly noted for their advanced drone designs and manufacturing, drone technology, and, in general, the design of UAV, or unmanned aerial vehicles. Beyond administrative functions, the unique contribution of the tower cluster is to create an environment conducive to stimulating, enhancing, and supporting creative technological invention and development. This intention to create "a unique workplace environment that embodies the spirit of invention and innovation" of the company was the motivation for the unique design.

The building's designers, Foster and Partners, have referred to this ambitious objective as establishing a "creative community in the sky." The three main means that are employed are:

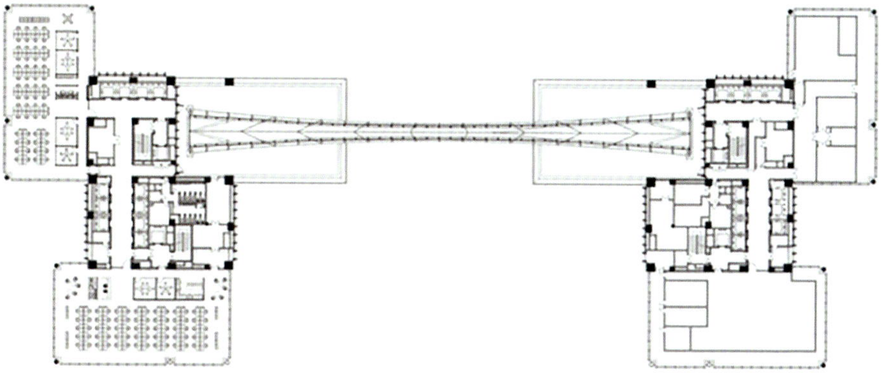

Opposite Page Duo, Singapore, environmental flows. Ole Scheeren @ Büro OS, 2018. Courtesy of Büro Ole Scheeren. **Bottom** DJI Headquarters, Shenzhen, China. Foster + Partners, 2016–2023.

Above DJI Headquarters, Shenzhen, China, plan. Foster + Partners, 2016–2023. Courtesy of Foster + Partners. **Middle Left** DJI Headquarters, Shenzhen, China, perspective. Foster + Partners, 2016–2023. Courtesy of Foster + Partners. **Middle Right** DJI Headquarters, Shenzhen, China. Foster + Partners, 2016–2023. Photo courtesy of Fangfang Tian. **Bottom** DJI Headquarters, Shenzhen, China. Foster + Partners, 2016–2023. Photo courtesy of Fangfang Tian.

- The establishment of a series of quadruple-floored labs, and experimental and operational display zones at the head of a vertical grouping of office floor slabs. This integration of one-story and four-story spaces is visible in the perspectives as the basic organizational module which is repeated throughout the cluster;

- The provision of a skybridge, which can be employed for testing and displaying drones in flight;

- The integration within the spatial order of the large structural modules of a broad set of amenities which are intended to stimulate reflection and creative thought.

b. Tower Cluster Duo: Program

Within the twin towers, advanced and sensitive research and development spaces are located in the east tower—due to the experimental and developmental nature of their functions, these spaces require privacy. The west tower provides for office and public functions, and contains the main entrance lobby. This entrance at ground level is the medium for security and access to both of the towers. The built area of the tower cluster is 160,000 square meters. The height of the tallest tower is 194 meters.

The organizational module of the multifloor spaces above single-floor spaces is also the structural support system in which a cluster of single-floor spaces are suspended from the four-story trusses ("mega-trusses") of the lab spaces through a structural suspension system that enables a minimum number of column obstructions on the office floors. The multifloor spaces also enable experimental and display zone flights. The labs provide for ongoing drone testing, allow column-free flight paths, and contribute to the experimental, futuristic, technological image of the headquarters. The skybridge can be employed to launch zone flights outside of the building.

The ground floor contains a major public exhibition space for product launches and for the display of media to demonstrate and illustrate the major technological achievements of DJI. There is also a theater which is frequently employed for the launching of new products.

c. Major Amenities: Program and Organization

Contemplative minimalist gardens based upon Zen gardens are located throughout the cluster. At ground level there are a series of gardens which relate the building gardens to the greenery of the surrounding area. On the rooftops of the floating modules are a series of private sky gardens as special contemplative private areas for the staff. Throughout the base of the tower cluster there are a large selection of staff facilities including gymnasia and fighting rings for robot combat.

d. Site (+ Extended Program)

The site area is located in the Nanshan District in the southwest of Shenzhen. The new building and its interior and exterior relationships with the

Opposite Page DJI Headquarters, Shenzhen, China. Foster + Partners, 2016–2023. Photo courtesy of Chao Zhang

site, its gardens, the green areas, and views are intended to be the heart of the developmental creativity of the company. Shenzhen, in general, and this area in particular is developing as a major site of high technological development.

e. Tower Cluster Contributions

- **From Traditional Office to Creative Community in the Sky**
  The cluster is organized by what appear to be floating modules. These modules are designed as environments to support processes of creative technological design innovation. Each of these modules also contains contemplative garden spaces to enhance creative thought.

- **Contemplative Zones for Refreshment Towards Creation**
  Both on the ground floor and on the module rooftops there are gardens to enhance reflection and creative thought. These are sky gardens of both the office and R&D environments.

- **Sky Labs for Testing and Display**
  The integration of multiple sky labs within the spatial order of the headquarters environment places both functional and visual emphasis on technological innovation as the heart of DJI.

- **Skybridge as Testing and Display Area: Skybridge Turned Zone-Launching Platform**
  The skybridge has unique functions in the tower cluster as an interface with the surrounding airspace and as a dramatic display area.

f. Special Amenities Provision: The Functional and Symbolic Role of the Tower Cluster
The symbolic form of the floating modules, the giant trusses, the suspended floors, and the steel construction expresses both a futuristic expression of form, as well as a unique emphasis of the flight of the mind as a metaphorical foundation of the activities of DJI.

2.6 Typological Anomalies

In this presentation and analysis of leading case studies of the tower cluster typology, we have observed both the exactitude of the typological definition and its concomitant flexibility. As defined in section 2.1, a tower cluster is a clustering of two or more towers that due to their size and density produce a situation in which it is possible to provide certain amenities such as garden space, urban plazas, etc., that might have been unjustified without the increased density. Usually the towers are multifunctional, and frequently they are linked by an articulated base, and possibly, in addition, a skybridge.

We have previously noted that the majority of the case studies have been designed, built, or in construction since the second decade of the current century. With respect to the tower cluster, the scale of typological innovation in this brief period has been extraordinary. In such a historically compressed term of highly innovative design, it is probable that the components of the typology can potentially be hybridized, or integrated in design with nontypological elements. For example, in this period we can observe designs that are mainly typological, but due to the elimination of a major typological indicator, do not exist in the design category of the tower cluster. We refer to this condition of the almost, but not quite, complete cases of the typology, as *typological anomalies.*

Among the dominant typological characteristics of the tower cluster are high-density development, multifunctionality, a public base area both interior and exterior which provides a significant public use interface, the presence of some form of skybridge, and others. The programmatic content that justifies such design characteristics are also generally common in the developing high-tech areas. Thus, we have also noted in our survey, developments that are similar to tower clusters and share these common tower cluster characteristics without actually being, according to the proposed definition, tower clusters.

2.6.1 A Duo That Is Not Quite a Duo: Leeza Soho, Beijing, Zaha Hadid Architects, 2015–2019

Opposite Page Leeza Soho, Beijing, China. Zaha Hadid Architects, 2013–2019. Photographs courtesy of Hufton and Crow. **Above Right** Leeza Soho, Beijing, China. Zaha Hadid Architects, 2013–2019. View of atrium walls with internal glass enclosure. Photographs courtesy of Hufton and Crow.

The tower is forty-five stories high and contains 172,800 square meters of built space. The building height is 200 meters. Leeza Soho in Beijing, China was designed by Zaha Hadid Architects during the period 2013 to 2019. It is a single tower which has a central atrium. At 194 meters high it is the

world's tallest atrium. Internally, the two sectors have glass enclosures at the atrium and independent means of vertical circulation. They are essentially two independent wings of the same building. Functionally, this creates a duo, or a building similar to a two-unit tower cluster.

The two sectors are joined by skybridges at four levels: 13, 24, 35, and 45. Since the building is built over the mass transit tunnels, the base is oriented in the direction of an underground service line of mass transportation; while the upper atrium is oriented in the direction of Lize Road. The atrium creates an internalized public square as a major civic space for the new Fengtai business district.

The tower is designed to provide small- and medium-sized office spaces for businesses seeking a high-quality location. The base has an internally articulated two-level area of shops, while the basement provides auto and bicycle storage and charging facilities for electric and hybrid automobiles. Leeza Soho is an internal duo, but misses, by definition, being a tower cluster.

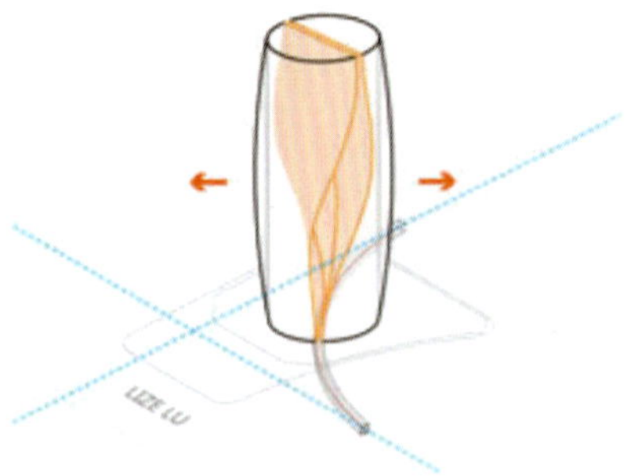

4. 扩大了切口的体量产生了中庭空间，为办公和大堂创造视野。进一步扩张的体量保持了楼板面积。

Widening of crevasse to increase atrium volume, create views for offices and liftlobbies outwards. Bulge volume to maintain gfa and create iconic silhouette.

5. 核心筒向上生长，在表皮上留下椭圆形“印记”，增加更多建筑面积。

Core offset growing upwards , leaving ellipsoid 'imprint' in facade surface, increasing GFA.

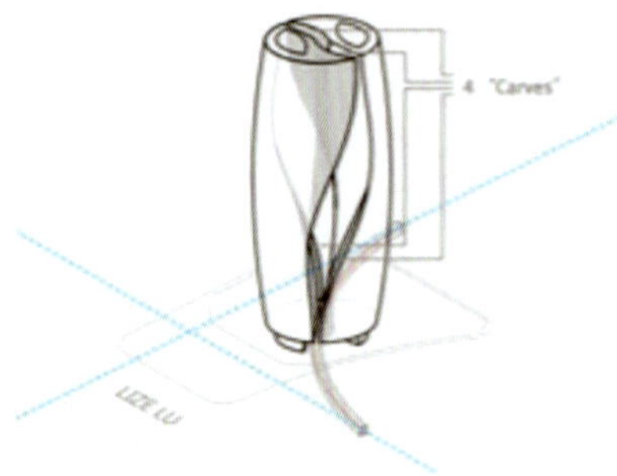

6. 削减4块体量以平衡建筑面积，并创造更多视角及首层大堂空间。

Carve out 4 conic volumes to balance GFA and create additional view situations and increasing ground floor lobby space.

MUTIPLE-UNIT PLAN

OPEN PLAN

Above Leeza Soho, Beijing, China. Zaha Hadid Architects, 2013–2019. Massing strategy of atrium form. **Bottom** Leeza Soho, Beijing, China. Zaha Hadid Architects, 2013–2019. Tower plan with multiple-unit plan and open-plan layouts.

Opposite Page Sky Soho, Shanghai, air view. Zaha Hadid Architects, 2010–2014. Perspective courtesy of Zaha Hadid Architects

2.6.2 Not Really Sky: Sky Soho, Shanghai, Zaha Hadid Architects, 2010–2014

Sky Soho is a cluster of four skybridge-linked slab office buildings located in the Hongqiao Business Zone. The development is close to the city center and airport. The site has access to subway and rail service. The buildings have eleven levels above ground. The program includes office space of 196,000 square meters; retail of 23,000 square meters; and space below ground level, including retail, for an additional 123,000 square meters.

The program includes designed gardens at the ground areas including significant garden developments plus waterfalls and ponds at ground and lower levels. The roof areas of the four slabs are also developed as large rooftop gardens. Thus, Sky Soho presents Shanghai with a civic gesture on a major urban scale as well as a walkable, multilevel shopping zone integrated within the parklike setting of the gardens. Again, this is an urban civic gesture on a grand scale.

Here we encounter one more case of the presence of almost all of the ingredients of the typological definition of the tower cluster, with the exception of one: the buildings are not towers. They are slabs—a type of which we have already encountered within the tower cluster definition, including the Grand Arche in Paris, and CCTV Headquarters in Beijing. Given the relatively low height and the strongly expressed horizontality, the project is distinctive, but digresses from the tower cluster definition. Despite this, as we have stated, the architectural and urban ingredients provide a profound urban statement. The definition and composition of these ingredients are perhaps among the major contributions of this emerging typology, and components of the vocabulary, such as skybridges, exist in many additional examples.

Above Sky Soho, Shanghai, entry-level view. Zaha Hadid Architects, 2010–2019. Perspective courtesy of Zaha Hadid Architects. **Right** Sky Soho, Shanghai. Zaha Hadid Architects, 2010–2014. View of base and underground levels. Perspective courtesy of Zaha Hadid Architects.

2.7 The Crystallization of the Tower Cluster: Summary

1. CCTV, Beijing, China, 2002–2012. OMA

Subtype: Geometrical Cubic Order of Double Tower Cluster
Function(s): Headquarters (Administration and Offices, Studios, Technical and Production Facilities, Exhibition, Broadcasting, Theater) of Chinese Central Television
Height: 51 Floors
Contributions: 4

2. De Rotterdam, Rotterdam, Netherlands, Design 1997–1998, Construction 2009–2013. OMA

Subtype: Tower Cluster of Three Adjacent Towers
Function(s): Offices (1.5 Towers), Residential (1 Tower), Hotel (0.5 Tower), Mixed-Use Base
Height: 44 Floors
Contributions: 5

3. CMG Qianhai Global Trade Center, Shenzhen, China, from 2016, Construction 2020. OMA

Subtype: Tower Cluster of Twin Towers Linked with Amplified Skybridge and Functionally Articulated Base: Micro-City
Function(s): Offices Above Shopping Base (1.5 Towers), Hotel (0.5 Tower)
Height: 54 Floors
Contributions: 3

4. VDMA Van der Meulen-Ansemsterrein, Eindhoven, Netherlands, Project, 2020. OMA

Subtype: Functionally Integrated Quartet
Function(s): Residential (4 Towers—2 High, 2 Low), Microforest, Low-Rise Offices for Start-Ups Plus Integrated Low-Rise Housing (Live-Work Environment), Shopping Base, Restored Buildings
Height: 30–40 Floors (approximation)
Contributions: 4

5. Marina Bay Sands, Singapore, 2010. Safdie Architects

Subtype: Linear Trio
Function(s): Hotel, Casino, Mall, Cultural Facilities, Sky Park, Mixed-Use Base
Height: 57 Floors
Contributions 9

6. Sky Habitat, Singapore, 2016. Safdie Architects

Subtype: Linear Duo
Function(s): High-Density Multistory Housing (2 Towers), Gardens and Rest Areas in Skybridge Links
Height: 38 Floors
Contributions: 7

7. Raffles City Chongqing, China, 2019. Safdie Architects with Chongqing Architecture and Design Institute

Subtype: Tower Cluster of Eight Linked Towers
Function(s): Residential (4 Towers), Serviced Residential Tower, Offices (3 Towers), Hotel, Private Club, Galleria
Height: 79 Floors
Contributions: 3

8. ORCA Toronto, Canada, 2021, Project. Safdie Architects

Subtype: Park-Oriented Double Tower Cluster
Function(s): TC 1: Residential (6 Towers), Offices (1 Tower) TC 2: Residential (2 Towers), Mixed-Use (1 Tower), Mixed-Use Base
Height: 43 and 46 Floors
Contributions: 5

9. Galaxy Soho, Beijing, China, 2009–2012. Zaha Hadid Architects

Subtype: Linked Quartet Courtyard Development
Function(s): Base Zone of Commercial and Entertainment (3 Floors), Mid Zone of Office Space (15 Floors), Upper Zone (Penthouse Level),Five Courtyards, One Central Courtyard
Height: 18 Floors
Contributions: 8

10. Wangjing Soho, Beijing, China, 2009–2014. Zaha Hadid Architects

Subtype: Clustered Trio
Function(s): Base Zone of Commercial and Entertainment (3 Floors), Office Space (3 Towers)
Height: 15 floors
Contributions: 3

11. Nanjing International Youth Cultural Center, Nanjing, China, 2011–2018. Zaha Hadid Architects

Subtype:	Linked Duo
Function(s):	Conference Hotel and Serviced Apartments (1 Tower), Hotel and Office Space (1 Tower), Base Zone Contains Conference Center with Auditorium and Three Multifunctional Halls, Commercial Area, Common Spaces with Lounges, Atria, and Terrace Spaces (5 Floors)
Height:	68 and 61 Floors
Contributions:	2

12. OPPO Headquarters, Shenzen, China, Project from 2020. Zaha Hadid Architects

Subtype:	Linked Quartet
Function(s):	Open-Plan Offices (2 Towers), Service and Circulation Functions (2 Towers)
Height:	42 Floors (Tallest Tower)
Contributions:	5

13. Tower C Shenzhen Bay Super Headquarters, Mixed-Use Complex, Shenzhen, China, 2021. Zaha Hadid Architects

Subtype:	Linked Duo
Function(s):	Hotel and Office Space (Taller Tower), Office Space (Lower Tower), Cultural, Entertainment, Leisure (Base).
Height:	78 and 68 Floors
Contributions:	5

14. Duo Twin Towers, Singapore, 2018. Büro Ole Scheeren

Subtype:	Tower Cluster Duo
Function(s):	Residential (Higher Tower), Hotel and Office Space (Lower Tower), Entertainment, Leisure, Shopping, Cultural (Lower Floors of Cluster), Landscaped Multilevel Pedestrian Area
Height:	49 and 39 Floors
Contributions:	3

15. DJI Headquarters, Nanshan District, Shenzhen, China, 2016–2023. Foster + Partners

Subtype:	Tower Cluster Duo
Function(s):	Research and Development (1 Tower), Office Space, Public Functions, Main Entrance (1 Tower), Theater, Public Exhibition Space (Ground Floor)
Height:	34 and 31 Floors
Contributions:	4

2.8 The Crystallization of the Tower Cluster: Conclusions

The fifteen case studies were selected through their appearance in major daily architectural internet sites. The research program was formally initiated in 2019, and this resulted in the identification and selection of a majority of the examples. In addition, four of the examples were added based on prior knowledge. These were two by Safdie Architects (Marina Bay Sands and Sky Habitat, both in Singapore) and two by OMA (CCTV Beijing and De Rotterdam from the Netherlands).

It is significant to clarify that the five architects emerged from a research process and were not preselected as case studies before starting the research. In addition, Ole Scheeren was formerly associated with OMA, and he had worked on CCTV which, it may be considered, reduces the number of architects even further. Two other projects were selected but not employed due to a lack of published information currently available on the projects. One of these is Zaha Hadid Architect's CECEP Mixed-Use Headquarters Campus in Shanghai, and the other is Studio Jeanne Gang's St. Regis, in Chicago.

Given that the selection was the result of a research-based process to select case studies rather than to select architects beforehand, it is clear that the crystallization of this new typology is associated with an outstanding group of architects distinguished by their innovative and often experimental architectural and urban design.

It is possible to tentatively summarize the findings of the research process so far. The tower cluster as defined in section 2.1 and as analyzed in the case studies has enabled the determination of an important set of its determinant characteristics.

- The typology provides a highly flexible mechanism for the design of multifunctional, high-density urban programs;

- It possesses multiple components such as tower number, tower types, skybridges (presence, numbers, and locations), and amenities, etc., each of which can be virtually programmed separately;

- The syntactical content of the typology is diverse and flexible enough to invite and enhance program invention and diversification;

- The ability to employ skybridges enables the possibility to enhance and implement interdepartmental connections in order to ameliorate segregation, which is frequently characteristic of vertical urbanism;

- The case studies have exemplified the high degree of both program, formal, and scalar flexibility that is characteristic of the typology;

- Of the fifteen cases, nine of them are located in China. Many of these are related to advanced technological industries. These and others of the case studies attest to the high level of programmatic flexibility as well as the potential power of urban-scale image generation.

- One may speculate that the open combinatorial character of the typology itself invites and promotes both formal and programmatic speculation and invention. For example, consider OMA's tower cluster in Eindhoven.

- There is a high degree of urban and landscape integration within each of the case study examples as well as with the surrounding urban environment. This may be considered the result of the high degree of flexibility of each of the horizontal zones that have come to characterize the horizontal stratification of the tower cluster. In the case of urban and landscape integration with the developmental characteristics of the urban site, this illustrates the particularly high degree of flexibility and importance related to the base zone of all tower clusters.

In the following chapters we will define and analyze the typology, its subtypes, components, and the emerging classes of *urban amenities* that are associated with this typology. We have already observed that between each subtype of the numerical organization of tower cluster there exists the ability to "host," or to support, the integration of amenities such as sky plazas, observation decks, sky pools, etc.

The form of the presentation and analysis of these characteristics and potential attributes of the typology will attempt to analyze and conceptually categorize certain of the creative architectural potential which is inherent in this emergent architectural/urban typology.

This may also enable us to define in which direction(s) this typology might lead from the point of view of future urbanism.

Above Model study of Hyperbuilding Bangkok. OMA, 1996. With the Hyperbuilding Research Committee Office. Photo by Hans Werelmann courtesy of OMA.

PART III

The Tower Cluster as a Flexible Mixed-Use High-Density Urban Building Typology

3.1 A Conceptual Definition of the Typology

> *Typology is concerned with those aspects of human production which can be grouped because of some inherent characteristics which makes them similar. The theory of typology is thus that of conceptualizing those categories.*
>
> —Micha Bandini,
> *Typological Theories in Architectural Design*

> *The tower cluster is a typology for the flexible, high-density multi-element design of tall buildings and urban habitat (CTBUH).*[10]

The tower cluster is a format for the *assembly of multiple high-rise buildings,* either towers or slabs, into a unified, high-density environment. In addition to the tall building elements, this assemblage is achieved with an additional set of conceptual components always to be integrated within the structural organization of the tower cluster syntax of parts. These conceptual components include the following four additional major syntactical elements:

Sky Elements

Horizontal elements such as skybridges, or sky plazas which accommodate *sky amenities.* These may occur on multiple levels, or multiple vertical zones in the tower cluster. Together they enable the potential to create a vertical campus. This important term denotes the intrinsic power of the cluster's unique characteristic vertical organization to overcome the traditional segregation and staff isolation which has been characteristic of the traditional skyscraper. Thus, as we have previously observed, the tower cluster has become a preferred architectural/urban design medium for the vertical organization of advanced companies of technological development.

Base Zone

The articulated multilevel base is generally employed for the accommodation of both public and private amenities.

Urban Landscape Zones

There exists a high degree of design potential for the integration within the overall structure of a tower cluster design for the integration with, and improvement of, contextual urban design and urban landscape design.

Optional Zones

These are structured horizontal zones for the potential addition of ancillary program(s) such as user amenities. They may also be considered zones for future expansion.

The tower cluster should thus be considered and designed as a *framework*, or *scaffolding*, for accommodating a multicomponent structure. The format is a vertical and horizontal syntax of parts for the five subsystems of the cluster. The major subsystem of high-rise elements is constructed of two or more high-rise components. This multipart scaffolding enhances the ability to respond to the requirements of complex circulation systems which are generally intrinsic to compact, high-density environments.

Employing this rich structural/organizational framework of the tower cluster, it is generally capable of satisfying a multifunctional program in diverse ways. With its particularized component syntax, it is particularly suitable for the accommodation of complex programs with multiple differentiated spatial, functional, and technical requirements. This has already proven the type to be highly malleable in the case of fulfilling the complex needs of emerging technological industries. The potential diversity of the framework's syntactical parts and relationships also renders it highly flexible for the integration of both public and private (industry-related) vertical amenity zones. Therefore, the structural and organizational flexibility of the conceptual typology of the tower cluster is emerging as a unique tool for the design of high-density urban accommodation of new technological industries, as well as for other complex urban functions. The scale of design flexibility of the type is very high and well-adapted to the design of complex, high-density urban programs.

The Sky Elements

Within the high-density spatial matrix of the tower cluster are integrated special structural zones for the provision of programmatic amenities, both public and private. These amenity strata may be single or multiple levels. They are located as base elements or sky elements. Sky elements such as skybridges and sky parks are located at various levels aboveground and potentially also include the upper levels within the cluster buildings as a penthouse. The unique visual presence of these sky elements integrated within an assembly of tall building elements has also instilled in this emerging urban typology a unique level of formal power and expressiveness. This high level of intrinsic formal malleability has enriched the typology with the ability to achieve powerful, even monumental, urban design solutions.

The Plinth or Base Structure

The plinth is usually an architecturally articulated structure. It generally serves multiple programmatic functions, including urban design, circulation, and the location of public amenities. The urban design program depends upon the site and particular urban situation. Among other factors, it must satisfy urban circulation requirements of the site including mass transit. Other aspects of circulation related to the base are the resolution of multiple requirements, particularly public and privacy requirements. The amenities frequently located in the base levels are generally associated with public access functions such as shopping and cultural facilities. In addition, exhibition and display functions and large facilities such as lecture halls—

all of which may be related to the occupants of the tall buildings—are frequently located in the base levels of the tower cluster.

The Urban Design Program

There are frequently urban design requirements that are incumbent upon the site and its urban location. These may include, among many others, the respect for, and response to, urban path systems, planting materials, and the existence of adjacent public spaces such as parks. This frequently imposes an additional level of complexity upon the design of the base elements as well as their intrinsic program requirements. Perhaps the most significant level of urban issue is that of the potential urban symbolism of the complex to be built. Should it, or can it, potentially express the symbolic importance of the main program of the tower cluster? Can the design of the cluster express a representation and function related to the urban location of the site? Such an expression might be that of a gateway. Both of these symbolic expressions have already occurred in the case studies. It is the high degree of both functional and formal flexibility of the tower cluster as a flexible ensemble of component parts that renders the type as such a highly malleable system of design.

Optional Zones

Optional zones are frequently possible within the limitations of the site size and geometry. These zones are generally employed to fulfill requirements for programs in addition to those of the main tall building functions. We have already observed that programmatic complexity is one of the characteristic factors for the emergence of the tower cluster as a highly adaptable framework of elements. Compositional diversity in response to program complexity is one of the great attributes of designing with a flexible matrix or parts designed, by definition, to create an integrated ensemble. Planning for future expansion is another reason for the a priori establishment of optional additional horizontal design zones.

3.2 Contributions to the Definition of the Typology

As defined above, the tower cluster is a componential, multi-element framework. Its high degree of flexibility derives from the potential for the variety of interaction and integration of the potential tower forms in relationship to the four additional subsystems described above. This contributes to the high degree of flexibility of form-giving that has been determined to be characteristic of the selection of case study samples.

Perhaps the dominant design intelligence derived from the case study sample is that the *typological knowledge* of this emerging urban type differs from the conventional interpretation of the concept of *type* in the sense of the existence of a series of related models containing certain similar familial characteristics. The tower cluster, being by definition an ensemble of five interacting design subsystems, is the particular characteristics of the subsystems that determine the *design subtypes*. Dominant among these as a characterizing factor is the *numerical character of the tall building components*. A secondary characteristic is the *number and distribution zones of the amenities*. Thus we can, for example, define a subtype as a linear trio slab organization of tall building elements with a major, dominantly expressed, linear sky-roof amenity component (Safdie, Marina Bay Sands). With respect to this particular example, the subtype description of the base element as being a linear atrium would further identify the subtype. Thus, the architect's contribution is the establishment of a unique development of the subtype. We have many such examples of the fecundity of tower cluster typological design among the case studies.

It is important to reiterate that the current objective of description here is *purely typological*. It avoids references to architectural style, or other significant descriptive aspects of actual projects such as the method of construction, the content of sustainability, and others.

Having stated that the typological case is always an ensemble of multiple tall building components combined with a zonal distribution of amenity elements, it becomes clear that the process of design of the tower cluster is that of the experimental testing and refinement of the *assembly* relative to site and program. We have observed in analysis that over and above considerations such as architectural styles, it is clear that we can distinguish each of our cases on the basis of their typological decisions regarding class and number of tall buildings plus the zonal distribution and, perhaps, subtype of the amenity zone. *It is the creation of an ensemble of these multiple component elements that produces the unique fundamental essence of the typology of the tower cluster*. As the design process of refinement relative to site and program is extended, the decisions regarding basic considerations such as tower number can be, sometimes dramatically, reinterpreted. See, for example, Hadid case study 4 and OMA case study 4.

Given the formal malleability of its subcomponents of the zonal structure of amenities, in both base and sky zones, the tower cluster as an urban design typology is responsive in a unique degree to urban design conditions. Within the case studies, virtually every case is remarkable for its response to urban environmental design conditions (Safdie 3, 4; OMA 1, 2, 4; Hadid 5; Scheeren 1). This obviously demonstrates the design ability of the architect, as well as the unique level of malleability and formal responsiveness of the urban typology.

The malleability of the matrix of parts, and particularly the flexibility of architectural representation of the amenity zones, enhances the architect's ability to achieve a statement of symbolic content at an urban scale. Such urban symbols are implicit in many of our case studies. See, for example, Safdie's "gateway" 3; OMA's "urban center" 1, "sea wall" or "precinct entry" 2, and others.

It is of great potential interest to urbanists and those environmental design professionals such as architects/urban designers that the tower cluster as a compound ensemble of high-density design elements is also relevant as a *tool for urban renewal*. Two of our case studies have demonstrated the formative ability of the tower cluster's capability in situations of urban renewal. OMA 4 in Eindhoven, the Netherlands, demonstrates the potential of the integration of building rehabilitation and restoration as a component integrated within the overall cluster of new buildings. In the case of Scheeren 1, in Singapore, the case study demonstrates the possibility for the insertion of a tower cluster within a neglected urban situation as a medium for the new modulation as the achievement of a holistic sense of relevant urban form. These methods of exploitation of the tower cluster typology as a potential medium for the urban rebirth of neglected urban areas are tremendously meaningful.

Tower clusters characterized by a *dominant base form*, for example, Hadid 3 in Nanjing, China, are characteristically appropriate when there is an extensive and diverse public program that demands a large site area relative to the base area of the cluster itself. Several of the case studies have demonstrated this situation.

The *dominant sky* condition occurs in our case studies in various situations in which amenities tend to be private with respect to usage primarily by inhabitants or employees of the cluster. These may take the form of usage of the upper levels of the towers as restaurant, bar, entertainment areas, etc., such as in Hadid 4 in Shenzhen, China. An alternative to this is the design strategy of the creation of a large-scale sky plaza such as in Safdie 1, in Singapore, or an elongated sky platform as in Safdie 3, in Chongqing, China, or OMA 3 in Shenzhen, China.

The ability to architecturally and structurally achieve large-scale structural elements such as the sky plaza, or the sculptural linear sky platform, enhances the possibility for the clustering of various program elements with a privacy requirement by means of such structures.

A place in the sky, or the urban symbolism which such structural sky elements add to the tower cluster, has become a highly significant characteristic statement of the typology.

In conclusion, the case studies have exhibited a group of sophisticated design solutions to a wide range of program requirements. Among these requirements are a good number of cases related to emerging technological companies, each of which has special types of requirements beyond that of a conventional office structure. For example, in Foster 1, in Shenzhen, China, certain manufacturing and experimentation facilities demanding multi-floor height spaces are integrated within the otherwise regular floor organization of the multiple towers. In addition, the skybridge between these towers is also employed for experimental and demonstration purposes.

All of the above demonstrates the amazing level of design flexibility and the high level of design enhancement that is characteristic of an architectural typology that is composed of an ensemble of components. Welcome to an intrinsically newly powerful architectural and urban design medium: *the typology as ensemble.*

Flexibility of the Tower Cluster

The functional program and site characteristics such as view and orientation are essential determinants of the design process. Building form is strongly influenced by these factors, and the design process cannot proceed without this knowledge. However, typological knowledge, the knowledge content of the building type itself, may be considered a form of *generic knowledge*. This knowledge seeks to identify what is innate in the type itself. Since the tower cluster is, by definition, a formally integrated grouping of multiple vertical elements, the number of elements, their base geometry, and their basic geometric relationships are such seminal factors in the determinants of the basic variants of the typology.

The number and geometry of the major compositional elements constitute the basic structural organization of the generic types of tower clusters, while the vertical and horizontal subdivision of the major elements constitute the basic syntactical elements, or constituent parts, of the design.

Functional Differentiation in Tower Clusters

Tower clusters are, by definition, a form of high-density organization. As an overall compositional principle, they are predominantly multifunctional, in which condition the towers themselves are both potentially monofunctional as well as multifunctional. In recent examples, the tower functions have been mainly housing, offices, dormitories, and hotels with the occasional horizontal introduction of specific horizontal strata containing special functions. The case studies have also demonstrated examples of multifunctional tall buildings.

As we have defined tower clusters, they are functionally diverse, dense, and compound typologically organized complexes. In general, the multiple towers of the complex serve repetitive functions such as housing, hotel, offices, and dormitories. The multiple towers may be of one function, e.g., all housing structures; or they may be of multiple functions, e.g., both housing and offices. However, the towers are always used to satisfy programmatic, high-density solutions of repetitive functions. Within the tower structure, the horizontal components, as opposed to the vertical, are generally collective, social, cultural or commercial functions. In addition, it is the horizontal strata that also potentially provide new forms of urban space.

Vertical Functional Mix

Where urban circulation systems are traditionally located on the ground plane, commercial or cultural functions are generally located on base levels. Certain cultural functions such as education may also be located at upper levels, such as on sky decks. Stepped towers provide the functional potential for observation decks and dining. Hotel dining frequently exists at roof level. Casinos can also exist at roof deck level, or at horizontal deck levels. Safdie 1 is an example of a casino housed in a major additional horizontal base zone located beside the main area of the towers.

Vertical Differentiation by Stratification

It is within this general principle of monotonic functionality in each of the multiple towers that the differentiation of function is usually introduced through the formal principle of stratification. In general, strata can be introduced by the staggering or staged reduction of dimensions, or by such movements as the breaking and shifting of sequential levels as the tower rises, as in OMA 4. The scale of the horizontally created strata can affect a single tower, multiple towers, or all of the towers.

It is the horizontal stratification in transforming sky decks into horizontal movement systems that introduces the potential for a new form of vertical urbanism. This also creates the theoretical possibility of the linkage of multiple tower clusters into larger urban groupings. We will resume this discussion in a later chapter.

Base, Median, Upper Zone, and Roof Zone Differentiation

It is now clear that stratification becomes the basic principle of joining in tower clusters, thus providing potential for the horizontal continuity of circulation. This creates horizontal zones within the dominantly vertical structure. Continuous horizontal strata create urban and communal areas and social spaces, while horizontal zones generally introduce larger-scale, generally horizontally continuous functions such as commercial functions. Continuous horizontal strata can also exist to provide continuity of circulation. Thus, the form of the tower structure, while possessing and exemplifying certain consistent formal principles, is strongly influenced by a formal code in which vertical represents privacy, while horizontal continuity enhances communality and freedom of continuous movement.

With respect to horizontally defined zones within the vertical structure of the tower cluster, there exist four basic zoning areas: the base, generally consisting of three to six levels; the median zone; the upper zone; and the roof zone. The base zone is generally a continuous urban and commercial zone providing horizontal continuity at various levels. The mid zone is generally discontinuous, while the upper zone and roof zone can potentially be continuous. While the roof zone can be potentially continuous, its functions may be semiprivate.

Rather than rules, these are generalizations based on recent practice. The stratification and continuity/discontinuity of the tower cluster is a function of program, site characteristics, and design objectives. Design within existing well-developed urban conditions and zoning may limit the potential for the upper-level horizontal continuity that we have referred to as vertical urbanism. This possibility may be very meaningful in a totally new urban condition in which there exists the potential for a new creative order of urban organization.

Urban Variables of the Typology

One of the most challenging questions regarding the brief history of the tower cluster is its relationship to urban design. Due to its diversity of scale (depending on the number of towers) and its compositional form, the tower cluster has up to now been adapted to diverse forms of existing urban fabric.

The tower cluster is a transitional scale between architecture and urbanism. As such, might it be considered as a seed of a future type of urban form? Given that the tower cluster is based on specific relationships between predominantly horizontal forms (layers and strata) and the predominantly vertical forms of the cluster groupings, does this emerging typology offer unique possibilities for the development of urban form in sloping urban conditions such as San Francisco and Hong Kong?

The tower cluster is a new urban medium that comes with *large-scale* programs, *high density,* and integrated *functional complexity.* Ultimately these characteristics lead to an urbanism based on complex and unique forms of stratification in which conventional forms of urban functions such as circulation and urban open space can now also exist in horizontal strata above the ground plane. The limitations of the ground plane as the grade of circulation become theoretically flexible within the definition of this new building form as the foundation of a spatially liberated form of urbanism. This building type, in engaging both the characteristics of the urban and the architectural, truly liberates the conception of urban form. It is potentially a medium for the integration of functional complexity, high-rise form, and perhaps also new media of urbanism.

The tower cluster is also a unifying force creating a sense of urban interiority, and thus, with the consideration of its diverse possibilities for compositional form, it creates a nexus of urban density. If we attempt to visualize a city of tower clusters, in what direction of urban form might this lead?

3.3 A Logic of Structural Organization: Numerical Subtypes

The Meaning of Numbers

One of the general observations derived from the analysis of the case study sample is that the high-rise building appears to be in the process of evolving into a new typology. One of the dominant variables of this typology is that of high-rise numbers in the subtype. This variable might be considered *the first variable of flexibility* in the typological construction of a particular design solution, or *partis.*

Under conventional logic, one might assume that this variable also increases flexibility—that is, the more high-rise vertical elements, the higher the level of flexibility. In point of fact, from observation of all of the cases, the type is extraordinarily flexible in the satisfaction of program as well as the generation of innovative form, irrespective of the exact number of high-rise elements.

The design process appears to offer insights into invention. From what might this push toward the extraordinary derive? It appears from the analysis of cases that each of the five subvariables of the typology that have been defined above in section 3.1. provides a wide range of design flexibility. This provides the high degree of what can be described as *composite creation* which derives from designing with a malleable ensemble of five sets of variable components.

It is the numerical decision related to the number of high-rise elements that is the initiator of the tower cluster design process. In the following section, we briefly review certain insights gained related to the general design significance of the numerical variables.

Duo

The duo, or two high-rise elements, is the first subtype of the tower cluster typology. The duo possesses two inherent symbolic poles: from static to dynamic. It is represented in six of the fifteen case studies: Safdie 2, OMA 1, Hadid 3 and 5, Foster 1, and Scheeren 1.

As observed in the case studies, the duo, in principle, has three conceptual subtypes. These are as Gemini, or the twins; or as a pair representing difference, for example, in size or in formal character. The third possibility is when the twins are connected by a continuous roof element (sky roof) to create a three-dimensional complex in open-ended cubic form.

The first of these, the twins, is represented by Safdie 2, Scheeren 1, and Foster 1. The second, difference, appears in Hadid 3 and 4. The third, a geometric, formal 3-D order, appears in OMA 1.

Twins order in Safdie's cluster and that of Scheeren have a certain degree of difference in the pair, but they are essentially the same. The towers of Hadid 3 appear to be formally different. OMA 1, which has a formal unification of the duo by creating an arch, or a ring structure, is a unification of the duo. This holistic approach to the duo also achieves a high-rise form which is unique.

Each of the duos succeeds in realizing the high degree of potential in the remaining four typological variables of base-form, sky-form, urban design, and landscape integration, as well as optional additional elements.

Trio: The Created Sense of Tower Cluster Dynamism

The trio, or three high-rise elements, is represented in four case studies: Safdie 1, OMA 2 and 3, and Hadid 2. The trio is a grouping of three towers. Such groupings are generally considered an irregular and unbalanced combination which is, by definition, dynamic. As such, unbalanced combinations are generally considered of good potential for interesting compositions of massing. This larger number of towers in the grouping generally offers an improved capability for supporting a broad and integrated functional program. It also potentially provides a higher degree of flexibility regarding unique forms for the integration and geometry of sky forms.

One of the most interesting case studies of a tri-tower grouping in high-density housing design is the previously mentioned Josep Lluís Sert's (Sert, Jackson and Gourley) Peabody Terrace Married Student Housing complex at Harvard University. In the case of this project, from 1963 to 1965, the towers are not clustered and the elements of the lower construction are dispersed over the large site around groups of courtyard spaces. Though this work is prior to the age of tower clusters, it does illustrate very well the potential massing visual dynamics of the trio organization.

As we have seen in the previous section, Safdie 1, Marina Bay Sands of 2010, is a trio-based grouping of a linear slab cluster. Among other things, it is remarkable for its exploitation of a sky-deck principle in order to, in effect, re-create a site for a functionally integrated hotel complex which had limited site area on the ground level.

The slab form and the linear organization are characteristic of a high-rise hotel program located on a site with one dominant view orientation. The linear organization of the cluster also enables a high degree of integration of the connectivity with ancillary program functions such as a linear commercial mall, a casino, large lecture hall, and others.

OMA 2, De Rotterdam, is also a linear trio on a somewhat constrained site. It achieves a high degree of functional integration of the tower function with the diverse public functions of the base levels. This is a compact linear arrangement which serves to strengthen its symbolic function of expressing the entry to an island area in Rotterdam after crossing a bridge from a main part of the city.

OMA 3, the CMG Center in Shenzhen, China, is basically a duo with an elongated sky element and an additional lower tower element located in the base adjacent to the twin towers. The state of the published drawings is rather early. As the project develops, we will be able to determine whether the subtype is a duo with additional vertical element or actually is a trio.

Hadid 2, Wangjing Soho, in Beijing, China, is a cluster of three elongated elliptical tower forms of different heights. They are arranged in a compact form that maximizes the spatial dynamism of the interspatial relationships. It also exploits the potential to establish ancillary independent forms associated with base-level commercial functions. This spatial dynamism of the trio is also a basis for the design of lower-level circulation, for the utilization of connectivity, for the formal arrangement of both landscape design and urban space design of the site development, and for scalar integration with neighboring developments.

Quartet

The quartet, or four high-rise elements, is represented in three case studies: OMA 4; and Hadid 1 and 4. The classical statement of the compact quartet is creatively represented in Hadid 1, Galaxy Soho, Beijing, China. The organization is essentially a four-square diagram treated as double pairs organized about an internal court, or atrium space. The towers are oval and each also contains an internal atrium. The base is essentially a multistory mall arranged around one major court and four minor courts. The shop arrangement within each of the towers is multistory. With respect to diagrammatic form and circulation diagrams, this is a highly classical example. In the actual design, the applied form has been geometrically modified and made more fluid than in the diagrammatic state.

OMA 4, the microforest in Eindhoven, Netherlands, is essentially a modified four-square diagram with a duo of tall towers, each element of which has an adjacent lower tower. Thus, it is a case of a paired pair of towers. As we have previously discussed, this project is distinguished by both its extended development on the site including the integration of existing restored buildings.

The final case of the quartet, Hadid 4, OPPO Headquarters in Shenzhen, China, is a highly original design of a quartet. Externally expressed as a quartet of four separate towers, it is essentially four vertical tower elements in one continuous exterior skin. The continuous open and minimally obstructed plan form, and the relatively detached relationship of office floor to external wall arrangement, achieves an extraordinary situation of multi-floor visual continuity. This unique structural/organizational arrangement of two of the towers, and the location of vertical circulation within the remaining two towers, demands the invention of new terminology in order to describe this continuously internally connected tower cluster. Does this possibly create a vertical megastructure?

Quintet

The quintet, or five high-rise elements, is not represented in the case studies. Safdie 3, Raffles City Chongqing, China, possibly offers some insights into the quintet, since its connected tower elements are a four-plus-two tower cluster arrangement.

Multiple High-Rise Elements

Multiple high-rise elements are represented in two case studies: Safdie 3 and 4. Safdie 3, Raffles City Chongqing, China, unites a linear grouping of cluster elements by means of an elongated sky element which functions as integration as well as symbolizing an urban gateway through the complex of buildings. The unifying factor of the large cluster of eight tower elements is the continuous, multifunctional base. The continuous base element providing commercial and entertainment functions also acts as a social integrator for the cluster. This medium has characteristically become a unifying strategy for tower clusters of various scales. Its efficacy in providing a significant functional provision as well as a malleable urban design variable and a symbol, has rendered it common to many, if not most, of the case studies. For larger-scale clusters the continuous base is virtually a necessity.

In Safdie 4, ORCA Toronto, Canada, both the skybridge and the continuous base are essential components of a large-scale, multifunctional, linear-organized cluster in a linear urban context of the city. Here too, the base functions as a medium of integration. On the one hand, it is an important element of connectivity of a longer linear development. In addition, it provides for the enlivening of the adjacent linear park, as well as for the important provision of shopping.

3.4 Design Intelligence of the Tower Cluster

This is perhaps one of the first examples of the definition of a typology as an ensemble of five relatively independent subsystems.[11] It is this characteristic of the four variant subsystems that can be sequentially added to the schematic cluster design in multiple cycles of the design process. This approach to *design with an ensemble* imbues the tower cluster with a remarkably high level of design flexibility and sequential adaptability. The tower cluster is therefore an *open system* of design.

The case studies have provided examples of these design attributes. Each of the five element subsystems (Towers, Base Elements, Sky Elements, Urban and Landscape Relations, Optional Site Zones) is not only a variable in design, but is *programmatically responsive*. In designing for such complex building programs as emerging, multifunctional, technologically innovative management, testing, and protoproduction facilities, this programmatic responsiveness is incredibly significant.

We have seen how this has proven a great advantage in all of the projects, for example, in maximizing team interaction in conception, design, and testing in Foster Architects' DJI Headquarters, and in enhancing the team creation processes among the staff of Hadid's OPPO Headquarters in Shenzhen, China. Emerging technologies are transforming the conventional range of program requirements of the traditional office building into a totally new and unusually diverse range of functions such as research, testing, experimentation, demonstration, and adaptation to processes of future change.

The ability to manipulate subsystem design variables in response to unique functional requirements such as multifloor relational connectivity, or to enhance or minimize connectivity, is the result of the sophisticated design intelligence derived from the design framework of *ensemble design*. The sequential process of design first defines the schematic design *partis* in response to program satisfaction relative to site geometry and contextual factors. During advanced stages of design, the variable subsystems are amenable to changes and refinements requested by the client in interaction with the designer.

Only a typological medium rich in design intelligence can suffice to enable responsiveness to the complex requirements of emerging intelligent industries. The concept of distributed amenities in a vertical campus also contributes a unique degree of responsiveness to the tower cluster typology as a design system. The tower cluster as a building type provides remarkable opportunities, both formal and functional, for the integration of amenities within the geometry of the tower cluster. These are among the reasons for the emergence of the tower cluster as a responsive design medium for a new age of technological innovation.

PART IV

Classes and Forms of Urban Amenities in Tower Clusters

4.1 The Uniqueness of Urban Amenities in the Tower Cluster

Amenity is defined as "a desirable or useful feature of a building or place." One of the unique characteristics of tower clusters is that they are of large scale, high density, and diversity of functional elements. This complex of characteristics means it is generally justifiable to introduce within them large, urban-scale, public spatial amenities such as sky parks. As the urban phenomenon of the provision of urban-scale cultural and social amenities within tower complexes becomes more common, there is emerging a broad new class of urban amenities as well as new forms of the organization of clusters of amenities in space. These *amenities clusters* are generally located either at the upper level of the cluster or at another significant nexus point within the syntax of the complex, such as the base. In this chapter we identify and describe the diverse classes of urban sky amenities that have been integrated into tower clusters and discuss the forms of amenities clusters and the implication of their potential locations within tower clusters. We will also discuss in section 4.2 the recent development by which the form of amenities clusters and their location within the tower cluster has become *a determinate formative element* in the design of the cluster.

The idea of amenities, both public and private, being associated with the development of the tall building is a well-accepted part of the history of the building type. With the relatively recent appearance of the typology of the tower cluster, *the grouping of multiple amenities within independent formal additions* to clustered high-rise building forms is becoming a characteristic of the tower cluster. In addition to this, larger groupings of amenities are beginning to appear in unique forms within the upper structural area of the tower cluster. There is a growing tendency to refer to such unique groupings of amenities as *sky amenities.*

It is the form, mix, size, combination, and organization of the grouping of sky amenities that make *amenity structures* in high-rise buildings unique. The case study sample has illustrated that tower clusters are generally multifunctional and frequently contain large-scale, relatively unique programs. Many of our cases are related to the new and special functional needs of the administrative, design, and testing facilities of emerging technologies. In such a situation, the unique level of design flexibility, and what has been described as the *programmatic responsiveness* of the typology as a system of multiple subsystems, can help to explain the rapid growth of the typology.

Though unrelated to high-tech industries, Safdie Architects case study 1, Marina Bay Sands in Singapore, provides excellent examples of emerging classes of sky structures, as well as the vertical and horizontal structural/organizational potential of highly varied multifunctional programs within the tower cluster itself and throughout the horizontal organization of the site.

The sky park at the 57th floor of Marina Bay Sands represents a unique form of tower cluster amenity structure. First of all, with water and tropical gardens as two of its characteristic design motifs, it symbolizes the *garden city* urban motif of Singapore. This sky park has an urban scale containing approximately 1.2 hectares of space. Its dimensions are 340 meters by 40 meters at its widest point. It is estimated that the park can accommodate approximately 3,900 persons.

The park is located approximately 200 meters above ground level. It contains an observation deck, jogging trails, gardens, restaurants, lounges, and an infinity pool. The pool itself is 145 meters long. The observation deck is cantilevered 65 meters from the edge of the north tower.

The Marina Bay Sands sky park is an outstanding early example of the concept of the amenities structure. It presents the ideational content of urban symbolism, diversity of multifunctional activities, grandness of urban scale, and iconic design image that has within the last decade made Marina Bay Sands one of the iconic visual symbols of Singapore.

From the case studies, we have observed that amenities structures recur vertically in most tower clusters, and create an order of amenities that are vertically connected. Such a vertical activity system, or the vertical campus, is located in design within the organizing structure of the tower cluster.

Having described certain principles of the organization of amenities within tower clusters, we now consider the possibility of an opposite logic of design in the tower cluster. Is it also conceivable that it is the system of the vertical campus that has become the *dominant design system* within which are integrated the high-rise elements?

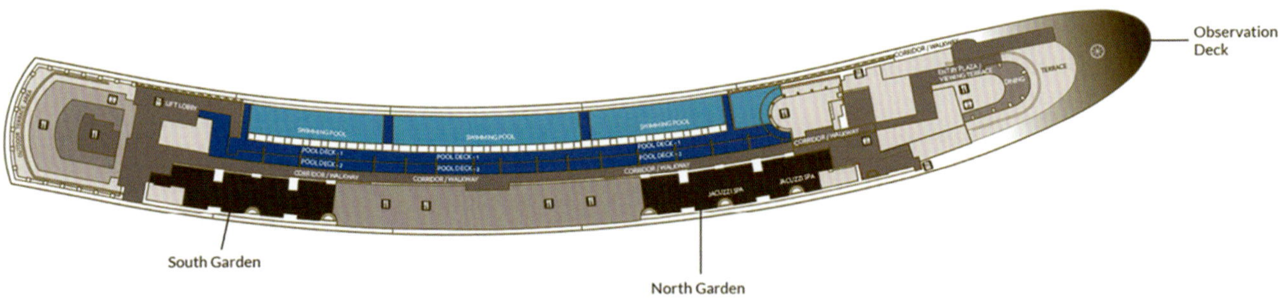

South Garden

- Floor area: 325sqm
- Up to 150 guests

North Garden

- Floor area: 450sqm
- Up to 250 guests

Observation Deck

- Floor area: 865sqm
- Up to 500 guests

Above Plan of the sky park, Marina Bay Sands, Singapore. Safdie Architects, 2010.

Opposite Page Mei'Lin Towers, Shenzhen, China. Safdie Architects, 2025. Rendering courtesy of Safdie Architects.

4.2 Amenities Structures as the Organizing Elements of the Tower Cluster

It is the vertically recurrent and connected structures of amenities within and between the high-rise elements of the tower cluster that can now be viewed as a *system of amenities structures*. Such systems are currently emerging as one of the dominant concepts for the design of the tower cluster. The tower cluster as vertical campus, or the recurrence of amenity structures as a vertical system within the height of a cluster, has emerged as both a potentially dominant formal element and a relatively independent visual element.

Safdie Architect's recent Mei'Lin Towers in Shenzhen, China is a circular-ordered grouping of a trio tower cluster. It is primarily a residential building which is currently under design and expected to be opened in 2025. The urban design concept which the architects refer to as the "three-dimensional city strategy" employs a tower cluster of three relatively slender towers in order to reduce the potential mass of a one-tower, or slab, solution. Relative to the case study sample, the unique approach to the design of this tower cluster is that the vertical amenity structure—or the vertical campus—appears also to be the geometrically ordering element of the whole project.

Rather than a design order in which the amenity structures are integrated within the geometric order of the towers, Mei'Lin presents a reverse ordering of the design of the tower cluster and amenities structures. A cir-

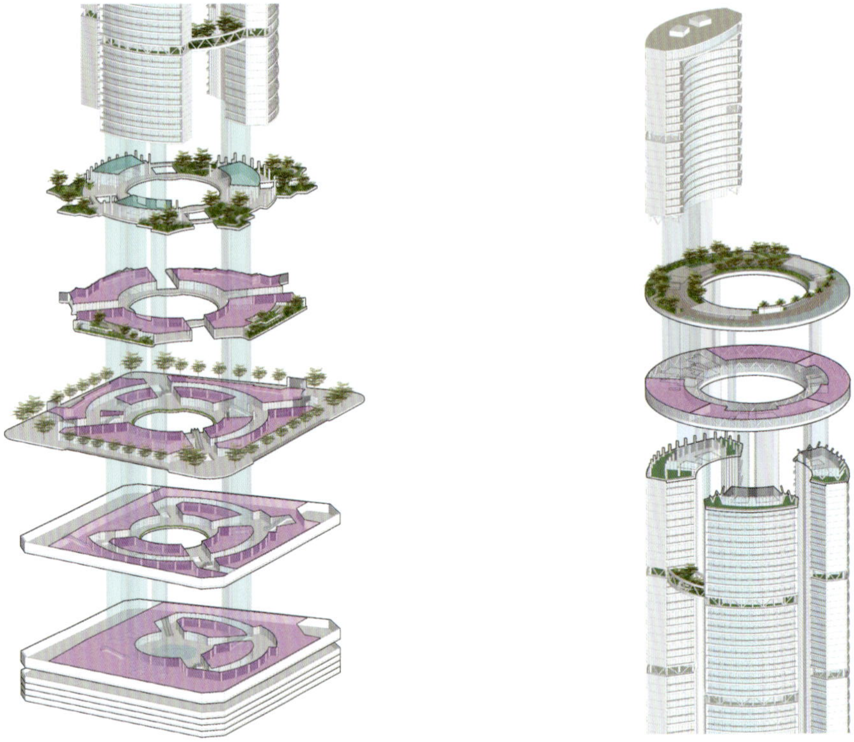

Above Mei'Lin Towers, Shenzhen, China. Safdie Architects, 2025. Diagram of amenity ring structures and towers. The ring-ordered vertical campus structure.

Opposite Page Mei'Lin Towers, Shenzhen, China. Safdie Architects, 2025. Base ring of shopping center courtyard. Rendering courtesy of Safdie Architects. Middle Mei'Lin Towers, Shenzhen, China. Safdie Architects, 2025. View of SkyLoop from upper tower. Rendering courtesy of Safdie Architects. Bottom Mei'Lin Towers, Shenzhen, China. Safdie Architects, 2025. Rendering courtesy of Safdie Architects.

cular geometry with a hollow center which is the ordering geometry of all amenities at multiple levels becomes the dominant design order into which the three towers of the cluster are integrated. In providing community amenities for the tower population of residents, such an ordering principle has important advantages. With respect to the potential for urban design integration with the surrounding urban context, there appear here to be certain disadvantages.

The ring-ordered vertical amenity structure can be seen in the above diagram. The multilevel base structure is shown on the left; the sky structure is shown on the right. The base structure contains a commercial and activities center designed around an interior court and tropical garden setting. This is illustrated in the rendering below. In the diagram, this is illustrated as a three-level series of rectangular floor plans, each of which has differing floor plans of internal circulation patterns in order to accommodate the diverse functions of the base. The commercial and activities center is organized around a circular garden court on the ground floor. Above this are two circular rings, the last of which is a garden plaza structure which also functions as the main entrance level to the three towers.

The diagrams on the right illustrate the vertical continuation of the three towers until they arrive at a completely circular two-level amenities structure which culminates in a level called the SkyLoop. This is another of the major public outdoor amenity functions; the SkyLoop serves the upper levels of the three-tower grouping, as well as the residences of the third tower, which rise 90 additional meters above the loop. The loop elevation is 200 meters; the third tower elevation is 290 meters.

In addition to the two major outdoor facilities of Towers Entry Garden and SkyLoop, there are two amenity levels beneath these gardens. In addition, there are a series of skybridges arranged as amenity arcs (not complete circles), partially indoor as well as outdoor. As can be seen in the first perspective, there are two arcs in the bottom three towers, and one arc in the upper tower. This divides the towers into subgroupings.

The skybridges and amenities located in these intermediate levels help to organize the vertical residential organization and to create a series of *vertical neighborhoods*. As can be seen in the first perspective, the lower towers have two intermediate amenity levels and the upper tower has one intermediate amenity level.

With respect to the relationship of the base to the surrounding urban design context, Mei'Lin is, in general, a relatively closed complex. It has one major street entrance into the commercial cultural functions of the base.

We can briefly summarize the diverse locations of amenities as they have appeared in the case study sample and in the recent sample of Mei'Lin. As we have seen, the multiple levels of amenities in the residential towers serve to divide them into smaller vertical neighborhoods. Consequently, there is in Mei'Lin a relatively high frequency of the vertical recurrence of amenity zones within the towers.

In summary, we can define the potential amenity locations within tower clusters as follows.

Potential Locations of Amenity Structure Zones in Tower Clusters

Base Zones (Base Structures in Single or Multiple Floors)
TC Base and/or Open Core of the Base
TC Base and/or Base Plus Continuous Horizontal Extension
Independent Ancillary Structures or Ancillary Towers Beyond the Base Area in Extended Zone(s) Beyond Base

Sky Zones (Sky Structures in Single or Multiple Floors)
Upper Base Level Skybridge(s)
Mid Tower Amenity Floor and/or Skybridge
Upper Tower Amenity Floor and/or Skybridge
Penthouse Amenity Floor and/or Skybridge
Roof Amenity Floor and/or Sky Plaza

We now begin to define the classes of vertical amenities.

4.3 Clustered Amenities: Sky Plazas, Sky Malls, Sky Spas

The sky plaza is a combination of amenities facilities. At Marina Bay Sands, amenities include a sky pool, various food service facilities, multiple gar-

dens, a running track, indoor meeting areas, and a large cantilevered observation deck. Being located there as a dramatically culminating facility above the three hotel slab buildings, it states by form and scale its importance in the complex as well as its symbolic significance as a large-scale unifying element of the tower cluster. At Marina Bay Sands, the architects call this multifacility structure a *sky plaza*. However, as we have observed in other tower clusters, such as in the SkyLoop of Mei'Lin, it is generally a one-level, partly open-air, partly enclosed combination of multiple functions. It is also commonly of grand scale and functions as a symbolic marker in the urban context.

The Crystal at Raffles City Chongqing is a ten-thousand-square-meter enclosed amenity sky spa facility. It contains gardens, multiple dining, bar, and event spaces, a hotel lobby, a members-only clubhouse, and a fifty-meter infinity pool.

The Crystal is, in the character of other rooftop sky amenities, large, and to some degree, monumental. In the urban context of Raffles City Chongqing, the positioning as a culminating element over four towers creates a visual metaphor of a symbolic gateway. That is to say, the scale and location of the sky plaza is such that they always have certain symbolic content. In addition to Marina Bay Sands and Raffles City Chongqing, both Mei'Lin Towers and CMG Qianhai Global Trade Center provide examples of sky plaza variations.

4.4 Connective Amenities: Skybridges, Skywalks, Skyways

As a connective medium, the skybridge is one of the most characteristic amenity structures of the tower cluster typology. As observed in the examples, the skybridge frequently provides a large range of functions in addition to connectivity. At Mei'Lin Towers, Safdie Architects has employed skybridges at multiple levels in order to provide gardens, sport facilities, and rest areas as communal meeting areas within a vertical residential community. Furthermore, the vertical structure of recurrent skybridges attempts to enhance the sense of community within the vertical city, to provide a network of connected public spaces, and to subdivide the vertical order into subcommunities of smaller vertical neighborhoods.

Above Marina Bay Sands, Singapore, view of the sky plaza. Safdie Architects, 2010. Perspective courtesy of Safdie Architects. **Middle** Raffles City Chongqing, Chongqing, China. Safdie Architects, 2019. The Crystal indoor sky spa. Perspective courtesy of Safdie Architects.

Opposite Page Petronas Twin Towers, Kuala Lumpur, Malaysia. César Pelli, 1996. **Above Right** *The Space Across* by Wood, Du, and Safarik is a major resource for knowledge regarding the skybridge. **Bottom** DJI Headquarters, Shenzhen, China. Foster + Partners, 2022. Skybridge rendering of original scheme. Perspective courtesy of Foster + Partners.

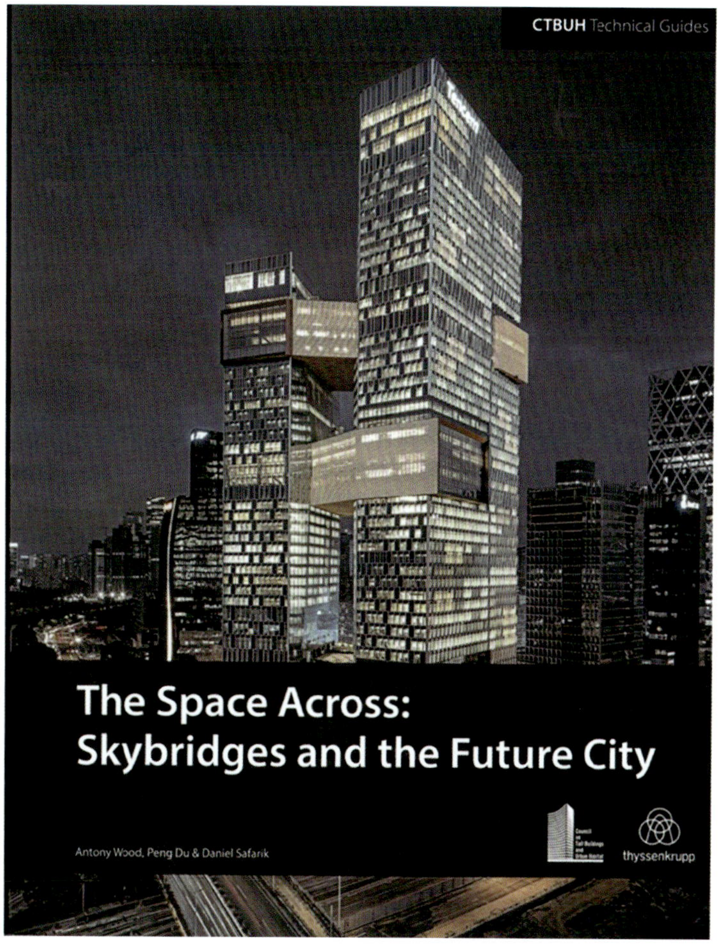
CTBUH Technical Guides
The Space Across:
Skybridges and the Future City
Antony Wood, Peng Du & Daniel Safarik
thyssenkrupp

In addition, we have seen skybridges employed as residential bridge areas which also provide horizontal connectivity (ORCA). Skybridges have also been used to link the social and entertainment functions of the penthouse (OPPO Headquarters), where they also link the areas of technological development and testing. At the DJI Headquarters it is employed as a medium for the testing and display of drones.

4.5 Sky Gardens

The *sky garden* as an amenity category is the attempt to re-create the lush verdure of a park within the realm of the sky. As such, it attempts to transpose the natural environment into the artificial. The principle of success of such transfers is ecological suitability, as well as the artful achievement of dramatic sensibility of the design.

There are many existing examples in both indoor and outdoor situations. Among the case studies, Marina Bay Sands in Singapore provides an example of the outdoor sky garden, two of which are located as part of the sky park. The vegetation of the gardens, particularly the palm trees, is also situated along the poolside lounging area.

An example from the case study of an interior garden is in the Crystal amenities structure at Raffles City, in Chongqing. From this photo, the garden area appears to accompany the lounging area adjacent to the infinity pool. On the interior, the structure is such that the garden receives adequate natural lighting. It consequently appears lush and verdant.

Right Marina Bay Sands, Singapore, sky gardens. Safdie Architects, 2010. Photo courtesy of Isnglobal.

Opposite Page Raffles City Chongqing, China. Safdie Architects, 2019. Interior view of the Crystal's pool and garden. Photo courtesy of Safdie Architects.

Both Marina Bay Sands's sky park and Raffles City Chongqing Crystal's sky garden also have an observation deck within the overall area of the larger amenity structure. However, in these two examples, the devoted observation area is not associated with the gardens. In the case of the following example, 20 Fenchurch Street, London, by architect Rafael Viñoly, the sky garden is within a three-story area at the top of the tower, which also contains an observation deck, a cocktail bar, and restaurants.

In the case of 20 Fenchurch Street, the large indoor observation area occurs on the top of the tower at the 35th floor. The sky garden is a stepped area at the rear of the observation area. The vegetation has been criticized as somewhat modest and unsuccessful. This may be a function of the overall design of the total amenity structure and the limited scale of vegetation in the planting plan despite the height of the room, as well as climatic factors.

In order to employ the term "sky garden," which conveys the promise of drama and induces a level of expectation, there is a responsibility to deliver a consequential experience. When the physical situation is more modest than the grand title of the space, it is frequently a cause for disappointment. The lack of success of the sky garden at 20 Fenchurch Street is one of several causes for which the tower has received both public and professional critique.

4.6 Sky Pools

If we view the panoply of recent sky pools throughout the world, most of them are rendered magical by their challenges of gravity as they invade the space of the sky. One is invited not only to swim in the sky, but to partake in a degree of magic.

In Bali, at the Como Uma Ubud Hanging Gardens Resort, the design reproduces the surrounding terraced levels of agricultural landscape. This

Right The Sky Garden, 20 Fenchurch Street, London. Rafael Viñoly, 2015. Courtesy of Wikipedia: Feature Picture Candidates.

Opposite Page Hanging terraced infinity pools, Como Uma Ubud Hanging Gardens Resort, Bali. Photo courtesy of Vincent Bretton. **Middle** Terraced gardens, Bali. Photo courtesy of Randolfo Santos. **Bottom** Marina Bay Sands infinity sky pool. Safdie Architects. Photo by Chia Ming Chen.

image has become the visual symbol of this fabled tropical landscape. Ubud's design of the hanging pools at its resort transfers the swimmer into the space of fable. It is the iconic poetic experience of the transfigured land.

Marina Bay Sands, with the world's longest elevated pool, at 150 meters, achieves this transformation from urban landscape to mindscape by the visual beauty of the grand sweep of its infinity waterfall as a tropical waterfall at the edge of the presence of the city center. It becomes a pool within a sky garden, within a sky park, all of which is a magical site within a magical city of tropical gardens.

At Marina Bay Sands, this dreamlike quality is also reinforced by the omnipresent drama of gambling. Here it is also the experience of danger in a beautifully romantic three-story space of dreams which is the casino. The pool is literally a reflective window at the edge of a world of drama and excitement.

The sky pool is a sports facility within an aboveground amenity structure which is frequently at the roof level of a cluster of tall buildings. But the sky pool is not simply a swimming pool in the sky. The sky pool comes into being only when a certain magic of symbolic transformation is achieved. This is the ultimate design challenge of the sky pool, as it is of all the tower cluster amenities structures.

The pool at Embassy Gardens Legacy Buildings in London is considered the world's first floating sky pool. These are residential structures in which the pool serves as both an athletic and community facility. The 25-meter pool is located at roof level of two residential structures and suspended between them at 115 feet in the air. It is accompanied at roof level by a rooftop

sky deck containing covered dining areas, a greenhouse, and entertainment/meeting areas with bar services. Here, transparency is the magic. The pool is constructed with reinforced Plexiglas, and it is suspended as a transparent and visually weightless environment hovering between ground and sky. The poetic transposition of the sky pool is shared both by the swimmers and by the street spectators who see the swimmers floating across the sky.

Above Embassy Gardens, London. HAL Architects and Eckersley O'Callaghan Engineers. **Middle** Embassy Gardens, London. HAL Architects and Eckersley O'Callaghan Engineers.

Opposite Page The Edge viewing platform, observation deck at 30 Hudson Yards, New York City. KPF Kohn Pedersen Fox Architects, 2020. **Bottom** The Edge observation deck at 30 Hudson Yards, New York City. KPF Kohn Pedersen Fox Architects, 2020.

4.7 The Observation Deck

Of all the amenities we have encountered in our study of the tower cluster, it is perhaps the observation deck that has the most integral relationship with the history of the skyscraper. In towers in general, it is the observation deck associated with grand dining experiences that are most frequently associated with the public experience of the tall building. It is the peak of the tower which has become associated with the peak of emotional experience.

Within the framework of the multiple peaks, so to speak, of the tower cluster, it is the skybridge which most naturally, through its very form, produces *the bridge to view*. Petronas Twin Towers of 1999 by architect César Pelli is perhaps the classic example of the skybridge as the generator of exceptional experience.

It is at Marina Bay Sands where we discover that the tower cluster can produce unique morphological opportunities for re-creating in differing forms the experience to the peak with its potential visual gifts of the experience of place as they are to be experiences in the age of the skyscraper. At Marina Bay Sands the whole of the sky park is, in effect, an observation platform.

Thus, we should not search for models of amenities. Rather we should consider the structural and morphological potential presented by the order of multiple towers. In each distinct subform of tower cluster, we are presented with unique possibilities for the new form of the tall building in the twenty-first century. It is within the unique range of subforms of the tower cluster that each presents us with a potential syntax which can be exploited in multiple ways for amenities programs such as observation. The tower form will generate the syntax of the distribution of amenities structures, wherever they may be functionally integrated. From the morphology of the tower cluster comes the opportunity to create integrated places of magical experience within the cluster.

However, it is appropriate to illustrate how this characteristic tower function is developing in our time. The following example is considered a contemporary classic. Despite the fact that the locale is within a conventional tower structure, the example is most illustrative of the new definition of the drama of the observatory experience.

The function of the contemporary observation deck is to provide a heightened and transfigured experience of both view and height. The observation deck that began its history as the public-access top story of the skyscraper is now also a site of magical experiences. The Edge is an observation deck located within the Hudson Yards Redevelopment Project on the West Side of Manhattan. The Edge is on the 100th floor of the North Tower. It juts out 24 meters from the side of the building at 1,120 feet, or 337 meters, above grade. The Edge is suspended in midair from the side of the building, and it has around its periphery a 9-foot-high glass railing which is tilted outward in order to enhance views of the ground. On the 101st floor there is also a bar and event space.

The Edge is the highest outdoor observation deck in the Western Hemisphere. It appears to the visitor to be a triangular platform floating in the sky. The projection from the tower enhances the possibility of 360-degree viewing. There is a 225-square-foot glass triangle in the floor through which one can see the ground below, which is part of the overall dizzying experience of the Edge.

4.8 Conclusions: The Significance and Design Potential of Sky Amenities

Tower cluster amenities require what we have termed *magical transposition*. As we have seen, this includes formal and symbolic considerations, contextual references, the symbolic content of materialization, and many other aspects of design. All of this new skyscraper content is being advanced by the amplified programmatic content of the tower cluster. New types of urban amenities are emerging, such as the sky park and new forms of amenities structures within the geometry of the tower cluster.

In most of our case studies, sky amenities are at the scale of urban amenities. These new urban elements can be integrated between, besides, within, above, and under tower clusters, as has been demonstrated in the detailed analyses of this chapter. How and where amenities are realized in design and construction depends on the interrelationship between tower cluster and amenity structures—where and how this integration occurs, and what experience is achieved as a form of dynamic balance.

The graphic analyses of mapping, massing, and magic have been selected to enable the study and understanding of the design potential for achieving magic within the framework of the numerical variables of tower cluster morphology through location, integration, geometry, and form within the cluster.

Opposite Page The Edge viewing platform, observation deck at 30 Hudson Yards, New York City. KPF Kohn Pedersen Fox Architects, 2020.

PART V

The Amenities Revolution and the Emergence of the Vertical Campus

5.1 Introduction: New Amenities in the Vertical Campus

We have observed through the analysis of case studies that the tower cluster typology is associated with complex, generally multifunctional programs, many of which have been designed for unique urban situations. It is within this dynamic background that the tower cluster has emerged as a flexible building type that can potentially respond both programmatically and symbolically to a range of newly emerging complex situations. The population size associated with multiple towers may also economically justify the inclusion of a certain enlargement of the range of amenities.

A segment of the responsiveness of the tower cluster has been its capability to accommodate and integrate a required range of new amenities within the vertical organization of its multiple towers. The ongoing increase of classes and quantities of amenities in tower design has accelerated in the age of the tower cluster. In this chapter we will consider the nature of the growth and improvement of amenities in tower cluster design. Amenities improvements in three basic functional classes of the tower cluster—residential, hotel, and office/high-tech office—are presented, and the significance of the improvements is discussed.

With the advancement of skyscraper designs in the 1950s and 1960s, there originally appeared a modicum of amenities that have accompanied the predominant quantitative presence of the main functional type, such as housing or offices. Depending upon the particular function, these amenities have always been motivated by the commercial norms of the field as existing within a particular real estate context. This relationship of major function and ancillary amenities organizations was, in general, fairly constant for a long period of time.

During the past decade, it has become possible to speak of a revolution in amenities content within tall buildings of all functional classes. As multifunctional tower clusters are beginning to emerge, their appearance is accompanied by an increase in the functional presence and architectural expression of a new range of amenities classes within the environment of tall buildings.

The quantitative revolution has been accompanied by a second important factor: this new range of amenities has become significant in the vertical organization of the tall building as well as in that of the tower cluster. So much so, that as we have observed at Mei'Lin, the vertical organization of the amenities has become an important organizational and formative factor in the design of the tower cluster. Furthermore, the vertical organization of the amenities, or the amenity zoning diagram (AZD), may continue to increase its role as a generative factor in the form and organization of tall buildings. We have referred to this vertical relationship of amenities within the tower cluster as a vertical campus. This new and unique concept has now become a typological determinant within the organization of tower clusters.

The classic AZD diagram presented in section 4.2 is accurate, with two exceptions.

1. In one tower amenity zone, for example, intermediary AZs may repeat themselves over the height of the building and thereby divide the vertical structure into vertical subzones, or subneighborhoods. This has occurred at Mei'Lin, among other cases;

2. In the case of multiple towers, there exist multiple AZDs—one for each tower. Within the differing towers of a cluster, the AZD may be the same. However, in the case of tower clusters in which there are significant differences of height between the towers, as at Mei'Lin, there exists a condition of vertically superimposed multiple AZDs. That is, the tallest tower at Mei'Lin has a *second base condition* which includes the sky park of the lower two towers. The highest tower of Mei'Lin has a *double base*, with one base at ground level and another base at the sky park atop the lower two towers.

With respect to the definition of the AZD, these two new conditions have now been defined:

1. In the AZD there can exist repetitive vertical subzones, for example, the vertical community subzones of vertical housing;

2. In the AZD there can exist repetitive sky zones, for example, one tower's sky park is the taller tower's base park, as at Mei'Lin.

An additional important concept related to the structural organization of amenities within tower clusters is that of the vertical campus. This concept defines the vertical relational structure of amenities within the tower's functional organization.

We will now define and discuss the newly emerging amenities revolution within tower clusters. This will be presented with respect to a range of three basic functional types. In the analytical context of current tower cluster designs, these functional types have been selected: residential, hotels, offices and high-tech office headquarters.

5.2 Residential Amenities in Tower Clusters

The range of new amenities within both rental and sale residential facilities is very extensive. To some extent it is the existence of these amenities that constructs the fiber of community in residential tall buildings. Thus, community facilities and their location and detailed content are significant to programmatic as well as to design decisions. These are the shared facilities of tall buildings. Their vertical locations throughout the building or the tower cluster construct internal social connectivity. In most of the following functional categories that are presented in part 5, we shall present a similar logic of categorization of amenities. We begin with major *shared amenities*, continue with *building location–oriented amenities*, and end with *technical amenities*. Within these three general classes, we create a more detailed schema which may be relevant for other functional categories as well.

This general schema of amenities in tall residential buildings is as follows:

Residential Amenities
Community Facilities
Sports/Gymnastics
Spas
Technical Amenities
Wellness-Related Technical Amenities
Smart Facilities

Residential Amenities Locations
Site Amenities
Base Amenities
Sub-Base Amenities
Mid-Story Amenities
Sky Amenities in Sky Parks, Skybridges, Sky Gardens, Sky Spas

Among the most significant architectural decisions is the nature of the integration of amenities within the vertical structure of the tall building, the architectural form of the amenities structure, and the contribution that they make in the creation of the vertical campus. What the vertical campus contributes to the tower and tower cluster in both form and function is a critical factor in the justification of the ever-expanding amenities revolution in tall buildings.

In each functional category of tower cluster, we will first present the amenities categories and then discuss the locational/formal considerations. Since the amenities revolution is in fact a revolution of quality, quantity, and technical invention, it is also hugely significant in its contemporary enlargement. The emphasis in the following presentation is to suggest the nature of current considerations regarding amenities in tower clusters as well as to provide some indication of the significance of locational factors in the design of the vertical campus as a seminal concept in the design of tower structures.

a. Community Facilities

Community facilities constitute the social fabric of the residential high-rise. Therefore, the selection, design, and location of these facilities are related to the vertical substructuring scheme of the tower cluster into horizontal subgroupings. Larger functional elements such as movie theaters and auditoria will usually occur in a concentrated single location. Generally, this will be the base structure so that it will also be available to visitors. Service areas such as package delivery rooms will also be concentrated and located in the base. Casual community spaces such as lounges, game rooms, TV rooms, and playrooms are generally distributed throughout the tower(s) at the intersections of vertical subdivisions of groups of dwellings. As a cluster of social functions, they would also presumably be repeated for each meeting of the vertical subdivisions. Coworking space(s) are a recent development after the rise of WeWork. This is a unique and significant function, and appropriate decisions regarding design and location are important.

Movie Theater
Meeting Rooms
Coworking Spaces (including conference rooms, snack/coffee facilities, etc.)
Game Rooms and Lounges
TV Rooms and Coffee Shop
Children's Play Areas and Study Areas
Mail and Package Room(s)
Package Delivery
Community Event Auditoria

b. Sports/Gymnastics

Sports facilities are relatively luxurious for residential buildings. Perhaps the most attractive and thus the most significant functions are various types of swimming pools. The potential location and detailed design are due to the size and character of the project site. Should an enclosed pool be desirable, a potential high-level site may be desirable, as at Raffles City Chongqing.

In addition to pools, there are four other classes of sports/gymnastics functions:

Court Games (such as basketball or tennis courts)
Gyms
Classes and Studio Rooms
Running Track

Gyms are beginning to be very popular functions for residential buildings, particularly in resort sites. They are frequently introspective and not necessarily oriented to view. Thus, potential locations in the upper level of the base are appropriate. Classes and studios could generally be appropriately linked to the gym area. Running tracks and court sports such as tennis are relatively unique within tall buildings. If required or desirable for special housing programs, site locations would be easiest to accommodate. However, there are currently various examples of building-accommodated running tracks, and also of building-integrated tennis courts.

Tennis Court(s)
Basketball
Running Track
Swimming Pool(s)
Fitness Classrooms
Yoga/Tai Chi Studio
Lap Pool (various other pool options such as heated pool)

c. Spas

Spas are relatively small functions and can generally be accommodated in internalized spaces. For potential public access, upper levels of the base are appropriate.

Hair and Beauty Salons
Pet Care Salons
Massage Rooms
Sauna

d. Technical Amenities

High-Speed Wi-Fi
Solar Panels on Roof
Intercom

e. Wellness-Related Technical Amenities

Touchless Entry
Cleaner Air Quality/Circulation Improvements
A.C. System Filtration (for improvement of air quality)
High-Quality Water Filtration
Hospital-Grade Air Filtration
Antimicrobial Gym Equipment
UV Sanitation Media for Elevators
Recycling Bins and Building Recycling Center

f. Smart Facilities

Smart Access Control
Smart Security Systems
Inclusive Smart Apartments (e.g., smart appliances, smart locks, smart thermostats, smart lighting controls)

Technical amenities, wellness-related technical amenities, and smart facilities are all essentially technical rather than spatial requirements. Their presence is highly desirable and attractive to potential residents.

Residential Amenities Locations

Site Amenities

Dog Park
Multiple BBQ Areas, Fire Pits, and Comfort Seating
Green Areas
Outdoor Grill Area
Community Garden (food and flowers can be grown)
Outdoor Children's Play Areas

Base Amenities
Shopping Centers
Malls
Commercial Facilities

Sub-Base Amenities
Auto Parking
Bicycle Parking
Electrical Vehicle Charging Stations
Storage Rooms

Mid-Story Amenities
Community Amenities
Sports Amenities

Sky Amenities
Observation Decks
Sky Parks (exterior or interior)
Sky Gardens
Sky Spas (enclosed)
Roof Track

Residential Amenities: Conclusions

There are three significant categories of improvements with respect to the provision of new amenities in high-rise residential structures:
Programmatic: There is an ongoing qualitative and quantitative increase in amenities in residential structures;
Technical: There is an increase in the provision of smart amenities and wellness-related amenities both in the apartments as well as in the overall buildings;
Architectural: New formal architectural elements such as sky parks, sky-bridges, and sky spas are emerging, which have introduced a formal statement of what may be termed an *architecture of the apogee*. This is a strong *formal statement of linkage* by aboveground bridging or decking, as at Marina Bay Sands.

5.3 Hotel Amenities in Tower Clusters

As is characteristic of residential facilities, there is currently a huge qualitative and quantitative increase in hotel amenities. Since hotels are constantly in a situation of competition, amenities content and form can provide a possible competitive edge in the market. The incentives are therefore to maximize amenities, to be inventive, unique, and expressive with regards to quantity, quality, and unique forms.

Regarding the emphasis on amenities in this building type, socially motivated community facilities are of lesser significance than amenities functions that grant a unique character to the hotel, such as the provision of coworking space. Among the services of the hotel, food service facilities, bars, coffee shops, and cafés (potentially being of unique character and visual interest) are very significant within the category of community facilities. Again, the uniqueness of associative functions such as casinos or art galleries can add a high level of distinction and attractiveness to a hotel. As with residential facilities, sky functions such as multifunctional sky plazas, and penthouse-related functions such as bars and dining rooms are highly attractive.

Among the amenities of the hotel, room-associated amenities are very significant and are also experiencing a high level of innovative expansion among newly emerging types of amenities. We will make some general reference to such room-related amenities, but will not deal with them in detail. The main emphasis here is to identify those areas and forms of change that affect building-scale vertical organization and physical form.

Hotels are highly site-specific. Given the particular characteristics of site, market, and associated functions within the tower cluster, there emerge certain emphases on desirable amenities. Certain formal qualities that can characterize the hotel, such as sky plazas, are very significant in providing visual emphasis on its unique attributes.

The hotel is experiencing a remarkable expansion and improvement of amenities at two scales of the classes of new amenities: the micro and the macro. In this case, the micro is the typical minimal space of the room/suite, and the macro is the assembly of the large-scale common facilities such as restaurants, bars, and other public amenities.

One example of the visual importance of the macro assemblage of special amenities is that of bold formal expression. The view of Marina Bay Sands, which has become the iconic image of Singapore, provides a perfect example of the *visual power of the macro*. In contrast to the high level of vertical distribution of amenities in high-rise housing structures as previously described, the emphasis of the visual distinction of the hotel is generally in the base and, primarily, in the upper sky sections of the building.

This having been said, tower clusters are generally multifunctional, and thus they are amenable, first of all, to the search for a newly expressive urban language. This search reaches in multiple new directions, from the Hugh Ferriss–like structuring of a new, continuous, urban, multilevel base structure, to a sky architecture, and beyond.

Room quality and in-room extras are important contributors to the hotel experience. While this is addressed below, the emphasis of the text is upon hotel-wide amenities and the potential significance of locational possibilities within the tower cluster.

Hotel Amenities

a. Type/Character/Specialization of Hotel

b. Commercial Facilities

Commercial facilities (such as malls or entertainment facilities)

c. Community Facilities

Dining and Bar Facilities (provision of variety, unique character, and special design emphasis)

d. Sports/Gymnastics

Sport-Themed Hotels (e.g., golf hotels; provision of game rooms)

Indoor/Outdoor Themes (for spatial organization and landscaping)

e. Spas

f. Technical Amenities

g. Green Hotels: Wellness and Sustainability-Related Technical Amenities

h. Smart Facilities, Smart Rooms, Smart Technologies

Hotel Amenities Locations

Site Amenities

Base Amenities

Sub-Base Amenities

Mid-Story Amenities

Sky Amenities in Sky Parks, Skybridges, Sky Gardens, Sky Spas

Hotel Amenities

a. Type/Character/Specialization of Hotel

This involves the clustering of special amenities and amenities that grant special functions such as sports orientation, or the provision of special services and character which provide new and unique classes of experiences such as wellness, outdoor activities, special tours orientation, gastronomy, sports, music and culture/art orientation. Branding is significant for new hotel types such as those which provide unique experiences, and combinations of experiences, e.g., combinations of vacation and work.

Provision of Rooms, Apartments, and Houses (as currently exists at the Mandarin Oriental and many other hotels)

Coworking Facilities and Remote Work Facilities

Coffee Culture Facilities

Pet Orientation Hotels and Facilities

Experiential Travel (e.g., yoga, surfing, horseback riding, etc.)

Music- or Art-Focused Hotels

Bleisure Hotels (blending business and leisure)

Glamping Hotels (blending glamor and camping)

Med-Hotels (provision for medical tourism)

Culinary Travel

b. Commercial Facilities

Commercial Facilities (such as malls, shopping streets, art galleries)

Entertainment Facilities (e.g., film screening)

Art Galleries

Casinos
Conference Facilities (including meeting auditoria and work areas)

c. Community Facilities

Dining and Bar Facilities (provision of variety, unique character, and special design emphasis)

d. Sports/Gymnastics

Sport Themed Hotels (e.g., golf hotels, provision of game rooms)
Fitness Hotels
Indoor/Outdoor Themes for spatial organization and landscaping
Fitness Rooms (e.g., provision in private rooms of Peloton bicycles, mirrors, etc.)
Gyms and Gymnastic Classrooms

e. Spas

Beauty Spas
Wellness Spas, Saunas

f. Technical Amenities

AI-Directed Hotel Experiences
Digital Room Selection
Digital Selection of Room and Hotel Add-Ons, Tours, Special Activities, Sports
Mobile Check-In
Mobile Booking
Robotic Room Services: Package and Meal Deliveries
Translation Apps
Automated Information Services
Digital Meeting Venues
Lobby Grab and Go: Self-Service Purchasing

g. Green Hotels: Wellness and Sustainability-related Technical Amenities

Vegan Menus and Meat Alternatives
Solar Power
Limited Use of Plastics
Motion Sensors for Automatic Power Control
Recycle Bins for Waste Disposal
Green Hospitality (e.g., skip housekeeping services)

h. Smart Facilities, Smart Rooms, Smart Technologies

There currently exists a uniquely high level of competition with regard to the provision of special apparatus that can achieve the distinctions of "smart rooms." Some such technologies, among a virtually limitless variety are:

Keyless Entry
Smart Room Controls (temperature, lighting, power)

Voice-Activated Controls (e.g., to request services such as housekeeping)
In-Room Tablet (for hotel information, music, menus, etc.)
Concierge Video Chat (via personal cell phone)
Smart Mirrors (TV Screen and Mirror: e.g., Savvy system by Electric Mirror)
Smart TV (provide hospitality services through streaming facility)
Wireless Cell Phone Charging Mats

Hotel Amenities Locations

The beauty, attractiveness, and uniqueness of amenities have a huge impact on the hotel experience. These are the premiums of each hotel and require great thought and imaginative design. Given that modern travelers are accustomed to receiving a broad range of advanced amenities, the programming of the list of amenities for a new hotel is almost as important as the effort and imagination to be invested in their design. One of the new evaluative criteria for the successful design of a hotel is the opportunities and situations for the implanting of amenities that the design enables. In this case, the tower cluster design itself can create the unique potential for distributing amenities through the vertical environment. Since view is enhanced by height, this invites new thought regarding the vertical distribution of amenities.

Hotels are highly site-sensitive with respect to climate, view, geometry, topography, size, and vegetation. These factors are obviously significant with respect to building design. They are also of importance in the distribution and design of amenities relative to the location and circulation patterns of the hotel facilities within the tower cluster. In general, there is a high degree of added value associated with the clustering of amenities within sky parks and sky spas. This value relates to the creation of commercial attractiveness as well as increasing the use value of the multiple functions of the sky park.

Site Amenities

Amenities of the site are dependent upon the location and the physical attributes of the site. The creation of visual and functional uniqueness is, as in all aspects of hotel design, a major potential consideration that will impact attractiveness and distinction.

Garden and Site Furnishings
Sports Facilities (e.g., tennis courts)
Pool Areas, Furnishings, Landscaping
Pet Park
Outdoor Dining

Base Amenities

Lobby Amenities
Casual Dining, Bar, Coffee Areas

Seating Areas
Meeting Rooms
Cinema Rooms
Fitness Areas (may also be in mid-story of sky amenities)
Commercial Facilities
Mall or Specialized Shopping

Sub-Base Amenities
Auto Parking
Electric Vehicle Charging Stations

Mid-Story Amenities
Interstitial amenities floors are potentially a significant means to distinguish and differentiate vertical zones of hotel rooms. (See also skybridges under Sky Amenities, below.)

Sky Amenities in Sky Parks, Skybridges, Sky Gardens, Sky Spas
Observation Decks
Sky Parks (exterior or interior) and Sky Gardens
Skybridges (linking towers of the cluster can provide indoor or outdoor amenity locations at selected levels)
Sky Spas (enclosed)
Roof Track

5.4 Offices and High-Tech Office Headquarters Amenities in Tower Clusters

In considering new amenities for office buildings as well as high-tech headquarters and administrative offices, we intend to provide those changes to the classical office building that will present a portent of the future of work. In the amenities that are being adapted in the special requirements of high-tech headquarters and administrative offices (for example, Foster Architects' project for DJI Headquarters in Shenzhen, China, or Zaha Hadid Architects' OPPO Headquarters, also in Shenzhen), we are witnessing the coming into being of new worlds of work.

Interactivity has become the formative principle of the new office. More interactions, particularly with respect to creative developmental work, have become necessary in the growing requirement for collaborative work. In addition to physical interaction, there is also a growing requirement for maximizing visual connectivity.

These design principles have created a general requirement for the transcendence of the classical concept of fixed workstations in favor of a more, or less, static environment. New concepts of flexibility are now in demand. Fixed office locations are often exchanged for open workstations. Rather than conventional conference rooms, more casual and flexibly organized and furnished breakout rooms have become desirable. These developments can be summarized as an evolution towards creating a situation of universal WeWork-like office environments. This includes more open-space organization to foster collaboration and an emphasis on coworking spaces.

Following successful developments of organization and amenities distribution in the hospitality industry, there may also be applied a higher organizational level such as a concept of neighborhoods, or work zones, which can provide areas for special work functions, or selective team work zones.

With respect to the provision, design, and location of amenities, five major principles of the future of work environments are emerging:

1. The guiding principle is the provision of *good experiential conditions.* This not only relates to place design, but also to the provision of options of choice that will support community development and networking, and provide maximum possible options for variety of experience. With respect to services, always provide choices between the informal and immediately available as opposed to more formal options. Satisfaction, it is hoped, will increase productivity.

2. Provide *collective space variations* from local (within the office space, or that of the neighborhood) to more formal, penthouse-type collective spaces and services.

3. Always provide *in situ service amenities*, as at WeWork facilities. Here there exists a great range of possible variations, for example, communal kitchens, pick-up and go food shops, etc.

4. *Use biophilic design principles.* Provide green spaces, courts, roof decks, etc. These should be well planted, possibly employ water design and pools, provide views, and supply appropriate furnishings for contemplation as well as small group conversations and even for working.

5. All design should be *wellness-inspired.*

The Transformation of the Office Building and Office Amenities: From "the Skyscraper Changes Work," to "Work Changes the Skyscraper"

In the mid-twentieth century there occurred a takeoff point with respect to the evolution of skyscraper office buildings. Lever House, which opened in New York City in 1952, and was designed by Gordon Bunshaft of Skidmore, Owings and Merrill, is a classic example. The tall office building became an urban medium for the systematized organization of the work environment. Characterized by division into managerial and work environments, the work environment became characterized by relatively fixed workstations, generally equipped with large and heavy electric typewriters. The work environment was a mass open space with fixed workstations. The tall office building had changed work.

Accompanying this new work mode was a relatively standard list of amenities. The building scale amenities usually included workers' cafes and rest areas at ground floor, and luxury restaurants located at ground level or at penthouse levels.

The typical work environment as seen in the photo above and the floor plans below, is relatively open, with workers generally located in fixed locations. The desk was the place of work.

By the late twentieth century, a new evolutionary period begins which transformed the tall building's work environment. The causal factor in this transition was the emerging cultural dominance of the computer age. The computer transforms the workstation into a more flexible work environment. As the computer also evolves to become lighter and more portable with the age of the laptop, and with workers becoming more digitally connected through the coming of the internet, traditional office work becomes potentially less dependent upon fixity of location. With this new period of flexibility, mobility, and lack of the need for stable and fixed locations, the skyscraper office building begins its current stage of evolution. These changes in work are now changing the form, organization, and contents of the office building.

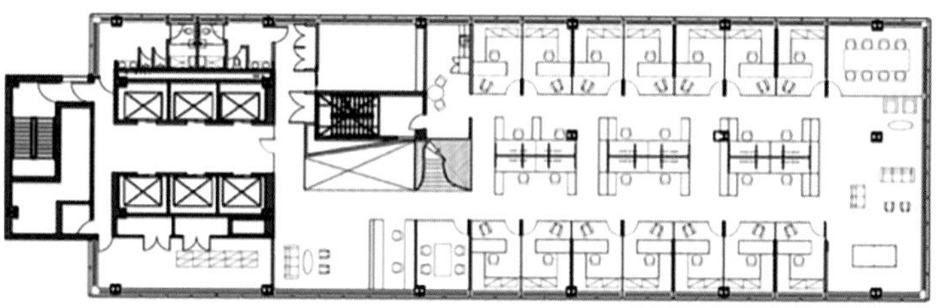

FIRST FLOOR

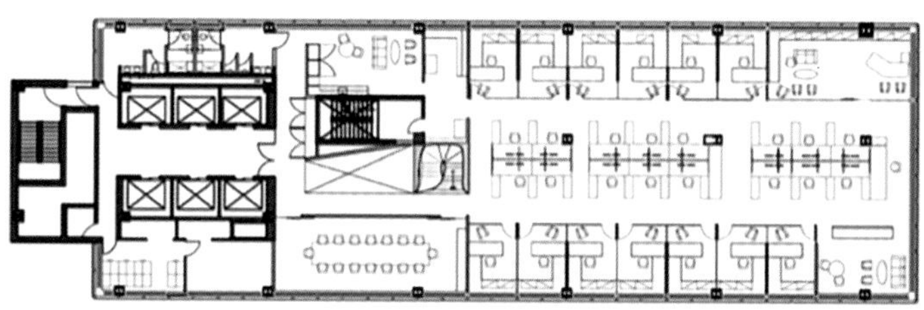

SECOND FLOOR

Left Lever House, New York City, typical floor plans. SOM Architects, 1952.

In the first phase of the evolution, the building influenced work. In this second phase, work influences the building. One of the causes has been the cultural emergence of the computer as the definitive medium of the late-twentieth-century work environment. What is the other major causal factor in the evolution of the work environment by the early twenty-first century?

The institutionalization of the flexible, computer-based, mobile workstation as a characterizing set of elements of the evolving office environment occurred in the last decade of the last century and the first decade of the current century. For example, in 2008, WeWork was established and its first coworking installation was opened in Brooklyn, New York. By 2022, the company had 756 locations in 38 countries. In certain respects, this symbolized the transformation of the work environment.

WeWork is a coworking environment that provides rentable, open-plan facilities in small quantities to small-scale office clients in the early, and often experimental, stages of their development processes. What is most relevant to us here are the typical characteristics of the WeWork environment. Workspace is completely open in plan form and there are large numbers of small amenities and services immediately available. In comparison to the somewhat compartmentalized openness of the mid-1900s, workspace is relaxed and provides great flexibility for the workers to communicate with one another, to move around, to take time for relaxation. This culture of openness in the work environment, with its enhancement of interactive work both individually and in groups, created fresh potential for flexible design for the new generation of office buildings.

The flexible core design principles of the WeWork environment have become absorbed within most new office designs. In the current period, the spatial design, vertical organization, and amenities distribution of the office building is treated as a mechanism for satisfying and optimizing the productive objectives of the company. Nowhere is this vertical design optimization process more experimentally explored than in current high-tech office and headquarters buildings such as that of the OPPO Headquarters building in Shenzhen, China of 2020, by Zaha Hadid Architects, or DJI Headquarters, Shenzhen, China, 2016 to 2023, by Foster and Partners Architects.

It is in programs such as those of high-tech office and headquarters buildings that newly articulated design characteristics emerge which become canonical contributions to the generic design of the vertical campus as the core generative form of the high-tech office and headquarters. These characteristics are becoming common to most contemporary office building design. The first similarity between offices and high-tech offices has been the evolution to highly flexible WeWork-like spatial design, as well as the distribution of minor amenities within the local office space environment. Beyond this significant change in the social environment of the office building, the high-tech vertical office has introduced several pronounced additions to programmatic content.

We have observed in our case study sample that a significant function incorporated within the vertical high-tech office is that of research, design experimentation on future products, and related testing and display of new products. It is characteristic of such functions that they may require unique ceiling heights, spatial organization, and services as in the case of R & D in the DJI Headquarters facility in Shenzhen, China, by Foster and Partners Architects. In that case, the special space contains a significant increase in height over the typical office floor height as well as the employment of skybridges for experimental purposes. There are other important organizational factors as well.

The first of these general characteristics is the attempt to optimize what might be called institutional creativity through emphasizing design for interactivity. Concomitant to this emphasis on interactivity, particularly in the R&D sectors of the building, is the need for privacy control for special creative and experimental work neighborhoods. Privacy control for these units is generally achieved through the *vertical privacy zoning* and control of circulation to these important sectors of the high-tech office. This is also characteristic of the general emphasis in current office design on the vertical zoning of diverse programmatic groupings that has appeared frequently in the recent design of the tower cluster. The tower is thereby divided into vertical subgroupings, which potentially simplifies traffic control.

Within this general growth of the vertical subdivision of the towers in tower clusters, there has been a general increase in the kind and quality of worker amenities and their frequent distribution in the actual work environment. The new condition is the control of movement *between* the vertical order of functional groupings and increased freedom of actual work *within* the newly adapted WeWork-like environments themselves.

Amenities, their availability, and location are site-sensitive. Is the site large enough so that beyond the towers there is additional space for amenities locations? Generally, with respect to tower clusters, site characteristics such as view and site space limitations generally require the incorporation of amenities within the tower cluster. In this situation, there are three general locational possibilities:

- incorporation within work neighborhoods;
- incorporation within base structures;
- incorporation within penthouses or independent sky structures.

Office Clusters and High-Tech Office Clusters: Amenities and Amenities Locations

Food Service

Local communal kitchens may be available in office work areas, particularly in special work neighborhoods. Coworking areas are generally amenity-rich directly within the immediate spatial environment.

Food service amenities such as cafés may be open all the time as well as at fixed hours. They may also be "pick-up and go" cafés at the level of work neighborhoods.

More formal restaurants and bars are usually available either in cluster base structures, in penthouse areas, or in independent sky structures.

Relaxation Spaces

Multipurpose Lounges

Community Facilities

Community facilities frequently exist in tech headquarter–type clusters. In such building types, community facilities are rich in variability. They may include such facilities as auditoria, cinemas, display areas both for exhibitions and product display, class and seminar rooms. Occasionally, in special circumstances, such as Nanjing Youth Cultural Center by Zaha Hadid Architects, they may include well-developed conference facilities.

Sports/Gymnastics

The most common office building sports facilities are workers' gymnasia.

These may be highly diverse in design and equipment. Cycling and electronic cycling (Peloton, etc.) are frequently provided beside the gym space(s). In addition, gym class spaces, for example, for group Tai Chi classes, may also be incorporated within gym clusters.

Swimming pools are very popular sports facilities.

Less common are running tracks, due to the difficulty of internal accommodation. Other facilities such as tennis courts, which have both scale and height requirements, are rare in internal environments.

Locker and shower Areas

Spas

Spas are special private room facilities in which health and beauty treatments including massages and hair treatment are given. These are common in hotel environments, but rare in current office facilities.

Technical Amenities

Tech-enabled conference rooms

Virtual coworking setups

Distance coworking environments

VR work and presentation environments

Executive Wi-Fi networks

Wellness-Related Amenities

Medical wellness office and services

Child Care

In-building child care

Smart Facilities

Application design in working group communication with AI and VR emphases

Smart facilities highly relevant for operational and micro aspects

Biophilic Design Principles and Places

Bring nature into work environment
Fresh air terraces
Roof gardens

Parking

Covered parking with electric vehicle charging
Bicycle storage with electric bicycle charging
Bicycle repair

Shopping

Highly relevant in large-scale, high-tech tower cluster facilities. This is particularly the case in developmental situations such as those in Shenzhen, China. Here there is a high priority on design emphasis on urban connectivity which increases the potential scale of customer population.

Special Care Service Facilities

Laundry and dry cleaning

Amenities Management

Team to manage services and amenities
Concierge to coordinate events and services

Office Amenities Locations

Site and Urban Amenities

Usually tennis and swimming facilities are site-located when possible.

Base Amenities

Base amenities, particularly in high-tech, include display facilities, auditoria, classrooms, etc. They would also include restaurants and shopping areas.

Sub-Base Amenities

Parking
Electric car charging
Electric bicycle charging
Showers and lockers
Auto washing
Air for tires and personal services

Mid-Story Amenities

Horizontal subdivision into work neighborhoods and research areas in high-tech headquarters tower clusters generates a structuring model for amenities of the local community. These include food service facilities, sports facilities, personal service facilities, and others.
Food services of various classes

Decks and other outdoor garden spaces and rest/recreation/small group interaction areas

Sky Amenities in Sky Parks, Skybridges, Sky Gardens, Sky Spas

As has been clear in the case studies, sky amenities are prestigious and generally large-scale. Of particular importance are sports facilities and restaurants/bars. Such sky-based facilities frequently exist in large-scale and uniquely shaped structural form, such as those at Marina Bay Sands in Singapore.

5.5 Emerging Amenities Structures in Tower Clusters

The vertical campus is a vertical structure of amenities distribution within the tower cluster. The vertical campus of hotels within tower clusters generally involves the development of architecturally significant emphases of sizable amenities clusters on the site, base, or sky areas. The result of this locational emphasis is that the vertical distribution of amenities structures and their formal design have become a very important part of tower cluster design. The case studies have also illustrated how these amenities structures have become an expressive architectural element of the design of tower clusters. There is a strong tendency for such physical, and often sculptural, amenity structures to be constructed into a vertical system, such as at Mei'Lin. Marina Bay Sands, with its sculptural sky amenity's structure, has become the iconic visual motif of Singapore. The concept of a bridging structure that spans the tower structure as at Marina Bay Sands, CCTV in Beijing, and at Raffles City Chongqing, has become a monumental one for the visual celebration of the scale and urban significance of the tower cluster.

The vertical campus, or structured amenities in tower clusters, has emerged as a major vertical organizational and formal factor of the most recent examples of the tower cluster. The vertical campus, the design of which began as a formally lower-level series of formal motifs that were integrated within the grouping of towers, now has potentially become the primary, rather than the secondary, order of the design of the tower cluster, e.g., at Mei'Lin.

Each of the classes of tower cluster that have been defined in part 3 provides differing potential for the provision of urban amenities within tower clusters. We analyze the ways in which these two factors: the morphology of tower clusters and the classes of urban amenities can be integrated. This study demonstrates the integration of different classes of urban amenities within the morphology of the classes of tower cluster.

PART VI

From Collective Form to Connective Form

6.1 Collective Form

We now consider the potential contribution of multiple tower clusters to a new urbanism. Among the basic questions is the extent to which the typology of functionally integrated tower clusters can become a universal model in the urbanism of new and existing urban areas. Given the potential existence of a city based on the repetition of tower clusters, what *consensual factors* such as the agreed-upon height locations for street connections from complex to complex are required so that a connective network of streets in the air and other phenomena of vertical urbanism can actually come into being? What are the preconditions for a city of vertical urbanism to come into being via the existence of a generally accepted new typology of large-scale, high-density urban tower clusters?

Diversity of Systems of Vertical Urbanism

The concept of vertical urbanism that we introduced in part 1 is a bold idea which implies that high-density, high-rise construction can potentially provide certain of the spatial and functional constituents of urban environments that usually exist only on, or directly connected to, the ground plane. First of all, vertical urbanism refers to the potential for the means of pedestrian and possibly also vehicular circulation to exist within the context of tall buildings as streets, or ways, in the sky. Secondly, the term refers to the potential for additional urban phenomena such as large public spaces and parks to exist within tall buildings.

Vertical urbanism is a new urbanism based on the tower city. It reflects the unique urban qualities of both interiority and dynamic continuity. It is the forms of spatial exploitation of the three-dimensionality of the tower city that render unique the potential urban contribution of the tower cluster to a completely new type of urban experience and future development. This is an urbanism that is spatially liberated from the historic dominance of the ground plane as the urban nexus.

Given that vertical urban phenomena such as sky parks might even exist as part of the public, or private, urban environment of tall buildings, theoretically this would produce the environmental conditions for new forms of vertical urban environments to also establish a sense of community. Thus, the existence of a common phenomenon of vertical urbanism can theoretically provide the potential for socializing the sky.

We will attempt to demonstrate how these phenomena already exist in virtually every instance of the emerging building type that we refer to as the tower cluster. The tower cluster, which is defined in detail in part 3, is, among other things, a form of high-density clustering of multiple towers. Within such building groupings there are integrated new forms of urban-scale social, cultural, and commercial activities, even at the upper levels of the grouping. Given that the tower cluster is also capable of supporting streets in the sky, as a new urban architectural type it has the potential to function as a *nexus structure* in a new form of urbanism. The generative ingredient of the tower cluster as a generator of this new form of urbanism is that it can potentially provide new layers of public urban space and functions and new media of circulation above ground level.

Can the tower cluster, with the rapidly evolving sophistication of its structures of amenities, be employed to create new principles of urban form? One key answer may reside in the conceptual framework of *collective systems.*

Collective Form

In 1964, the Japanese architect Fumihiko Maki published an essay entitled "Investigations in Collective Form." In the introduction, he postulates that there is always a raison d'être for the grouping of the components of what will become a *connected grouping*. This reason may be spatial, social, or functional, such as a horizontally connective commercial zone. Such linkages are typical causal factors in the creation of larger urban groupings. He goes on to define three classes of collective urban form:

Compositional Form

These are buildings that are in group form due to a *compositional approach*. The buildings may be created, or designed, individually. However, there may be a reason to connect them, such as the creation of a desired type of urban form, or spatial experience, or symbolic effect. This is the most natural causal approach to creating collective form, since it is essentially architectural; it creates form from a series of given components. It is therefore the most popular and common situation for the generation of connected urban form. Examples of compositional urban form given are Rockefeller Center in New York City, Chandigarh Government Center in India, and the city of Brasília in Brazil.

Megastructure Form

Megastructure form is achieved due to a *structural approach*. The megastructure is a physical infrastructure in which various functions may be incorporated, or in some way plugged in. Generally, the megastructure incorporates multiple and diverse components, the combining of which into one large framework is viewed as a positive factor. It is considered one efficient means to achieve a massive grouping of diverse functions, and is considered highly attractive to urban designers. As an example of megastructure urban form, Maki proposes Kenzo Tange's proposal of 1960 for the extension of Tokyo into Tokyo Bay. In that experimental urban design scheme, the multistory residential buildings are the major urban components that are inserted into the urban infrastructure of circulation media. In addition, the multistory housing structures are themselves organized as infrastructural frameworks, or megastructures, into which individual housing units may be plugged. This principle of the hierarchical ordering of frameworks that can accommodate a subsystem of component infill can be employed at various hierarchical scales. In megastructure design the hierarchical principle of the grouping of multiple systems becomes the means for the creation of collective form at a large urban scale. It has been for this reason a prominent urban design principle in the second half of the twentieth century.

Maki proposes three significant advances for the megastructure concept. Firstly, it potentially enables the emergence of large-scale *environmental buildings* which enable the interaction of large-scale structural designs for the purposes of future environmental engineering. Such structures might be designed, for example, to achieve large-scale mechanisms for climate control. Secondly, as the need for *large-scale multifunctional structures* becomes necessary, the megastructure principle offers an approach to their realization. Finally, the approach may be applied in situations in which urban infrastructure is a form of public investment. Here, I believe that it is important to quote Maki. "Substantial public investment can be made in infrastructures (the skeleton of megastructures) in order to guide and stimulate public structures around them. This strategy can be further extended to a new three-dimensional concept of land use where public agencies will maintain the ownership and upkeep for both horizontal and vertical circulation systems."

This rationale of the content of the quotation will continue to be highly relevant to the later development of concepts of infrastructural connectivity as a means of the establishment of urban connectivity in tower structures.

Group Form

Group form is based on the existence of a *generative system* employing repetitive elements in space in order to create a systematic urban order. Examples given of such historic developments are medieval European cities as well as regionalist urban form created by residential-scaled units in coordination with a spatial system for circulation and public spaces, such as is common in the Greek islands.

Among principles involved in group form, the definition of typological and organizational rules of order in the making and repetition of basic elements is the most fundamental rule set. This understanding may be informal, or actually defined in law. This rule system always includes as well *principles of systematic linkage*.

In comparison to the smaller-scale generative elements of the repetitive system in group form, in megaform the basic elements tend to be of large scale. In the case of contemporary application of these principles in the establishment of urban spatial systems, it is theoretically possible to employ in tandem multiple approaches to the creation of collective form and, potentially, also connective form in urban environments.

Linkage in Collective Form

Linkage is the articulation of rules of combination of the elements of an urban order of collective form. This involves both the definition of how links may be achieved as well as how and when these rules may be applied in order to achieve a desired urban order.

Any system of urban linkage rules may also define multiple forms and media of linkage such as "ground-based" streets as opposed as "elevated

bridge systems." Linkage systems may also be two- or three-dimensional systems. In an era of high-rise urbanism, it is inevitable that we approach the concept of urban connectivity as a matter of three-dimensional connectivity. Given that the city is a dynamic cultural entity, any system of connectivity there, must be a means to achieve connectivity between the existing and the future elements to be linked. That is to say, there must be a system of *open linkage*.

Maki has stated that "there are five *basic linking operations*: to mediate, to define (boundary conditions), to repeat, to make a sequential path, and to select."

- *Mediation* is to connect with intermediate elements, or to define a potential for connection;

- *Definition* is to identify a boundary to, or from, which connection can be made. This is not necessarily a physical boundary such as a wall, but some element that defines a linkable site;

- *Repetition* is to repeat and identify one common element in each of the linkable components of an urban system. In his definition, this need not necessarily be physical, but can be something such as a repetitive spatial hiatus between buildings;

- *To make a sequential path* is to create a meaningful, potentially useful path between multifunctional elements of the collective grouping. Then there is the need to reinforce the path by such means as landscape design, which will move people through the connective system. This combination defines a three-dimensional activity sequence;

- *To select* is to establish potential unity in the operations of the linking process in the appropriate selection of the site, the attributes of which, such as topography, or views, will enable the potential success of linked urbanism.

6.2 From Collective Form to Connective Form: Berlin Hauptstadt—Alison and Peter Smithson with Peter Sigmond-Wonke

The British architects Alison and Peter Smithson were discussed in part 1 with regard to their important professional contributions to postwar high-density residential design in Great Britain. Among these contributions was the formulation, propagation, and practical realization of the concept of *streets in the air*, or *streets in the sky*. Their own work and the work of their students in the realization of this concept at urban scale makes it possible for us to consider them among the significant postwar architect/urbanists of the practice and theory of *linked urban form*. Their realizations

Above Antonio Sant'Elia, *House with External Elevators*, 1914. Connective tissue integrated in architectural form.

Opposite Page Economist Buildings, London. Alison and Peter Smithson, 1959–1964.

of the concept of streets in the air was an early form of connective urbanism. In other professional work, they engaged in the application of the linkage principle in the design and construction of what may be considered a proto-tower cluster.

Between 1959 and 1964, they designed and built a project for The Economist journal on an urban site in London. They designed a complex of buildings including an office tower for the magazine, a private residential building, a private club, and a bank building. This urban complex of four buildings is clustered around an open courtyard. The courtyard provides entry into the main buildings and is located at an intermediate elevation between the upper entry and the lower entry. Below the complex there is underground parking. As can be seen in the architect's visualization below, the complex has many of the characteristics of the tower cluster. It is multifunctional and has a strong consistency in the formal and material language of the project. As the courtyard is also an expression of buildings organized as a cluster on an urban pathway, it may be considered an early case of the expression of a tower cluster as a component of connective form in the city. The project is currently considered an urban legacy.

Berlin Hauptstadt: Alison and Peter Smithson with Peter Sigmond-Wonke

Due to the wartime devastation of Berlin, the government, which in 1957 had made Berlin the capital of the Federal Republic, announced an international competition for the reconstruction of the central area of the city. Among other things, this was to be an attempt to unify the divided city. The competition entry of Alison and Peter Smithson along with Peter Sigmond-Wonke exemplifies and further enhances the potential application of the concept of urban connectivity. In this scheme, a low-rise base structure of continuous nodes and bridges is proposed as an urban planning principle to be applied over a large site with provisions for the separation of pedestrian and vehicular circulation through a multilevel, geometrically layered pattern.

The proposed platform network maintains the existing street network with the superposition of an additional pedestrian network integrated within the existing block structure. The new layered proposal for the southern area of the plan creates an irregular pedestrian pattern superimposed on the regular pattern of vehicular circulation of the existing urban plan. Parking garages were to be located at the periphery of the layered city. The irregular layered pattern which was the heart of the plan was a novel approach to the attempt to create an additional urban form based on pedestrian movement and landscape systems. This is an attempt to return pedestrian movement to the central focus of the modern city.

The diagrammatic organization of the plan located governmental and municipal administration on the north of the plan running along an east-west axis in relationship to the path of the river. South of this is located

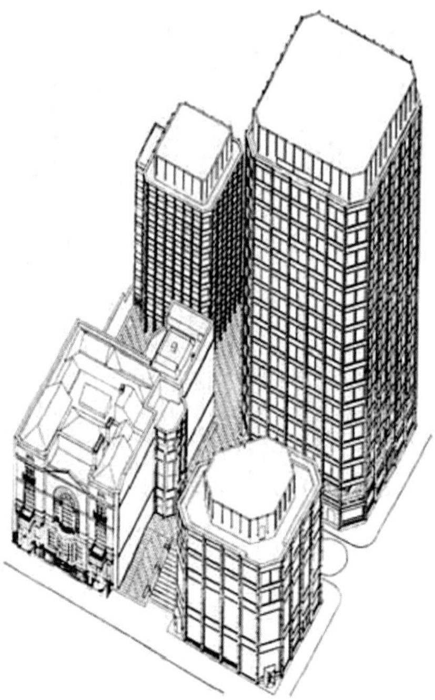

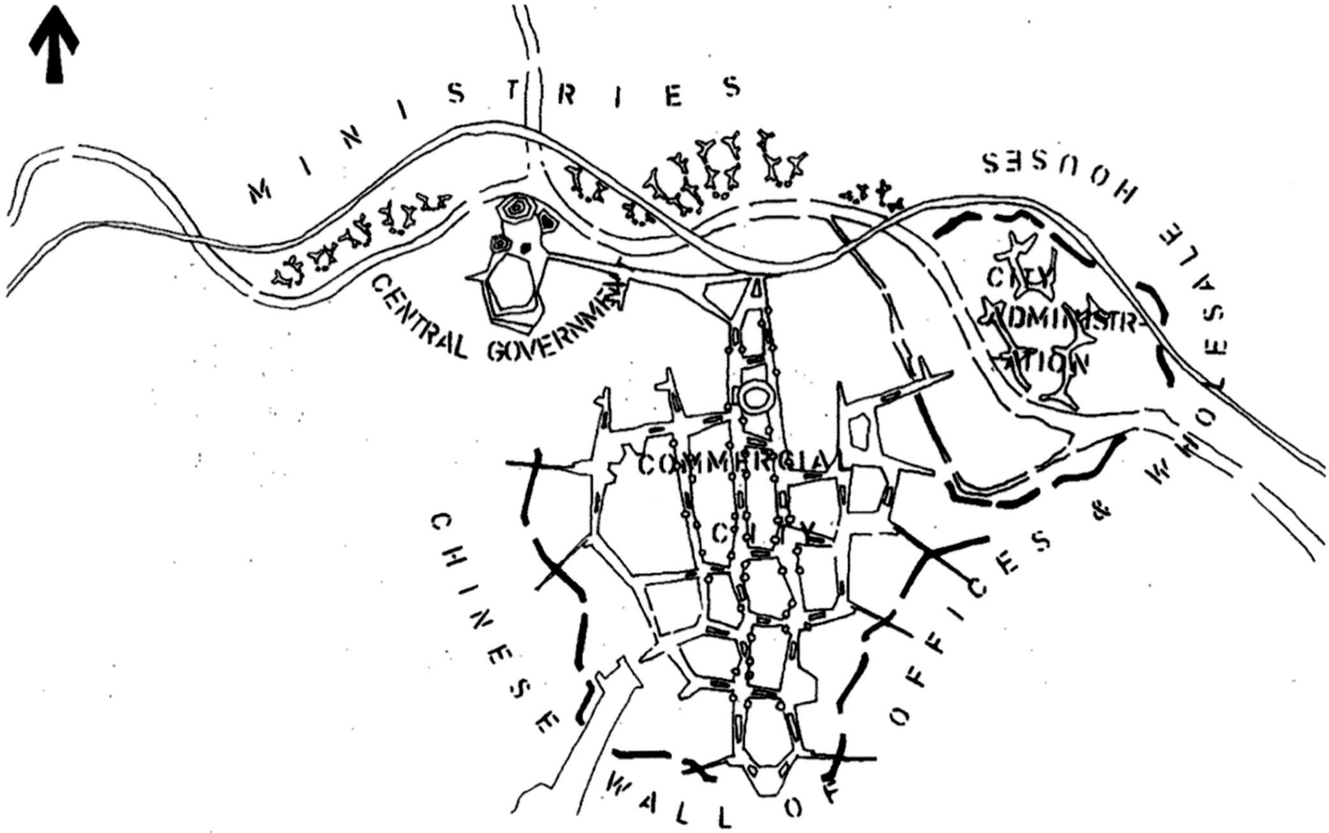
MINISTRIES
CENTRAL GOVERNM
CHINESE WALL OF OFFICES & WHOLESALE HOUSES

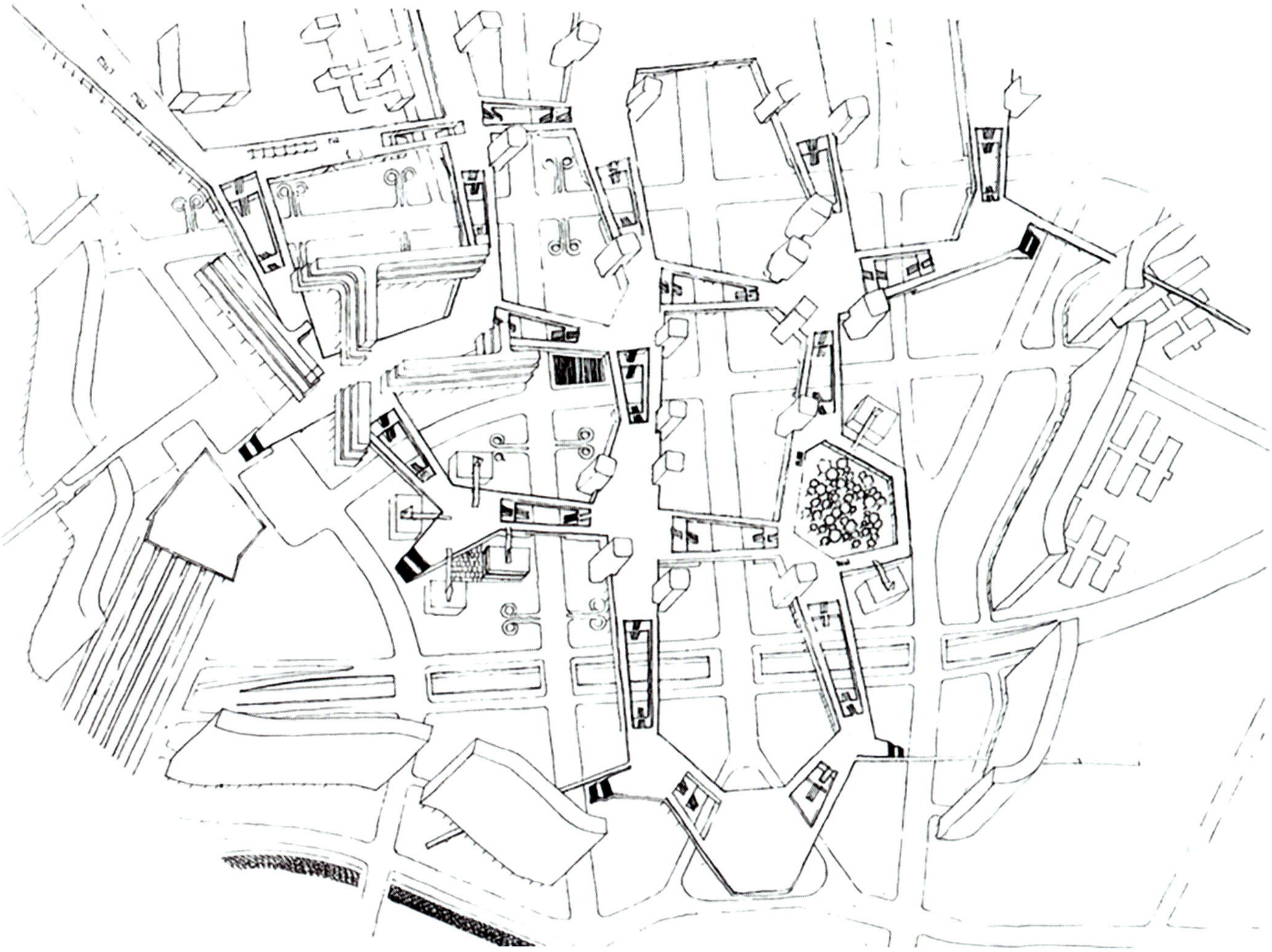

Opposite Page Alison and Peter Smithson with Peter Sigmond-Wonke. *Project for the Berlin Hauptstadt Competition*, plan diagram, 1958. **Bottom** Alison and Peter Smithson with Peter Sigmond-Wonke. *Project for the Berlin Hauptstadt Competition*, urban plan, 1958.

Above Alison and Peter Smithson with Peter Sigmond-Wonke. *Project for the Berlin Hauptstadt Competition*, 1958. Aerial projection of the commercial pedestrian network with skybridges and towers. **Bottom** Alison and Peter Smithson with Peter Sigmond-Wonke. *Project for the Berlin Hauptstadt Competition*, sketch, 1958. Separation of movement systems in commercial center.

the new network of commercial facilities and pedestrian movement layered above the ground plane and creating a connected city. The dark linear elements surrounding the layered pattern and the municipal administrative precinct was to be a linear organization of high-rise housing and office buildings. The towers surrounding the junctions of commercial areas are tower clusters of offices for the businesses. There are other tall buildings such as hotels located in the network. This project specifically illustrates the urban potential of tower clusters to create a city of connective urbanism.

6.3 The Networked City of Connective Urbanism

> *Footbridge networks throughout the city that grew piecemeal, built by different parties at different times, to serve different immediate needs, eventually formed an extensive network and became a prevailing development model for the city's large-scale urban projects.... The ground plane remains a reference point for cultural life. Hong Kong enhances three-dimensional connectivity to such a degree that it eliminates reference to the ground altogether.*
>
> —Frampton, Solomon, and Wong, *Cities Without Ground*

Hong Kong as a city without ground is also defined as a city without figure-ground relationships. That is, it is a city of direct skybridge relationships from building to building, or from cluster to cluster. This urban situation of ultimate linkage is based on two characteristic urban factors of the city's urban development: high density and the steeply sloping terrain. The result is that skybridging is an ad hoc process which serves to create a complex, three-dimensional order of spatial relationships in a continuous state of urban creation. Nothing is the result of an overarching plan. There is a sense of virtually continuous mass in which functional continuity in space is made possible by bridge connectors and vertical transitions mainly by escalators.

There are three typical classes of movement space: street level, underground, and overground. There is a hierarchy of pedestrian movement possibilities in the city. The primal order of pedestrian movement is the ground plane. The preferred medium of pedestrian circulation is the continuous system of bridges, escalators, and passages through buildings, lobbies, or malls. That is, what has become the cognitive movement system of the walker or shopper in the city are these three-dimensional, multimedium, interlocking passages and transitional places which create the complex infrastructure of circulation that is the city of continuous linkage. There is no repetitive pattern, nor is there a particular, well-defined system of goal objects that create the linkage mechanism of the walker in the city. The city of modernity, once formalized by Walter Benjamin, has evolved into a dialectical system in which the *flâneur* can become forever lost in this three-dimensional continuous space of linkage and transitions.

Beyond this linked, internalized system, there also exist other media of movement and circulation. These include, among others, buses, trains, trams, ships, ferries, and airplanes. So any typical continuous path on any typical day is generally a multimodal experience. There is no repetitive pattern, no main streets, no directional system, no simple basis for orientation. With respect to spatial experiences, the major characteristic spaces of the city are train stations, office lobbies, or shopping malls and atria.

Since there is much redundancy in the network, there is often no functional fixity to various places. Activities such as political activity may occur in various types of functional spaces such as on public streets, just as diverse, nonshopping activities may occur in shopping malls.

There are currently approximately seven hundred skybridge footbridges in Hong Kong. This multilevel pedestrian system is the most extensive in the world, and one of the most complex and sophisticated networks of a combination of movement systems including elevated walkways, skybridges, escalators, elevators, and spatial transitions like deck-access plazas and podiums, as well as multiple bridging conditions such as over-air bridges and bridge networks. Into this three-dimensional system of interior and exterior linkages new components still continue to be added as extensions to the interconnected urban system.

These two approaches to the connective city, one a theoretical project, the other a series of practical strategies for dealing with a complex existing three-dimensional situation, differ significantly in site conditions, urban situation, and design approach. Hong Kong presents the antithesis of the preplanned, single bridging level of the Berlin project, which is essentially on a flat site. Hong Kong demonstrates the possibility of the application of three-dimensional above-grade circulation systems in urban locations of irregular site conditions and complex topography in order to produce ad hoc solutions to the development of a network.

The diagrams below represent the connectivity in the area of the Central Railroad Station. Among other circulation media in this site, the diagram illustrates the half-mile-long system of covered escalators and elevated walkways in this area and the approximately 443-foot descent to the station.

Historically, the networked city of skybridge links and the tower cluster have a parent-progeny conceptual relationship. Theoretically, one would assume that this relationship develops from micro to macro. However, the historical relationship very possibly had its origin in the three-dimensional urban developments in Hong Kong. Because Hong Kong's transformation into a three-dimensional networked city began around 1963, it is the urban realization of the networked city that stimulated the emergence of the tower cluster there, rather than vice versa. This is certainly the case with the prominent emergence of the typology during the process of the contemporary industrialization of China, in this case, following upon the first decade after the millennium.

In Hong Kong, it is the network of skybridged pedestrian connectors that has socialized the sky. This has enabled the viable ad hoc construction of a complex, dense urban network of skybridge connectors that has made pedestrian circulation feasible in a city with a naturally steep topography. Since this process began when the first elevated footbridges were constructed in 1963, which is much earlier than the present phenomenon of the tower cluster, it is the urban skybridge network that preceded the tower cluster. It is highly likely that at least in China the skybridge city influences the relatively recent emergence of the tower cluster.

In any case, there is a communality within the urban and architectural relationship of these two architectural concepts. The networked skybridge city and the tower cluster as a systematically ordered relationship of the eight factors defining the typology of the tower cluster:

- A related close-grouping of multiple high-rise buildings;
- A formal ensemble of interconnected vertical and horizontal architectural elements;
- A multifunctional program;
- A structured distribution of amenities, some of which may be public-access amenities;
- A connective plinth, or base, element as well as potential additional upper-level skybridge connectors;
- Large-scale public urban spaces vertically integrated within the cluster ensemble which creates the potential for vertical urbanism;
- Vertical urbanism as the creation of spaces of urban experience such as public plazas above ground level;
- Vertical urbanism can be fully realized as both the vertical distribution of urban experience within each tower cluster as well as the *potential urban connectivity* between tower clusters.

So how can this potential theoretical development achieve its fullest realization in terms of urban development? As the tower cluster potentially advances in design sophistication, can it possibly be the source of a new urbanism? Can it possibly evolve from a skybridge architecture to a skybridge urbanism? If so, what is the constellation of preconditions that might foster such an evolution?

The tower cluster creates high-density nodes that intrinsically invite three-dimensional urban interconnectivity. This becomes more realistic when the cluster's density and nodes of urban resources, and the potential system of tower clusters, are dense enough to justify networked pedestrian circulation. This becomes realistic when sufficient commercial, cultural, urban, landscape, and other potential public resources become available throughout the network.

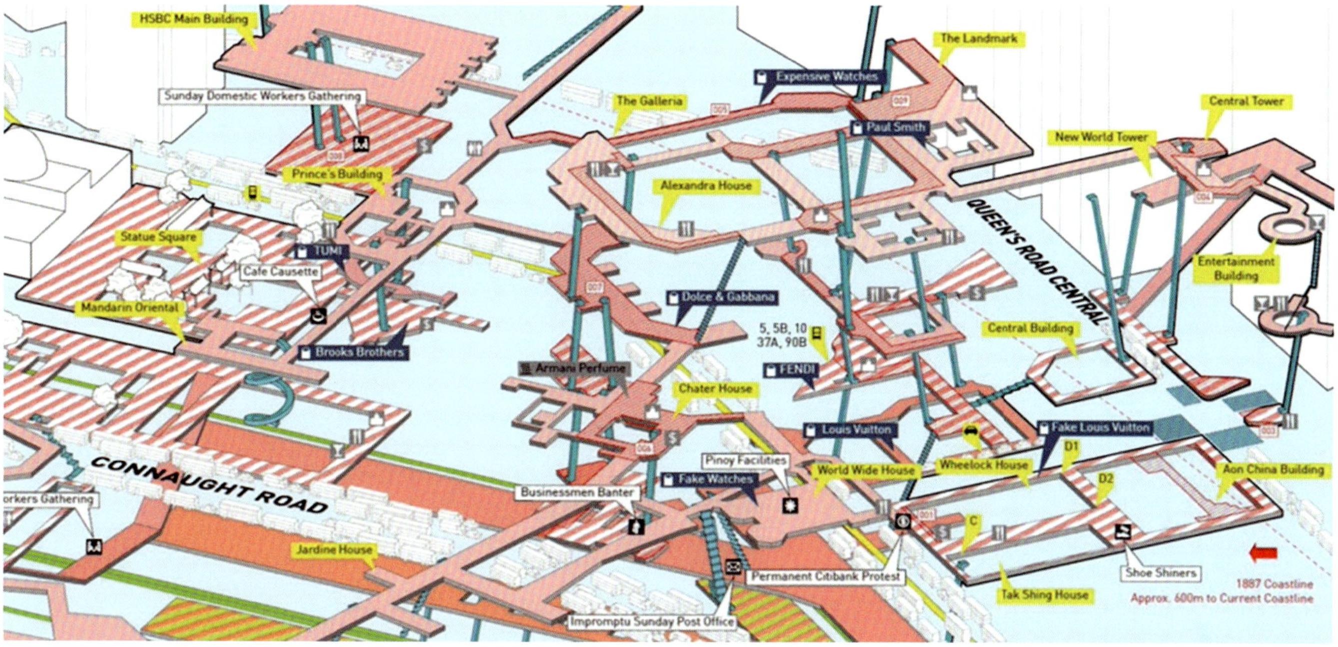

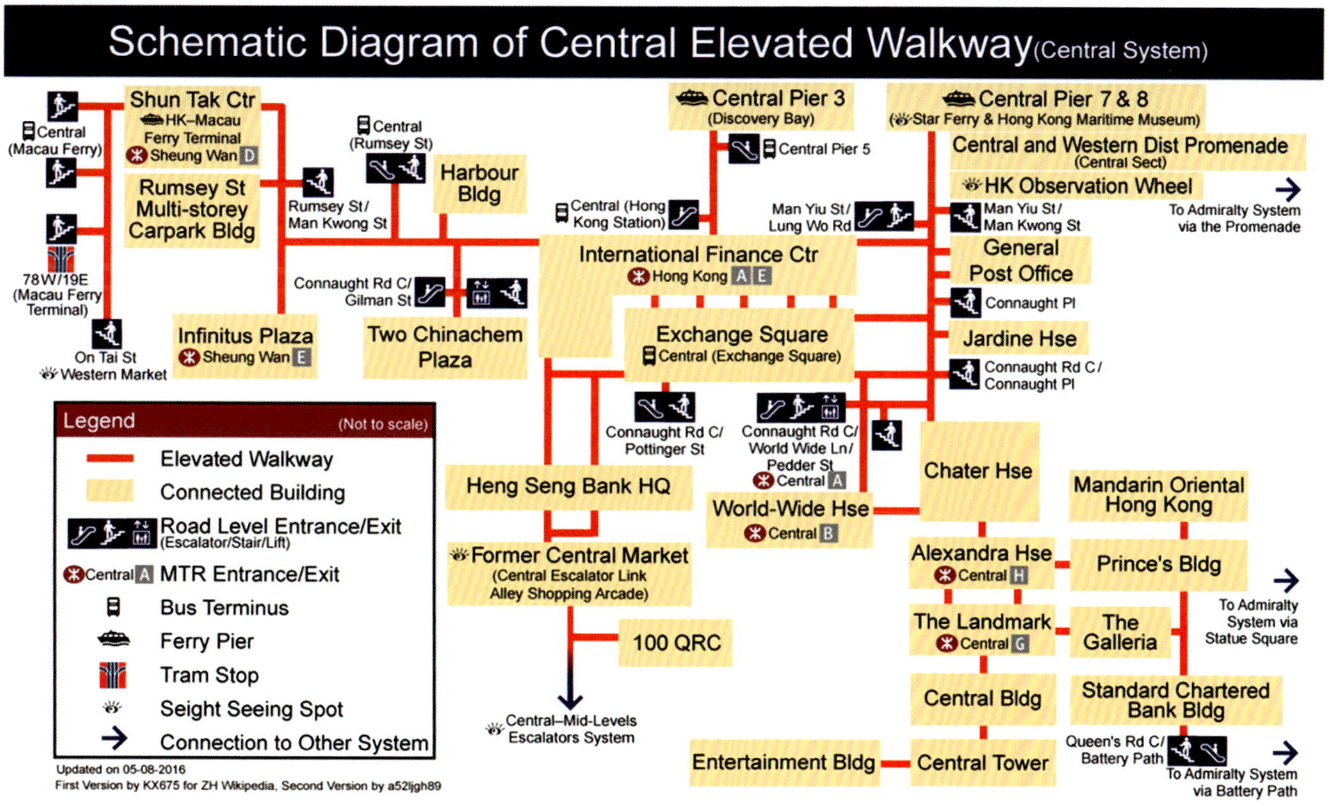

Above Hong Kong Central Station, diagram of connectivity in the Central Station area. Courtesy of *Cities Without Ground*. **Bottom** Hong Kong Central Station, diagram of connectivity in the Central Station area.

PART VII

On Socializing the Sky

7.1 The Tower Cluster and the Networked City

This research has led to the discovery of a series of powerful contributions to both architectural and urban knowledge. Such contributions can be evaluated only on the basis of their contributions to future environments. It is therefor, in the end, valid to attempt to recover those multiple theoretical discoveries and attempt to assemble them into a foundation of thought for potential futures in an urban world of great density as well, as one of diversity, cultural richness, and social brilliance.

Contributions to knowledge as well as to the transcendence of typological limitations can be viewed as a means of elevating the discipline as well as contributing to newly elevated models of what quality of environments may eventually be achieved. Herewith, four territories of newly engaged ideas may be approached:

- **The Tower Cluster and the Networked City**
  This speaks to the uniqueness and potential creative power of a new urban architectural typology. The creative potential of the concept of the tower cluster is discussed, and an attempt at evaluation of that potential is presented. The multifunctionality and increased density of the tower cluster is seen as justifying the existence of increased physical packaging and structuring of amenities. Such characteristics can further lead to the creation of three-dimensional orders of networked cities;

- **The Syntax of Amenities Structures in Tower Clusters**
  The systematized distribution of the elements of the vertical campus of each tower cluster now acts as a node of urban attraction in three dimensions. Density of the tower cluster has resulted in a high level of provision of facilities such as cultural and commercial attractions. This increase in functional provision establishes a pressure for formal expression as a sign of the unique allure of what is asking to be visually expressed as the visible structure of amenities. Inevitably, as we have already witnessed, this can and will lead to the multiple horizontal connectivity of cluster to cluster, or to the networked city.

- **The New Architecture of Amenities Structures**
  The increased provision of amenities within tall buildings for residential, hotel, office, high-tech headquarters, and other multifunctional tall buildings is contributing to the creation of new urban models. What has been referred to as the revolution of amenities provision furthermore stimulates the coming into existence of the vertical campus, that is, a circulation-integrated structured system of amenities, as well as a potentially formally rich world of attraction, utility, and experience that is distributed vertically throughout the height of the tower cluster.

- **Socializing the Sky**
  We have witnessed the potential, in Berlin and Hong Kong, of two

approaches to the coming into being of the three-dimensionally, freely-distributed in space networked city. One of these is consensual, that is, preplanned and relatively ordered in advanced by planning, agreement, and/or building code. In the case of Berlin, the proposed system was three-dimensional, but relatively fixed in terms of its multistory potential. It is also limited to interconnection only by bridging. In the case of Hong Kong, the model is potentially much more open and dynamic in means, place, and time. The linkage mechanisms, beyond those of bridge structures, include many options such as plazas and podiums, high-bridge networks, and others. Hong Kong is a model that has freely evolved in three-dimensional urban space. We will briefly consider certain models of complex 3-D urban interconnectivity

7.2 The Syntax of Amenities in Tower Clusters: The Vertical Campus

The *syntax of amenities structures* describes the elements, vertical ordering, and relationships of syntactical elements within the vertical order. The typified ordering of these relationships is referred to as the vertical campus. That is, a vertical ordering of amenities grouping of different functions the access to which is controlled by the system of vertical circulation.

The diagram below illustrates a potential ordering of special amenities elements and their possible locations of vertical distribution. It is important to note that the ordering and distribution of amenities will differ according to the nature of the major functions of the tower cluster. Secondly, depending upon the nature of the function, the amenity floor(s) may be repeated over the height of the high-rise tower(s). For example, in residential structures, floors containing collective amenities may be repeated over the height of a grouping of floors, thus creating a system of vertical neighborhoods. In high-tech headquarters office buildings, there may also be repetition of floors, including amenities, for special activity groups.

Starting from the top of the diagram and working down to the base elements, the order is as follows:

Super Structures: Sky Plazas/Sky Spas

Generally, this is an elongated amenity structure superimposed upon all towers of the cluster. External structures are referred to as sky plazas. These generally contain multiple functions. When enclosed, they are referred to as sky spas. The architectural form as, for example, at Safdie Architects' Marina Bay Sands (sky plaza) or Raffles City (sky spa), is generally uniquely sculptural forms and therefore adds significant formal impact to the cluster.

Penthouse / Connected Penthouses

The upper levels of the towers are expressed as the cluster terminus. There is no superimposed unifying element. Instead, the towers receive a special formal expression, such as multistory spaces. These multiple penthouses of the cluster may have skybridge interconnections, as at Galaxy Soho, for example.

Upper-Level Special Functions: Experimental

Depending on what the function of the building is, it may have special requirements for functional elements and their distribution throughout the building. For example, in Foster and Partners' DJI Headquarters, there is a requirement for multistory experimental spaces used for research and development. Please note that, in addition to these spaces, there is a unique skybridge also employed for experimentation and demonstration.

Syntax of Amenities in Tower Clusters
The Vertical Campus

Super Structures: Sky Plaza/Sky Spa

Penthouse/Connected Penthouses

Upper-Level Special Functions
Experimental

Intermediary Sky Plaza

Intermediary Amenity Floors
Intermediary Amenity Decks

Internal Sky-Bridge Connectors

Upper Level of Base
Potential Sky-Bridge Connectors
Articulated Base Levels

Sub-Base Amenities

Left Diagram of possible layout of zones of amenities within the tower cluster.

Intermediary Sky Plaza

If the towers within the cluster are of differing heights, such as at Raffles City, the sky plaza/sky spa may be below the height of the upper towers. This also occurs in the Mei'Lin residential tower cluster project in Shenzhen, China.

Intermediary Amenity Floors / Intermediary Amenity Decks

The vertical distribution of amenity services such as gyms and other athletic and social spaces may occur multiple times over the height of the vertical subgroupings, which potentially create vertical neighborhoods in the sky. This occurs at Mei'Lin. Intermediate amenity decks are also vertically distributed through OMA's Micro Forest Project in Eindhoven, Netherlands.

Internal Skybridge Connectors

We must differentiate between intracluster sky connectors and intercluster sky connectors. Intrastructure connectors are within the cluster, uniting the towers of the cluster aboveground. This occurs in almost all of the case studies. Intercluster skybridge connectors occur in the Berlin Hauptstadt competition project of the Smithsons and Sigmond-Wonke, discussed in section 6.2. It is also one of the main connective circulation means of the Hong Kong 3-D interconnected city.

Upper Level of Base Structure: Potential Skybridge Intercluster Connecters at the Top Level of the Articulated Base Structure

Tower clusters generally have an articulated base structure that is occupied by an important series of levels of cluster amenities. This structured base is between three and five levels in height, depending upon the extent of the program. Its upper level provides a potential level(s) for intercluster urban connectivity.

Sub-Base Amenities

The sub-base always exists in the tower cluster as a linking function providing a broad range of amenities that have been discussed in the amenities section.

7.3 The New Architecture of Amenities Structures

What began initially as a cluster of towers with multifunctionality and flexibility of internal suborganization, soon evolved, along with the amenities revolution, into a truly novel urban typology. The provision of large groupings of amenities in tower clusters over the past decade has resulted in the emergence of a *new architecture of amenities structures*. This phenomenon describes the physical and organizational structuring and formal expression of the vertical campus. The ability to flexibly program and design this newly emerging high-density organizational system has rapidly attracted new uses such as high-tech administrative headquarters, especially in China.

The new functional applications and multifunctional realizations have, in turn, expanded the applications of the vertical campus and its integration within the tower cluster. Furthermore, this new prominence of amenity structures as an integral component of the tower cluster has created a totally new design condition in which the organization of the vertical campus has become a prime determinant in the vertical organization of the tower cluster.

Each tower cluster and its amenities structures now represent a dynamic urban nexus attracting urban circulation and public use. Given that the assembly of amenities structures is a public attraction, the appearance and formal character of the structure of amenities has become a critical challenge in what may be termed the new architecture of the vertical campus. The architecturally bold display of form and scale of the vertical campus and its elements has come to characterize the recent design of prominent international tower clusters. One of the conclusions of the research is that the architecture of amenities structures is rapidly developing as one of the most significant design characteristics of the tower cluster. The more the tower cluster boldly displays the unique scale, contents, distribution, and design of the vertical campus, the more successful it will be both functionally and commercially. It will attract and satisfy not only the urban public, but new employees as well.

The architecture of the vertical campus is now the formative design element of the tower cluster. Will this urban architectural design challenge potentially achieve the recognition of urban place and places? The research indicates that the relative scale of the amenities structures within each vertical campus may become a significant urban attractor within its urban situation. Should the degree of public attraction of such urban facilities be sufficient, they may succeed in stimulating the potential for intertower cluster connectivity.

7.4 Socializing the Sky

7.4.1 Socializing the Sky: The Walker Returns to the City

With the rapid development of the skyscraper by the beginning of the twentieth century, the vision of the future existence of streets in the sky had become a well-accepted image of the future of the modern metropolis. We have observed that early modernist architectural theoreticians such as Hénard, architectural renderers such as Ferriss, as well as illustrators in magazines and journals, began to develop a range of visionary expressions of the "city in the sky." It was a vision of elevated roadways and walkways as part of a totally new urbanistic architecture of the new metropolis.

This body of concepts and images remained visionary and exclusively the subject of illustrations until what might be thought of as a new direction for their potential realization. The source of this realization came within what is considered the first major high-rise post–Second World War residential structure in southern France, Le Corbusier's Unité d'Habitation building, in Marseilles, of 1947 to 1952. Here began the impulse to employ circulation ways as the basis for instigating socialization between neighbors even within high-rise housing, as well as employing this medium for sharing new social and cultural attributes by implanting them within the organizational structure of tall buildings. In the case of the Unité d'Habitation, many of Le Corbusier's main concepts were repeated in his buildings elsewhere in France. Among others, these involved an open-roof plaza established on the top story of the building containing facilities such as a kindergarten. Here, perhaps, the first modern sky plaza on a tall building was created.

This became a potential source concept well-established in the hearts and minds of architects in the twentieth century. It was among other locations to recur again in the coming into new realization in the brief history of the tower cluster, much of which we have recorded here. In addition to the grand roof terrace, the Unité building also included a modest shopping facility and parking beneath the building's *pilotis*, or open-column floor. We may also consider this, among its other theoretical contributions, the beginning of the independent physical realization of amenities as a visible structural component of the high-rise building.

Within the design of the building there were other seminal design concepts that became the source of conceptual progeny which was later realized by future generations of architects. The sectional design of the building illustrates an important concept which was to become the source idea of streets in the air. In the Unité building, the sectional concept has two important contributions. The first is that of the treatment of the interior corridor as an "interior street" (*rue interieure*). This means that the corridor must be widened in order to support certain furniture and activities, as well as the spontaneous meeting and interaction of neighbors.

The second important idea is that of the duplex, or two-level apartment. In section, one apartment is interlocked with the apartment above. That is, the L-shape section of one duplex interlocks with the reverse L-shaped section of the unit above. This leaves a space in the center of the three-story section that becomes the interior street. This became a generative sectional concept that employs a three-level planning module in section. This translates into an elevator situation termed a *skip-skip-stop*, in which the elevator stops only on each third floor.

These were magnificent design concepts that carried into the future and produced an important body of planning ideas for future high-density high-rise residential structures. What was missing? Le Corbusier's so-called street in the air was an interior street—no view, no daylight, no fresh air. The younger generation of European (mainly British) architects, solve the problem by maintaining most of Le Corbusier's idea, but changing the interior street into a broad exterior street. The true street in the sky actually came into being in postwar British mass housing.

These brilliant buildings later failed due to other social causes, and most were eventually demolished. One of them, Lynn and Smith's Park Hill in

Sheffield, England, still exists in remodeled condition as the grandest urban rendition of the streets in the sky concept, and as one of the seminal concepts of the three-dimensional connective city. So how do we transition from here to the foundational concepts of the connective skybridge city?

The first great transitional move is towards the typology of the tower cluster. It will become an intermediary concept by demonstrating the potential for sky plazas and/or skybridges to act as elements of potential foundational linkages in the (ultimately) connective city. The prescription will be to build from one tower to several as a connective element which will potentially lead to a connective city.

7.4.2 Typological Definitions

The tower cluster type is a potential theoretical foundation for the 3-D networked metropolis. Firstly, it has a scalar level of increasing density over that of the individual tower. Within the basic framework of two or more towers, it also has an articulated base structure, a clearly formulated and well-articulated structures of amenities, and, potentially, a connective superstructure. It is these three programmatic elements and their publicly accessible contents which constitute urban attractors. The variable design components are both flexible in design and outstanding in formal potential.

The case studies have indicated the potential diversity and richness of the typology. This architectural and urban flexibility derives in part from the high degree of compositional flexibility resulting from a theoretical system derived from the assembly and composition of multiple component elements. It has also been possible to observe from the case studies that there exist in tower clusters two major developmental and expressive tendencies. The first of these is the assembly of the towers into a compositional ensemble in which each of the towers is expressed individually. In this condition, the physical and functional integration into a unity is generally achieved either through the existence of a large-scale, continuous base structure, or through a superstructure. The Nanjing International Youth Cultural Center, in Nanjing, China, by Zaha Hadid Architects, is unified by its multilevel base structure, while Marina Bay Sands, in Singapore, by Safdie Architects, is unified by its superstructure.

The second significant compositional approach is that in which the towers or slab elements are tied into a unified geometric figure such as an open cube. The CCTV building in Beijing, China, by OMA is an example of the second tendency. Given the relatively brief history of the typology, we expect that other compositional approaches will develop over time.

According to both of these models, the tower cluster as a typology is a tightly packed ensemble of multiple towers which is consolidated by a prominent base element, and is vertically integrated both functionally and formally by an articulated structure of amenities from base to superstructure. In addition, it has the potential for horizontal urban linkage by means of skybridges.

The historical derivation of the typology and its two models has theoretical origins in the 1960s. In 1969 a study of the urban design potential of certain important sites in Manhattan was produced by the Regional Plan Association, a nonprofit citizen's research and planning organization. Consultants for this study were urban design consultants Rai Y. Okamoto and Frank E. Williams. It should also be noted that during the sixties, urban design as a professional subject was emerging. The first educational program in urban design was also developed during this time by Josep Lluís Sert at the Harvard Graduate School of Design where Sert was dean.[13]

In the report of 1969, there is a study of the midtown area of Manhattan which includes a case study of Forty-Second Street. Along this access, a site is selected for the prototypical design of a new office cluster. This is illustrated in models and plans and is discussed in the text. What is presented is a large tower cluster, connected at the base and upper levels, providing horizontal interconnection of multiple towers that are organized into a larger multicluster grouping around two intersecting streets and several courts and landscaped gardens at multiple levels. This appears historically to be one of the urban proposals closest to the proposed definition of the tower cluster.[14]

Beyond the 1960s, there exist several emerging prototypes for the tower cluster. The text of part 2 presents and discusses a model for the geometric approach in La Grande Arche in Paris, 1982 to 1989, and in the classical, numerical approach found well articulated in Moshe Safdie's urban design proposal for Columbus Center in Manhattan, 1985 to 1987. From 1996 to 1999, the Azrieli Center in Tel Aviv, Israel, is a triple-tower cluster with a large commercial-cultural-public circulation base structure, and multifunctional program in the towers.

Following this conceptual progression and period of typological theoretical development, there emerged the two models of the tower cluster that are highly clear and well articulated in their components. One of these, which opened in 2010, was Marina Bay Sands in Singapore. Approximately contemporaneous was CCTV in Beijing which is dated from 2002 to 2012. Following this origin of the typology in construction, the documentation of the case studies has illustrated and defined the continuity and continuous development of the typology until today.

This typological evolution has repeatedly articulated the constancy and change possible within the prototypical characteristics of the typology:

- It is a system of parts organized into a formal ensemble that provides a high degree of typological flexibility for transformation while still maintaining the central concepts;
- It is a related close grouping of interconnected towers;
- It possesses a multifunctional program;

- It contains a series of vertically distributed amenities which are organized into a visually prominent structured order—this expression of vertically distributed urban-scale elements within the tower cluster is referred as the vertical campus;

- It possesses a connective plinth structure and may also have a vertical distribution of skybridges;

- It enhances urban integration through public circulation, plazas, and landscape design;

- It has the potential for intercluster urban connectivity through horizontal bridge pedestrian connectors; these skybridges can be potentially located at upper levels of the base structure, or above, by bridging from the upper levels of the towers.

This definition of the typological elements of the tower cluster has continued until today to demonstrate its great compositional, programmatic, and urban flexibility, as well as its stimulative creative force to advance the evolution of the typology.

7.4.3 The Creative Role of Typological Design

The more the architect is aware that this is a well-defined existing building typology, the more likely he is to participate in its future development. The more aware each designer becomes of its several major formal subtypes, the more likely the potential for innovation in each evolution of the type. If it is clear that design, in this case, involves primarily the architecture of amenities structures, then it becomes clear at the outset that the amenity structure and its overall design is a significant element of the architect's contribution to the future development and formal expression of the typology. That this structure has a significant role in the design and refinement of each building form provides a potential advancement in the typology. Well-articulated typological knowledge establishes the cultural situation in which creative theoretical contributions can clearly emerge from each project.

The typology currently possesses two major organizational subtypes: *classical assemblage*, which is tending towards open assemblage, versus the geometric completeness of the *totalizing geometric approach* as one of the forms of knowledge relative to tower cluster typology. That it is a typology currently in the process of extension and refinement, and that its present level of knowledge and definition is known and understood, increases the likelihood that each architect can become a contributor to the historical evolution of this type, and potentially to the future of the city as navigable network. Each architect must also be aware that externally this is a new archetype of urban form, but that this is also the case internally. It is also an amazingly flexible and expressive typology for certain technological building functions, such as the high-tech headquarters building with its uniquely sophisticated demands for programmatic tunability, or refinement, of each particular case.

Given the relative youth of the typology, these important characteristics of this particular typology, and the unique nature of typological design, these facts may sometimes be overlooked in the search for other, perhaps more recognized architectural values, such as formal innovation.

There is here, in this design medium called typological design, a vehicle for the architect to exhibit a great level of creativity in the creative lifetime of the building. This particular typology is a unique set of typological components that can be assembled to support the long-term creative functioning of the building organization. It has the potential to enhance functions such as office forms in enhancing communication, interaction, collaboration, and, thereby, also creativity. In such emerging building functions as the vertical high-tech office, including research and development activities, this building type has already demonstrated itself to be a working mechanism for developmental creativity.

The amazing rate of industrialization in China and other countries of the East has acted as a growth platform for a new vertical medium of compact urban organization that might fulfill such a sophisticated range of operative requirements; and together with these demands, it also requires it to become a potentially meaningful module in the making of intelligent and sustainable urban environments.

Typological innovation is one of the highest and most intellectual levels of architectural creativity. In the case of the tower cluster, as in that of all great inventions, the typology enhances rather than inhibits the flexibility and freedom of the architect to freely explore its potential. OPPO Headquarters by Zaha Hadid Architects and Mei'Lin of Safdie Architects are two diverse visions in the service of two differing functions. One senses that in both cases—one with sensible internal differentiation; the other with visible external differentiation—the typology has enhanced the potential for creative design.

It is now essential to define and critique this typology—its characteristics, its support for creative design, its achievements, and its future developmental possibilities. This is the first step towards defining a new architectural/urban typology. May this professional discourse encourage experimentation as well as expanded discourse.

There are by now several more recent tower clusters on the architectural horizon. This book is intended to provide a structured and organizational description of the typology as well as a history of its recent growth and refinement during this important period of the emergence and development of the typology. It also provides certain guidelines for future refinement of the tower cluster as well as its potential influence on emerging concepts of connective urbanism.

This has been an attempt to define the working model of an emerging urban typology and the sketching of certain potential future urban developmental implications. As we observe these international processes on a

Opposite Page St. Regis, Chicago, Illinois, 2016–2020. Courtesy of Studio Jeanne Gang.

daily basis, we rediscover multiple instances of the type as well as its powerfully generative role.

7.5 The Unification of the Tower Cluster

Before the close of this work, it is essential to reiterate and clarify the unique quality of formal and functional unification that is achieved by the typology of the tower cluster. Within the limitations of structural stability and safety, there are three main formal media of unification:

Base: The base is well articulated formally as one integrated unit;

Bridge: The skybridge can be articulated formally as a connecting and integrating element;

Sky Element: A sky element such as a sky plaza can function formally, functionally, and as a unifier. Depending upon the geometric regularity of the design, the sky element may also achieve a sense of geometric unity as well as providing formal and functional unification. We have observed this, among other projects, in Safdie's Marina Bay Sands of 2010, and Mei'Lin of 2025. In OMA's CCTV Headquarters of 2012, we have observed how the sky element has been employed to create both unification and geometric regularity.

There are also the following additional concepts that are causally related to the expression of unification:

Combination of Unifying Media: As we have already observed in the illustrated examples of tower clusters, the three tower cluster unifying media may be employed in combination. For example, Safdie Architects' project for Marina Bay Sands has an articulated base as well as a sky plaza;

Scale of Unifying Media to Achieve Unification: Occasionally, bridging may be excessively long, or the base may not be articulated. For example, the excessive length of a skybridging functional element may weaken the formal expression of unification. In Steven Holl's otherwise important project Linked Hybrid in Beijing, China, 2009, the skybridges are relatively long and create a sense of distancing between the tower blocks, which in themselves are also limited in vertical height. In addition, the formal articulation of the base element is less pronounced than in all of the other examples. Thus, this example has been located at the edge, or limit, of the formal qualities of the definition of unification.

Obviously, the formal expression of unification is a major consideration in the definition of the tower cluster. In contradistinction to Wood, Du, and Safarik (2020), here the unifying element is *not* limited to the skybridge. This is an important distinction. A bridge at the upper level of the base element can also be considered, and can function in all respects as a skybridge. It can provide an effective connection as well as a formal expression of unification. While skybridges are formally distinctive and dramatic connectors, they are usually also structurally difficult connectors.

> *Tower cluster typology can achieve the physical, formal, functional, and symbolic creation of unification. It is a high-density urban type which can potentially provide a design medium for urban interconnectivity by employing the tower cluster as a flexible architectural and urban design base module.*

POSTSCRIPT

On Typological Evolution and the Creative Role of Typological Knowledge

The Nature of Typological Evolution

Research has demonstrated that in recent decades a new typology of the tall building has emerged. This new typology is a striking transformation from what might be termed the origin of the modern high-rise during the period of the 1920s and 1930s. In the formally explorative experimental designs of Mies van der Rohe during this period, for example, the Friedrichstrasse Project of 1921 was a completely glass-sheathed building with a steel structure. In 1922, his second project for a glass skyscraper begins to exhibit the characteristic emphasis on the expression of an unlimited verticality of the glass structure, which becomes characteristic of the accepted expression of the skyscrapers of the 1930s and beyond in the United States's rapid development of the modern high-rise structure. This source connotation of an endless vertical structure with unlimited verticality is transcended in the tower cluster typology, which introduces a new high typology that is much broader as well as conceptually richer in its definition as an urban, multifunctional, high-density typology of a newly emerging vision of the high-rise.

Above Mies van der Rohe, *Glass Skyscraper Project*, 1922. Courtesy of MoMA. **Left** Seagram Building, New York City. Mies van der Rohe and Philip Johnson, 1958. Photo courtesy of Butterpaper.

The tower cluster, as we analytically articulated in part 2, is defined by eight component elements:

- A formally and functionally related close grouping of interconnected high-rise elements;
- An ensemble of both vertical and horizontal components;
- A multifunctional program;
- A series of vertically distributed common amenities;
- A connecting plinth and potential upper-level bridge connectors between towers;
- Urbanistic integration;
- The potential for vertical urbanism;
- The potential for intercluster urban connectivity.

As has become historically clear during the first and second decades of the twenty-first century, the tower cluster is a unique and flexible urban typology. During this period, the new typology has proven capable of generating a broad range of new and remarkably emergent conceptual and formal typological subtypes. A subtype is a significantly unique case of either the interpretation of one of the typological components, or the relationships among certain of the eight typological components, in order to justify the establishment of the class "subtype."

The purpose of this postscript is to determine what is and what isn't a unique subtype, and what might be the recurrent stumbling blocks to using a typology creatively. This will help to understand, at least in the case of the tower cluster, what constitutes creative design in the evolution of the typology.

Subtypes in the Tower Cluster

In general, the clarity in understanding the definition and functioning of the typology is a major prerequisite to its successful and creative application in particular sites and programmatic situations. Once this is achieved, experimental development can exploit the potential of multifunctional integration and design with new forms of amenity structures (types and organization of groups of amenities), new approaches to vertical urbanism, and new types of landscape urbanism.

Also of great significance in each instance of typological design of new tower clusters is to constantly be aware that new worlds of urban architecture can come into being through multitower cluster urban developments as well as new types of urban design creation exploiting, or inventing, rich concepts of landscape urbanism.

Resulting from such knowledge-based design processes of typological evolution is the potential achievement of new exemplary forms of urban development. Such intellectual content in the design process is particularly relevant in urban situations of high-density integrated living, working, and commercial environments.

The Creative Role of Typological Knowledge

Therefore, of major importance to the future relevance of the design knowledge achieved through this research is the identification, definition, and exemplification of this emerging typology which has achieved the articulation of design knowledge in a clear formulation that may be exploited in future design.

And so, does there exist a form of architectural knowledge that can be termed typological knowledge, and if so, what might be its unique value to the design process? It would appear to be a possible conclusion from this research that what has been analytically demonstrated is that typological knowledge provides a depth of design understanding that can be endowed distinctively through this class of deep design knowledge.

As we potentially acquire deep knowledge of the type, our ability to invent new dimensions of the type—subtypes—becomes immeasurably enriched. So, to enter the anatomy of this high-density, multifunctional type is to become newly enlightened as a designer. Now that you have traversed these pages and considered the embodied reasoning, you may have discovered new keys to the relationship between architectural knowledge and design knowledge.

We are left then with the question of what the nature of architectural creativity is. This seminal question grows in its significance to the profession as it touches upon the relationship between architecture and urbanism, a problematic which is today at the pinnacle of domain activity. It appears obvious from the investigation of new cases of the design of tower clusters that the pursuit of superficial aesthetic effect, or what might also be termed aesthetic innovation, appears to be a shallow approach to fulfill the important role of environmental designer, a role that has come to represent the breadth of the profession's domain knowledge.

Today we, the architects, face a deeper and more fundamental initiative when we begin to conceptualize problems in the domain of the tall building in dense urban situations. It is here, perhaps, that we encounter the need for engagement with the very source material of the role of architecture. In this realm of design problem there must occur an engagement with *typological creation,* which must be considered the very source material of truly architectural creative achievement.

Among the complex of design problems which appear when one attempts to conceptually approach the future of skyscraper cities is the attempt to redefine the very nature of human habitat in emerging situations of vertical urbanism. In arriving at the conceptualization of a typology here termed the tower cluster, we have discovered the problematic of programs: human dwelling, office-research environments, technological design, research, and manufacturing complexes that are now, by definition, emerging elements of the urban condition.

We have sketched the architectural history of the coupling of designing density and the humanization of the skyscraper as it became an integral component of the urban environment. Intellectually and conceptually, the historical research of this current volume has been bottom-up in scale:

from streets in the air, and from Le Corbusier's focus on complex vertical, multifunctional situations in the Unité building in Marseilles, to Safdie's Habitat in Montreal, and beyond, to Koolhaas's attempt to redefine the very conceptualization of the skyscraper in Beijing, we have entered the new domain of the tower cluster with its profound definition as a potential source element of urban design. So it is the tracing of the process of the conceptual history of the discovery of a new body of architectural knowledge that we have attempted to document here.

We have also discovered that designing in the realm of high density, or what we might now term super-tall/super-dense, is by its very nature totally integrated with urban design. How then is it possible for architecture to approach the problem of humanizing vertical density—the future of skyscraper cities? It appears that such a monumental question is at the very periphery of architectural knowledge and even beyond experimental designs such as the work of the Smithsons and Sigmond-Wonke in Berlin, which were barely at the fringe of the process of problem definition.

So here we as a profession approach the edge of our knowledge. What is the morphological potential of these emerging human forms of high-density and super-tall, and how do we approach such questions? This again brings us to the territory of the question of the sources of architectural creativity and innovation. This time perhaps the design investigation should be top-down. To enter this new design territory, we have the knowledge of the tower cluster to accompany and guide us.

NOTES

1. See *Future City 20/21: New York Modern*, the Skyscraper Museum. https://old.skyscraper.org/EXHIBITIONS/FUTURE_CITY/new_york_modern.htm

2. A. Moustaka, "Re-scripting the Streets in the Sky: Shifts in the Typology of a Listed Building in Park Hill, Sheffield," Salford University, Manchester, UK, 2019. Available at: http://usir.salford.ac.uk/id/eprint/49114/

3. It is important to note that we diverge slightly from the logic of the important CTBUH technical guide of Wood, Du, and Safarik, *The Space Across: Skybridges and the Future City*. (Chicago: Council on Tall Buildings and Urban Habitat, 2020). In their work, the study relates to the skybridge as a unique potential medium for the connective city. We view skybridges as potentially also existing at the top of the tower base structure as well as at various levels throughout the tower cluster. There are also other differences.

4. See the KPF video of the proposed new tower for the Azrieli Center tower cluster in Tel Aviv at: https://www.kpf.com/projects/azrieli-tower. Also see *Spiral Tower Tel Aviv* on YouTube.

5. See Moshe Safdie, *Beyond Habitat by 20 Years* (Tundra Books, Special Anniversary Edition, 1986). See also, Myron Goldfinger, *Villages in the Sun* (New York: Praeger Publishers, 1969), Introduction, 9–24. The introduction presents an overview of village morphology and its contemporary evolution as a housing high-density morphology from the 1950s onward. This introduction contains examples relevant to the application of typological models influenced by Habitat, including a project by Robert Oxman and Francisco Javier Blanco (illustration 36–37, pp. 18–19).

6. It is clear that Safdie had already at Columbus Center been aware of the urban and architectural potential of an integrated composition of architectural elements. In fact, the composition of the tower cluster was very likely the result of site and program as well as the awareness of new typological concepts for the urban complex. It does, however, appear clear that the Singapore project evoked a singular synthesis and formal order that truly celebrates the design potential of a new urban typology.

7. On the OMA website, it is noted that the project was led by Rem Koolhaas, former OMA partner Ole Scheeren (until 2010), OMA partner David Gianotten, and project manager Dongmei Yao. Three additional partners at OMA are listed as "close collaborators." These

are Shohei Shigematsu, Ellen van Loon, and Victor van der Chijs. For this building, the structural engineering function was highly significant to the design team due to the structural irregularity of the building form. These services were led by Cecil Belmond, the noted engineer and theoretician, and by the office of Arup. Illustrations of the building also appear on the website of the office of Ole Scheeren.

8. TVCC (Television Cultural Canter) is an ancillary thirty-four-story building on the main site of CCTV. It functions as a public service facility for the main production building, providing a hotel, theater, studios, and other functions.

9. I have been academically connected with the Technical University of Eindhoven (TUE) since 1983. From 1994 to 1996, I held the Chairs of Design Methods and Computer Aided Design at TUE. I am well acquainted with this site area.

10. CTBUH, or Council of Tall Buildings and Urban Habitat, is an international organization located in the United States that promotes research and the exchange of information on the subject through conferences, workshops, the publication of research works, and documentation.

11. For those interested in further insights into flexibility and adaptability in ensemble systems, please refer to the works of John Habraken and SAR (Stichting Archiktekten Research) on support structures, in such sources as John Habraken et al., *Variations: The Systematic Design of Supports* (Cambridge, MA: MIT Press, 1976).

12. Tange's 1960 unrealized plan for the extension of Tokyo into Tokyo Bay is a very well-known and theoretically important project. Among many other sources on the project and its influence in Japan see Rem Koolhaas and Hans Ulrich Obrist, *Project Japan: Metabolism Talks* (Los Angeles: Taschen America, 2011).

13. Apropos of the contemporary history of the emergence of urban design as a professional field as well as an educational discipline, see the excellent history by Eric Mumford entitled *Defining Urban Design: CIAM Architects and the Formation of a Discipline* (New Haven, CT: Yale University Press, 2009).

14. See Regional Plan Association, *Urban Design Manhattan* (New York: Viking Press, 1969), 96–104.

BIBLIOGRAPHY

a+t Architecture Publishers. *Hybrid Building Index*. Vitoria-Gasteiz, Spain: a+t Architecture Publishers, 2022.

Böck, Ingrid. *Six Canonical Projects by Rem Koolhaas*. Berlin: Jovis Verlag GmbH, 2015. "The Outdated Typology of the Skyscraper," pp. 307–313.

CTBUH. *Council on Tall Buildings and Urban Habitat* Journal, Issue III. *Special Edition: Skybridges*, 2020.

Frampton, Kenneth. *Modern Architecture: A Critical History*. London: Thames and Hudson, 1980.

Frampton, Adam, Jonathan D. Solomon, and Clara Wong. *Cities Without Ground: A Hong Kong Guidebook*. San Francisco: ORO Editions, 2018.

Franck, Karen A., and Lynda H. Schneekloth, eds. *Ordering Space, Types in Architecture and Design*. New York: Van Nostrand and Reinhold, 1995.

Hou, Jeffrey. "Vertical Urbanism, Horizontal Urbanity: Notes from East Asian Cities." In Bharne, Vinayak, ed., *The Emerging Asian City: Concomitant Urbanities and Urbanisms*, pp. 234–243. London and New York: Routledge, 2012.

Koolhaas, Rem. *Delirious New York*. New York: Monacelli Press, 1997.

Koolhaas, Rem, and OMA. *Content*. Köln, Germany: Taschen, 2004, pp. 450.

Majerowitz, Merryan, and Yael Allweil. "Housing in the Neoliberal City: Large Urban Developments and the Role of Architecture." *Urban Planning* 4, no. 4 (2019): pp. 43–61.

Maki, Fumihiko. *Nurturing Dreams: Collected Essays on Architecture and the City*. Edited by Mark Mulligan. Cambridge, MA: MIT Press, 2012.

Selected articles included in above: "Investigations in Collective Form: Preface," pp. 40–42; "Investigations in Collective Form: Three Paradigms of Collective Form," pp. 44–56; "Linkage in Collective Form," coauthored with Jerry Goldberg, pp. 57–65; "Time and Landscape: Collective Form at Hillside Terrace," pp. 68–79. The first two parts originally appeared in a pamphlet published by the Washington University School of Architecture in 1964.

Mulvey, Christopher. "The Three-Dimensional Urbanism of Raffles City Chongqing." *CTBUH* Journal, *Special Edition*: *Skybridges*, 2020, pp. 12-19.

Murphy, Douglas. "Notopia: The Fall of Streets in the Sky." *Architectural Review*. London: 9 June, 2016.

Peckham, Andrew, and Torsten Schmiedeknecht. *The Rationalist Reader: Architecture and Rationalism in Western Europe 1920-1940 / 1960-1990*. London and New York: Routledge, 2014.

In the above, on the subject of typology, see: Vidler, Anthony, "The Third Typology," pp. 221–27; Oechslin, Werner, "Premises for the Resumption of the Discussion of Typology," pp. 242–47; Bandini, Micha, "Typological Theories in Architectural Design," pp. 248–55; Francescato, Guido, "Type and the Possibility of an Architectural Scholarship," pp. 256–60; Rossi, Aldo, "The Architecture of the City," pp. 262–68; Krier, Rob, "Typological and Morphological Elements of the Concept of Urban Space," pp. 274–76.

Regional Plan Association. *Urban Design Manhattan*. New York: Viking Press, 1969.

Safdie, Moshe (in conversation with Michael J. Crosbie). *With Intention to Build: The Unrealized Concepts, Ideas, and Dreams of Moshe Safdie*. Melbourne: Images Publishing Group, 2020.

Safdie, Moshe. *If Walls Could Speak: My Life in Architecture*. New York: Atlantic Monthly Press, 2022. Ch. 9, "Megascale," pp. 248-83.

Wood, Anthony, Peng Du, and Daniel Safarik. *The Space Across: Skybridges and the Future City*. Chicago: Council on Tall Buildings and Urban Habitat, 2020. Case study 3.13, Raffles City Chongqing, pp. 130-39.

Yoos, Jennifer and Vincent James. *Parallel Cities: The Multilevel Metropolis*. Minneapolis: Walker Art Center, and New York: Distributed Art Publishers (DAP), 2016.

Internet

Berlin Hauptstadt Competition:
https://en.wikipedia.org/wiki/Hauptstadt

City of London Pedway Scheme
https://en.wikipedia.org/wiki/CityofLondonPedwayScheme

De Rotterdam, OMA:
https://en.wikipedia.org/wiki/De_Rotterdam

De Rotterdam, OMA:
https://www.oma.com/projects/de-rotterdam

De Rotterdam, OMA
https://www.theguardian.com/artanddesign/2013/nov/18/rem-koolhaas-d

De Rotterdam, OMA
https://www.nytimes.com/2005/03/20/travel/rotterdam-a-city-designed-around-design.html

De Rotterdam, OMA
https://www.dezeen.com/2013/11/21/oma-completes-de-rotterdam-vertical-city-complex

DJI Shenzhen, China. Foster and Partners
https://www.youtube.com/watch?v=7Gf2lk3d_vM

DJI Shenzhen, China. Foster and Partners
https://www.dezeen.com/2018/05/10/foster-partners-architecture-dji-robotics-drone-offices-shenzhen-china/#:~:text=The%20Foster%20%2B%20Partners%2Ddesigned%20building,by%20architectural%20photographers%20and%20filmmakers

DJI Shenzhen, China. Foster and Partners
https://www.fosterandpartners.com/projects/dji-headquarters/

DJI Shenzhen China. Foster and Partners
https://www.youtube.com/watch?v=7Gf2lk3d_vM

DJI Shenzhen, China. Foster and Partners
https://www.archdaily.com/894239/foster-plus-partners-unveil-images-for-towering-dji-robotics-headquarters-in-shenzhen

DJI Shenzhen, China. Foster and Partners
https://www.skyscrapercenter.com/complex/3728

Duo Twin Towers, Singapore
https://buro-os.com/news/buro-ole-scheeren-completes-duo-twin-towerssingapore#:~:text=DUO%2C%20a%20large%20scale%20sculpted,the%20two%20Southeast%2DAsian%20countries

Duo Twin Towers, Singapore
https://www.archdaily.com/890312/duo-twin-towers-buro-ole-scheeren

Duo Twin Towers, Singapore
https://www.skyscrapercenter.com/building/duo-tower/14823

Duo Twin Towers, Singapore:
https://en.wikipedia.org/wiki/DUO

Duo Twin Towers, Singapore
https://www.dezeen.com/2018/03/06/buro-ole-scheeren-architecture-duo-skyscrapers-singapore-gardens/

El Lissitzky and Mart Stam, Volkenbügel
https://thecharnelhouse.org/2014/03/07/lissitzky-wolkenbugel-1924/

Galaxy Soho, Beijing:
https://www.zaha-hadid.com/architecture/galaxy-soho/

Galaxy Soho, Beijing:
https://en.wikipedia.org/wiki/Galaxy_SOHO

Galaxy Soho, Beijing:
https://www.dezeen.com/2012/10/29/galaxy-soho-by-zaha-hadid

Galaxy Soho, Beijing:
https://www.youtube.com/watch?v=vvA5F5KhiD0

Galaxy Soho, Beijing:
https://www.archute.com/galaxy-soho-zaha-hadid/

Galaxy Soho, Beijing:
https://www.zaha-hadid.com/architecture/galaxy-soho/

Hauptstadt Smithson/Sigmond
https://urban-sphere.tumblr.com/post/79189249529/alison-and-peter-smithson-with-peter-sigmond

Hauptstadt Smithson/Sigmond:
https://en.wikipedia.org/wiki/Hauptstadt

Hauptstadt Smithson/Sigmond—Urbansphere Drawings
https://urban-sphere.tumblr.com/post/79189249529/alison-and-peter-smithson-with-peter-sigmond

Hauptstadt Smithson/Sigmond—Text Arquigraph
https://arquigraph.tumblr.com/post/162856642432/architecture-politics-hauptstadt-berlin

Marina Bay Sands Hotel and Sky Park
https://en.wikipedia.org/wiki/Marina_Bay_Sands

Marina Bay Sands Hotel and Sky Park
https://www.safdiearchitects.com/projects/marina-bay-sands-hotel-and-skypark

Marina Bay Sands Hotel and Sky Park
https://en.wikipedia.org/wiki/Marina_Bay_Sands

Moses King:
https://en.wikipedia.org/wiki/Moses_King

Nanjing International Youth Cultural Center
https://www.zaha-hadid.com/architecture/nanjing-culture-conference-centre/

Nanjing International Youth Cultural Center
https://www.archdaily.com/907145/nanjing-international-youth-cultural-centre-zaha-hadid-architects

Nanjing International Youth Cultural Center
https://en.wikipedia.org/wiki/Nanjing_International_Youth_Cultural_Centre

Nanjing International Youth Cultural Center
https://www.swagroup.com/projects/nanjing-international-youth-cultural-centre/

Nanjing International Youth Cultural Center
https://www.dezeen.com/2016/09/27/zaha-hadid-architects-nanjing-international-youth-cultural-centre-skyscraper-china/

Narkomfin Building:
https://en.wikipedia.org/wiki/Narkomfin_building

Observation Deck:
https://en.wikipedia.org/wiki/Observation_deck

Observation Deck:
https://en.wikipedia.org/wiki/SkyPoint_Observation_Deck

Observation Deck
https://en.wikipedia.org/wiki/One_Liberty_Observation_Deck

Observation Deck:
https://en.wikipedia.org/wiki/Burj_Khalifa Section 4

Observation Deck:
https://en.wikipedia.org/wiki/SkyPoint_Observation_Deck

Observation Decks: 30 Hudson Yards
https://en.wikipedia.org/wiki/30_Hudson_Yards

Observation Decks
https://en.wikipedia.org/wiki/Observation_deck

Observation Decks: The Twelve Highest Observation Decks in the World
https://thetowerinfo.com/highest-observation-deck-world/

Observation Decks: 10 Best Observation Decks in the USA
https://www.attractionsofamerica.com/travel/best-observation-decks-usa.php

Observation Decks: The World's Best Observation Decks
https://www.cntraveler.com/galleries/2015-05-22/the-worlds-best-tallest-observation-decks

Offices: New Amenities
https://www.fooda.com/blog/10-must-have-commercial-building-amenities/

Offices: New Amenities
https://leverage.com/assets/new-york-city-office-luxury-amenities/

Offices: New Amenities
https://www.edenhealth.com/blog/office-amenities/

Offices: New Amenities
https://mcphersonarchitecture.com/blog-post/office-building-amenity-trends/

Offices: New Amenities
https://www.gensler.com/blog/what-is-the-future-of-workplace-amenities-corenet-global

Offices: New Amenities
https://www.localeadvisors.com/new-amenities-in-commercial-real-estate/

Offices: New Amenities
https://blog.getspiffy.com/amenities-of-the-modern-office

Offices: New Amenities
https://www.nanawall.com/blog/workplace-design-the-rise-of-amenities-in-office-buildings

Offices: New Amenities
https://plandesignbuild.ucsd.edu/_files/planning/UCSanDiegoAdministrativeSpaceUseGuidelines.pdf

Offices: New Amenities
https://www.workdesign.com/2019/09/how-cre-experts-are-approaching-building-amenities/

Offices: Lever House
https://search.yahoo.com/yhs/search?hspart=blender&hsimp=yhs-002&p=Lever+House+Typical+office+floor&type=2608149564

Offices: WeWork
https://www.google.com/search?q=wework+wikipedia&rlz=1C5CHFA_enUS850US851&oq=WeWork+W&aqs=chrome.1.69i57j0i512j69i59j0i512j0i433i512j0i512l2j69i60.19016j0j4&sourceid=chrome&ie=UTF-8

Offices: WeWork
https://www.wired.com/story/wework-coworking-office-spaces/

OMA: CCTV Headquarters
https://en.wikipedia.org/wiki/CCTV_Headquarters

OMA: CCTV Headquarters
https://www.nytimes.com/2011/07/13/arts/design/koolhaass-cctv-building-fits-beijing-as-city-of-the-future.html?pagewanted=all

OMA: CCTV Headquarters
https://www.oma.com/projects/cctv-headquarters

OMA: Beijing CCTV
https://en.wikipedia.org/wiki/Beijing_Television_Cultural_Center

OMA: CMG Global Trade Center
https://www.oma.com/projects/cmg-qianhai-global-trade-center

OMA: CMG Global Trade Center
https://www.archdaily.com/939327/construction-begins-on-omas-cmg-qianhai-global-trade-center-in-shenzhen-china

OMA: CMG Global Trade Center
https://www.metalocus.es/en/news/cmg-qianhai-global-trade-center-erasing-boundaries-between-building-and-urban-context-oma

OPPO Telecommunications Headquarters
https://www.zaha-hadid.com/architecture/oppo-headquarters/

OPPO Telecommunications Headquarters
https://www.skyscrapercenter.com/building/oppo-headquarters/36867

OPPO Telecommunications Headquarters
https://www.designboom.com/architecture/zaha-hadid-architects-oppo-headquarters-shenzhen-china-01-28-2020/

OPPO Telecommunications Headquarters
https://www.archdaily.com/932720/zha-wins-competition-to-design-oppos-new-headquarters-in-shenzhen

OPPO Telecommunications Headquarters
https://www.dezeen.com/2020/01/31/zaha-hadid-architects-oppo-headquarters-shenzhen-china-architecture/

Petronas Twin Towers:
https://en.wikipedia.org/wiki/Petronas_Towers

Safdie Architects, Raffles City, China
https://www.youtube.com/watch?v=nLtXnw5Ir3g

Safdie Architects, ORCA Toronto
https://urbantoronto.ca/news/2020/06/moshe-safdie-retained-updated-orca-project-concept

Safdie Architects, ORCA Toronto
https://www.safdiearchitects.com/projects/orca-mixed-use-development-park

Sant'Elia, Antonio
https://www.tiscali.it/antonio_santelia/images/galleria/093a.jpeg

Sert, Jackson and Gourley, Peabody Terrace, Harvard University
https://www.archdaily.com/486015/ad-classics-peabody-terrace-sert-jackson-and-gourley

Skybridges: Ten Fascinating Skybridges
http://www.theworldgeography.com/2013/08/skybridges.html

Skybridges: Welcome to the Skybridge Renaissance
https://www.youtube.com/watch?v=oY1E4gMQ7fA

Skybridges: Skyway, Skybridge, Skywalk
https://en.wikipedia.org/wiki/Skyway

Skybridges: CTBUH: Skybridges of Significance
https://www.skyscrapercenter.com/skybridges

Skybridges: 14 Aerial Structures That Span Skyscrapers
https://weburbanist.com/2013/09/16/skybridges-14-aerial-structures-that-span-skyscrapers/

Sky Gardens: 10 of the world's best high-rise and rooftop green spaces
https://www.cnn.com/travel/article/amazing-gardens/index.html

Sky Gardens: Gardens in the Sky: The Rise of Green Urban Architecture
https://www.cnn.com/style/article/green-skyscrapers-roofs-city-architecture/index.html

Sky Gardens: Gardens in the Sky: The Many Benefits of Green Roofs
https://www.urdesignmag.com/architecture/2019/09/17/gardens-in-the-sky-the-many-benefits-of-green-roofs/

Sky Gardens: 20 Fenchurch Street, London
https://en.wikipedia.org/wiki/20_Fenchurch_Street

Sky Gardens: Featured Picture Candidates
https://en.wikipedia.org/wiki/Wikipedia:Featured_picture_candidates/Sky_garden_at_20_Fenchurch_Street

Sky Gardens
https://en.wikipedia.org/wiki/Wikipedia:Featured_picture_candidates/Sky_garden_at_20_Fenchurch_Street

Sky Habitat, Singapore
https://www.safdiearchitects.com/projects/sky-habitat-residential-development

Sky Habitat, Singapore
https://www.archdaily.com/781936/sky-habitat-singapore-moshe-safdie

Sky Habitat, Singapore
https://www.dezeen.com/2016/02/09/sky-habitat-moshe-safdie-architects-singapore-housing/

Sky Soho, Shanghai, China:
https://www.youtube.com/watch?v=36QaQ--sxTY

Sky Soho, Shanghai, China
https://www.zaha-hadid.com/architecture/hongqiao-shanghai/

Sky Soho, Shanghai, China
https://foursquare.com/v/sky-soho-%E5%87%8C%E7%A9%BA-soho/5458c8f4498e4a34f7ba2c91

Sky Park: Marina Bay Sands, Singapore
https://www.dezeen.com/2014/10/11/moshe-safdie-on-marina-bay-sands-habitat-67-skyscrapers-lego/#:~:text=World%20Architecture%20Festival%202014%3A%20architect,(%2B%20interview%20%2B%20slideshow)

Sky Pool: London
https://en.wikipedia.org/wiki/Sky_Pool,_London

Sky Pool: Embassy Gardens
https://www.embassygardens.com/sky-pool/

Sky Pool:
https://www.architecturaldigest.com/story/sky-pool

Sky Pool: A World Tour
https://www.theatlantic.com/health/archive/2012/08/pools-in-the-sky-a-world-tour/260978/

Skyway:
https://en.wikipedia.org/wiki/Skyway

Tower C Shenzhen Bay Super Headquarters
https://www.architectmagazine.com/project-gallery/tower-c-at-shenzhen-bay-super-headquarters-base_o

Tower C Shenzhen Bay Super Headquarters
https://www.dezeen.com/2021/01/13/tower-c-supertall-skyscrapers-zaha-hadid-architects-shenzhen/

Tower C Shenzhen Bay Super Headquarters
https://www.archdaily.com/954800/zha-wins-competition-to-build-tower-c-at-shenzhen-bay-super-headquarters-base

Tower C Shenzhen Bay Super Headquarters
https://www.skyscrapercenter.com/complex/4783

Tower C Shenzhen Bay Super Headquarters
https://www.designboom.com/architecture/zaha-hadid-tower-c-shenzhen-bay-super-headquarters-base-01-11-2021/

VDMA OMA
https://www.designboom.com/architecture/oma-eindhoven-van-der-meulen-ansemsterrein-micro-forest-11-22-2019/

VDMA OMA:
https://www.oma.com/projects/vdma

VDMA OMA:
https://www.oma.com/projects/vdma

Vertical City:
https://misfitsarchitecture.com/2017/09/24/the-vertical-city/

Wangjing Soho, Beijing:
https://en.wikipedia.org/wiki/Wangjing_SOHO

Wangjing Soho, Beijing:
https://www.zaha-hadid.com/architecture/wangjing-soho/

Wangjing Soho, Beijing:
https://www.dezeen.com/2015/05/19/zaha-hadid-completes-pebble-shaped-wangjing-soho-towers-beijing-offices-retail/

Wangjing Soho, Beijing:
https://www.skyscrapercenter.com/building/wangjing-soho-t3/13006

WeWork:
https://www.wired.com/story/wework-coworking-office-spaces/

World Trade Center (2001 to present)
https://www.google.com/search?q=world+trade+center+(2001%E2%80%93present)&rlz=1C5CHFA_enUS850US851&oq=World+Trade+Center+(2001&aqs=chrome.2.69i57j0i512l2j0i22i30l7.13211j1j4&sourceid=chrome&ie=UTF-8

World Trade Center One, otherwise known as The Freedom Tower
https://en.wikipedia.org/wiki/One_World_Trade_Center

Videos

Galaxy Soho, Beijing:
https://www.zaha-hadid.com/architecture/galaxy-soho/

INDEX

ADDENDA

List of Contributions

CCTV Headquarters OMA

- **The Tower Cluster as Symbolic System**
  The unique formal character contributes considerable symbolic power to this important public facility. Here the tower cluster form provides multiple and different possible interpretations. However, no other contemporary building has so strongly come to symbolize Beijing's movement into the future.

- **Amenities in Ancillary Building**
  TVCC is an adjacent building which was a part of the original program. The intention of this adjunct is to provide special facilities for, among others, visitors to CCTV. Among the functions are a hotel and other functions that do not normally relate to the ongoing functions of the building.

- **The Tower Cluster as Multiple Privacy Paths**
  The tower cluster can provide a medium of multiple circulation paths throughout the facility. These generally function to provide differing access throughout for different employee classes.

De Rotterdam OMA

- **The Tower Cluster as a Vertical City**
  The tower cluster exemplifies both formal and functional diversification represented by a large sampling of high-density urban functions of the modern city. Despite this diversity, there is a formal unanimity achieved through the use of a unifying skin solution for all of the diverse masses.

- **Unity in Diversity**
  This is a dialogue of independent, interactive masses. This same degree of interactive diversity appears in the overlapping multiple circulation systems provided for the diversity of users as well as urban visitors.

- **The Plinth as Collective and Public Amenity**
  The multiple functions of the plinth as a multifunctional and multiuser amenity of this collective skyscraper are given expression in seeking a complex formal language of intensified diversity in a place of spatial and formal harmony. Again, this is an architecture of challenging sensibility.

- **Beyond the Skyscraper**
  As exemplified by CCTV, above, De Rotterdam is also an experiment in the extension of the conventional definition of the skyscraper beyond the aspect of extreme height.

- **Multiple Towers as a Modulated Unity**
  De Rotterdam is a unified totality of indefinite number. It is a single building that reads as several, and a multiplicity that reads as one.

CMG Qianhai Global Trade Center OMA

- **The Urban Crafting of the Organizational Structure of the Base**
  *Base contextual interaction*s, in this case by geometric and organizational response to access vectors, is a major typological contribution of this case study. The commercial, cultural, and special office program of the base is designed to integrate with contextual connections and orientations. The base structure is treated as a flexible organizational and geometric model free of the dominant potential influence of the tower forms and geometries.

- **The Interlocking Duo as Classical Tower Structure Circulation Model**
  The *interlocking duo with major extended skybridge* appears to be emerging as one significant classical typological model of the tower cluster typologies. Interlocking vertical and horizontal loops of circulation also appears to become a characteristic form of circulation model in this subtype.

- **Separation of the Two-Loop Circulation System from the Contextual Complexity of the Base Structure**
  The interlocking vertical and horizontal circulation loops are geometrically regular and independent from the geometrical complexity of the base elements.

VDMA Van der Meulen-Ansemsterrein OMA

- **Tower Cluster as Compound Medium of Urban Renewal**
  In VDMA the typology provides a highly flexible medium for urban renewal in an urban situation with multiple, diverse historic and programmatic conditions.

- **Tower Cluster as a Medium in the Construction of Social Democracy**
  The towers integrate solutions for various socioeconomic groups, and the tower cluster provides common community amenities.

- **Tower Cluster Integrates Work-Live Environment**
  A novel WeWork-like environment is integrated as a significant component within the cluster.

- **Stratified Differentiation of the Tower Program**
  Diverse program functions are implemented within the stratified modularity of the architectural solution of the towers.

- **Creation of New Urban Sector of the City**
  The MBS complex establishes a new urban area opposite from the central city location. The concept of the new urban medium as a vehicle of urban development becomes a significant ingredient contributing to its international success in the second decade, and we believe, in the future. The tower cluster here in Singapore becomes a tool of large-scale urban design.

- **Major Precedent for Establishment of the Typology**
  The intricate formal, functional, and organizational integration exemplified by MBS becomes a model for future tower cluster developments. Creates the linear trio subtype of the typology.

- **Establishes Sky Park and Linear Atrium as Prominent Urban Amenities**
  The uniqueness and formal/functional/spatial significance of the monumental connective base element and the unique program and form for the multifunctional sky park are early precedents for the tower cluster's newly emerging compositional definition. This definition establishes the typology as including the multiple elements of towers plus urban attributes.

- **Interconnectedness at Ground Level and Upper Level (Sky Park)**
  The tower cluster is an urban design medium for the creation, or enhancement, of urban interconnectivity. This interconnectivity occurs both within the tower cluster, between the tower cluster and its extended program, and between the tower, the complex, and the city. This urban interconnection can occur at various levels and by various design media, such as continuous multifloor base or sky structures, e.g., the sky plaza or skybridges. These design principles of urban interconnectivity will be extended and further developed later in the decade as we will see below.

- **Circulation System Designed for Extension of Tower Cluster Programs**
  MBS's internal circulation system is expandable for the future addition of major new architectural/urban programs. See, for example, the 2019 hotel complex extension below.

- **Connection to Mass Transit and Bus Transport**
  MBS is connected to both bus and rapid transit public transportation.

- **Connection of Outdoor and Indoor Spaces**
  Throughout the complex there are multiple opportunities for connection with exterior spaces and functions.

- **Tower Cluster as the Architecture of Amenities**
  The architecture and the organization of the tower structure provides for an architecture of amenities. The distribution of the amenities within the organization of the tower cluster becomes a strong statement of the

conceptual basis of the tower structure. This is another important contribution of Marina Bay Sands as a precedent. From that project, we have also learned how the pattern of circulation can become the basis for the extension of additional programmatic elements added beyond the tower structure.

- **Tower Cluster as the Architecture of Integration**
  The typology of the tower cluster in general, and MBS in particular, is distinguished by a complex integration of elements: functional, formal, constructive, spatial, and urbanistic. Ideally, this characterizes all architecture. However, at MBS we have observed how complex and intricate this can be to achieve. Here the orchestration of spatial and experiential integration is an extraordinary experience. One can sense the potential richness of the experience of clustering. By definition, therefore, the successful design of the tower cluster constitutes a high level of architectural/urban achievement.

Sky Habitat Safdie Architects

- **System of Streets in the Air**
  Interconnection through skybridges provides access for all units to all amenities and communal functions.

- **Stepped Towers Create Special Units**
  The duo subtype supports diverse tower accommodations. The geometry of the towers—in this case through stepping—creates the potential for the accommodation of special dwelling shapes and functionality. For example, in the case of Sky Habitat, larger units are created that also have multiple orientations, which is an advantage for solar and breeze orientations.

- **Stepped Organization Creates Tall Atrium at Ground Level**
  The stepped section of the lower housing group of the lead tower creates a covered atrium-like space at ground level.

- **Gardens in the Sky: Multiple Skybridges for Socializing the Sky**
  The skybridges are used to provide a new kind of public realm for the inhabitants. On two of the three skybridges, this is used to create public gardens in the sky.

- **For Every Man a Garden**
  The stepped units (one-third of total) have large terraces and potentially large private gardens.

- **Special Amenities Provisions**
  At the meeting of the three skybridges with the floors of the towers, the spaces are devoted to a wide range of public functions, including sports functions, a gym, tennis court, function rooms, etc.

- **Tower Cluster in a Park**
  The tower cluster is sited in a private park situation which creates the possibility for the establishment of a large selection of private amenities for the inhabitants.

Raffles City Chongqing Safdie Architects

- **The Symbolic and Civic Role of the Tower Cluster**
  The structure and form of the tower cluster elements form a monumental symbolic gateway for pedestrian movements through the site towards the square. Viewed from the main section of the city, the slightly bowed shape of the towers suggests a group of sails upon the waters of the two rivers.

- **The Tower Cluster as Three-Dimensional Urban Design**
  The structured form of the tower cluster organization canalizes the pedestrian movement system through the galleria and down to the square.

- **Socializing the Sky by a Major Community Function Skybridge**
  The Crystal skybridge becomes a major sky-based location of community amenities and social interaction.

ORCA Safdie Architects

- **From Identity Park to Identity Mall**
  The base structure is a multilevel commercial mall which is integrated by landscape design with the linear park. Exterior space connects by axes in the north-south direction with the interior mall, which is planned to be a linear atrium space covered by a transparent, operable vault.

- **Tower Clusters as Connective Urban Tissue**
  Due to the multilevel integration of park-mall circulation and transportation in ORCA, the project illuminates the function of tower clusters as an effective urban design medium of connectivity.

- **Inhabited Skybridges**
  In addition to providing shared collective space for communal services and activities, at ORCA we observe the multiple potential uses of the skybridges. In this case they are also used for residential space in addition to providing interior space for communal uses.

- **The Connected Community**
  As compared to the "streets in the sky" corridor medium for enhancing social interaction, the tower cluster provides for enhancing community at a higher scalar level of the community, or the subcommunity of multiple floors in multiple buildings. Tower clusters are the tools of urban community. In this case, they are employed to create an urban park–oriented social community.

- **The Cultural Orientation of New Urban Communities**
  The cluster community is culturally integrated with multiple society, work, commerce, and cultural functions. This is a new, unique form of cultural interaction which may also become a new model of urbanism.

Galaxy Soho Zaha Hadid Architects

- **The Tower Cluster as Spatial Continuum**
  Through organization of spatial elements and design of circulation and building geometry, the tower cluster has been transformed into the experience of movement through space as a continuum. Furthermore, this continuum is flexible (i.e., it can be modified over time) and discretionary (i.e., the user can select various potential continuous paths).

- **A Double Duo**
  The four core atria can be organized as a double duo, or continuous space containing two core areas. There is further possible flexibility of core space organization (e.g., at the penthouse level).

- **Spatial Organization/Circulation as Flexible Matrix Optimizing the System of Connectivity**
  There exist multiple possibilities for the organization and experience of the core sequence.

- One Base Space: the major atrium
- Double Bridge Connectors: the office stratum at plan 4
- Three Spaces Linked: penthouse restaurants and bars
- Four Linked Spaces: route of the tower atria
- Five Linked Spaces: the commercial/entertainment continuum

- **The Base Aligned Skybridge**
  The major skybridge connections exist at the upper level, or just above the highest floor of the main base layer. In the case of Galaxy Soho, this constitutes one of the levels of intersection between mainly public and mainly private circulation. This location constitutes a potential level for intercluster urban connectivity.

- **A Colony of Atria/Linked Atria/Multiple Core Spaces**
  In Galaxy Soho each of the towers contains an atrium. The main public route for the connection between atria is on the main entry floor. On the fourth floor and penthouse floor, there exist multiple routes for the connection of atria.

- **Multiple Interrelated Skybridge System**
  There exist multiple routes at level 1 and multiple skybridge access points at levels 4 and 15 for alternate routes of connection between the towers.

- **Tower Cluster Linkage**
  The flexibility that is achieved by planned redundancy in the connection system provides for the strengthening of the linkages between specific units. Thus, this contributes a medium for the enhancement of connections for interaction or, in the case of the commercial areas, attraction. This case thus introduces the concept of and media for planning of connectivity between multiple towers, or other parts of the tower cluster.

- **Special Amenities Zones**
  Vertical zoning creates vertical amenities zones in the tower cluster. In addition to the atria and special amenity zones of the base and upper levels, there exist many outdoor plateau spaces throughout the building.

Wangjing Soho Zaha Hadid Architects

- **Major/Minor Tower Cluster Elements through Ancillary Structures**
  Ancillary structures have been built that employ geometric and formal characteristics similar to the major tower structures. In the case of Wangjing Soho, this tower cluster subsystem is used to provide for the expansion of the base-located commercial space in order to accommodate major brand-name clients.

- **Major/Minor Theme**
  The major/minor tower cluster theme can be applied to a variety of potential tower cluster subsystems, such as providing space for alternative program functions. They can also be applied as media for expansion.

- **Scale Transition Methods**
  The addition of elements of moderate scale at the periphery of the tower cluster can be employed as a means of reducing the large-scale impact of the cluster on neighboring developments.

Nanjing International Youth Cultural Center Zaha Hadid Architects

- **Plaza-Oriented Integration of the Tower Cluster and Its Amenities**
  The tower cluster is integrated with, and serves to provide various facilities for, a cultural center.

- **Special Amenities Provisions**
  In the case of Nanjing Cultural Center, the tower cluster is, in effect, in partnership with a more or less independent series of functions that constitute the cultural center. Many of the tower cluster functions, such as serviced apartments and the five-star hotel, are independent.

OPPO Headquarters Zaha Hadid Architects

- **Tower Cluster of Multiple Towers in Single Envelope**
  The glass envelope is continuous over four towers without interruption. The conventional definition of a tower cluster is of multiple, joined, independent towers.

- **Tower Cluster as Symbol of Advanced Technology**
  The smooth geometry and minimalist effect of the glass envelope, which without interruption wraps the four towers, creates a symbolic impression of an object of high technology.

- **Multifloor Open-Planning System to Encourage Interaction**
  Visual interaction within and between open-plan floors is optimized by withdrawing the slab ends from closing off at the curtain wall. The geometry of plan form also enables some visual interaction with successive floors.

- **Uninterrupted Visual Contact by Displacement of Cores**
  There is a subdivision of servant and served space. Vertical services and vertical circulation are located in separate towers in order not to impede visual contact and interaction.

- **Reduction of Plan Size at Base Increases Size of Public Exterior Space.**

Tower C Shenzhen Bay Super Headquarters Zaha Hadid Architects

- **"The Multidimensional Vertical City"**
  The term is that of the architect. Here, in combination with the following two typological contributions, the tower cluster becomes a vertical nexus among a collective of urban clusters, each of which is integrated with the movement paths, public transportation system, green axes, and spatial systems of the city.

- **The Open Heart**
  The spatial core of the cluster is open to the public, which is invited to use its spaces and facilities. The medium of spatial integration is a series of green terraces that invite the public to enter the core and participate in its spaces, facilities, and activities. Each vertically developed core can thus become part of a continuous urban spatial system.

- **Events on the City's Green Axis: Unification of the Urban Landscape**
  The design system of terraced green cluster spaces is functionally and formally integrated physically within the city's green-space system. It is designed to be part of a public, urban spatial continuum.

- **Skybridging Internal Functions Creates Sky Plazas and Sky Gardens**
  The internal functional system of collective commercial, entertainment,

and dining functions is roofed by plazas and green terraces. Public facilities perform the function of bridging.

- **Precedent Making and the Power of Connectivity**
  Create an idea that can become a precedent for other tower clusters of various numbers. Such an idea is the concept of the open heart in the core of the tower cluster and the development of the open heart and the further use of that core as a medium for public-accessed landscape terraces. These terrace clusters can potentially be connected from one cluster to another, thus creating a system in which the landscape becomes a medium of urban connectivity.

Duo Twin Towers Büro Ole Scheeren

- **Tower Cluster Design as Medium for Urban Renewal**
  The transformation of an existing neglected urban environment has been achieved by the uniquely instrumental design of the Duo tower cluster.

- **Potential for Urban Space Design**
  The design of the physical dimensions and geometry can influence and/or transform the spatial quality and character of the urban environment of the tower cluster's site.

- **Creation of Urban Space System for Pedestrian Use**
  The design of landscaping amenities such as gardens and plazas within the site area of the tower cluster has been a motivating factor of several of our prior case studies. In the case of Duo, this has been extended to the design and creation of such landscape amenities in the larger total urban spatial context of the site.

DJI Headquarters Foster + Partners

- **From Traditional Office to Creative Community in the Sky**
  The cluster is organized by what appears to be floating modules. These modules are designed as environments to support processes of creative technological design innovation. Each of these modules also contains contemplative garden spaces to enhance creative thought.

- **Contemplative Zones for Refreshment Towards Creation**
  Both on the ground floor and on the module rooftops there are gardens to enhance reflection and creative thought. These are sky gardens in both the office and R&D environments.

- **Sky Labs for Testing and Display**
  The integration of multiple sky labs within the spatial order of the headquarters environment places both functional and visual emphasis on technological innovation as the heart of DJI.

- **Skybridge as Testing and Display Area:**
  Skybridge Turned Zone-Launching Platform
  The skybridge has unique functions in the tower cluster as an interface with the surrounding airspace and as a dramatic display area.

AUTHOR'S BIOGRAPHY

Robert Maurice Oxman
Professor and Dean Emeritus
Professor of Architectural and Design History and Theory
Faculty of Architecture and Town Planning
Technion: Israel Institute of Technology

Robert Oxman is an architect, educator, writer, and researcher in the fields of architectural design histories and theories. He was educated at Harvard College (BA Magna cum Laude) and the Harvard Graduate School of Design (M. Arch), where he studied with Sigfried Giedion, Josep Lluís Sert, and Fumihiko Maki.

After graduation, he worked in two distinguished practices before opening his own professional office. The first of these offices was the Cambridge 7 of Cambridge, Massachusetts, where he worked on the design and construction of the New England Aquarium in Boston, and on the US Pavilion at Expo 1967 in Montreal Canada.

The second office was that of the famed landscape architect Hideo Sasaki. The office was one of the first integrated practices of Architecture, Planning, Landscape Architecture, and Urban Design in the world; it was named Sasaki, Dawson and DeMay, and later, Sasaki Associates. There, Oxman worked on numerous projects of campus planning including planning and design at the University of Virginia and in the master planning for the new campus of the University of New York at Buffalo. In addition, his master planning work at Sasaki included work on the planning and site development for the National Center for Atmospheric Research in Boulder, Colorado. His architectural work at Sasaki included, among other works, the complete design and construction work on the Tobin School at Fresh Pond in Cambridge.

He is currently Professor and Dean Emeritus at the Technion Israel Institute of Technology. Professor Oxman has also held the Chairs of Design Methods and Design Computing at the Technical University of Eindhoven, the Netherlands. He has been Professor of Architectural and Design History and Theories at the Shenkar College of Engineering, Design, and Art in Tel Aviv, where he was the founding Dean of Graduate Studies. There he also engaged in developing a unique program of graduate education which integrated design, technology, and industry.

His work in Architectural Design History and Theories since 1945 has been published internationally. He has written seven books. He is currently involved in researching and writing in three subject areas: *Emerging Architectural and Design Theories*; *Architectural Knowledge and Design Knowledge*; and *Design Concepts: New Conceptual Foundations of Architectural Theory since 1945*. In addition, he is currently working on an edition of the essays of Professor Rivka Oxman on Design Cognition and Design Computation, entitled *Theory and Design in the First Digital Age*. His most recent publication is *Socializing the Sky: The Typology of Tower Clusters*.